Global Health Partnerships

Global Health Partnerships

The Pharmaceutical Industry and BRICA

Mei-Ling Wang
Associate Professor, University of the Sciences in Philadelphia, USA

First published 2009 by
PALGRAVE MACMILLAN

Palgrave Macmillan in the UK is an imprint of Macmillan Publishers Limited, registered in England, company number 785998, of Houndmills, Basingstoke, Hampshire RG21 6XS.

Palgrave Macmillan in the US is a division of St Martin's Press LLC, 175 Fifth Avenue, New York, NY 10010.

Palgrave Macmillan is the global academic imprint of the above companies and has companies and representatives throughout the world.

Palgrave® and Macmillan® are registered trademarks in the United States, the United Kingdom, Europe and other countries.

ISBN-13: 978–0–230–51560–4 hardback
ISBN-10: 0–230–51560–6 hardback

This book is printed on paper suitable for recycling and made from fully managed and sustained forest sources. Logging, pulping and manufacturing processes are expected to conform to the environmental regulations of the country of origin.

A catalogue record for this book is available from the British Library.

Library of Congress Cataloging-in-Publication Data

Wang, Mei-Ling, 1960–
    Global health partnerships : the pharmaceutical industry and BRICA / Mei-Ling Wang.
        p. cm.
    Includes bibliographical references and index.
    ISBN 978–0–230–51560–4
    1. Pharmaceutical policy. 2. World health. 3. Public health – International cooperation. 4. Pharmaceutical industry. I. Title.

RA401.A1W36 2009
362.17'82—dc22   2008041055

10 9 8 7 6 5 4 3 2 1
18 17 16 15 14 13 12 11 10 09

Printed and bound in Great Britain by
CPI Antony Rowe, Chippenham and Eastbourne

For my brother Yazhou and sister Yuhua,
who believe in my ability and support me wholeheartedly

Contents

Acknowledgments

For the completion of this book, I would like to pay tribute to Dr William Hsiao, Professor at the Harvard School of Public Health, for his reminding us of the importance of examining health system issues from a comparative perspective. I am also grateful to Dr Marc Roberts, Harvard School of Public Health, for providing us the tools to analyze health care issues from a supply and demand perspective. I am always grateful to Dr Deborah Prothrow-Stith, Harvard School of Public Health, for her emphasis on improving social determinants in generating global health solutions.

Special thanks go to Dr Margaret Chan, Director of the World Health Organization, for her insights about the need to listen to each other and work together among all stakeholders to resolve global health challenges. Her leadership and approach to global health represents a new model of generating global health solutions.

I am also grateful to my colleagues in China, Ms Shuo Zhang, Dr Wei Zhang, D. Xiaowan Wang, Dr Hsu Hua, and Y. Zhang, for their insights about China's pharmaceutical industry. Special thanks also go to the staff of the Chinese Embassy in Washington, DC.

I am most grateful to Raoul Silva for his insightful analyses of the pharmaceutical industry in Brazil in relation to global stakeholders. My thanks also go to my Brazilian colleagues who are involved with quality control issues in Brazil. Special thanks also go to Paul Thomas, Intel, and Emerging Markets Group, for their assistance about multi-sector partnerships.

My gratitude goes to the reference librarians at the Harvard School of Public Health Library, the University of Pennsylvania Library, and the University of the Sciences in Philadelphia Library. I am also grateful to Stephanie Lassarat and Adam Clark for background information about global health partnerships by Novartis. On partnership building, I am particularly thankful to Mr Bob Laverty of Novartis for valuable information about the coartem partnership. I would also like to thank Elizabeth Ziemba for the framework of partnership building; Shadab Mahmud, of Grameen America, for integrated partnership; Sam Abbenyi for the International Trachoma Initiative; Dr Vinand Nantulya for the Stop TB Initiative and initiatives by the Global Fund as well as pharmaceutical access in Africa; Women's Agenda for Change about pharmaceutical access to HIV for the vulnerable population in Cambodia; Medical Sisters Mission about pharmaceutical access in Peru; and Kim Bouldin-Jones, KBJ Consulting, and Ashley Gasque, Management Sciences for Health, about strategies to improve pharmaceutical access in Africa. I am especially thankful to Aravind Eye Hospitals for being an inspiring example that synergizes the strengths of public health skills and business efficiency. Their work in India shows that as long as there is a will and a partnership, there is a way to better global health.

I would also like to thank the staff of the World Trade Organization, the World Intellectual Property Rights Association, the World Health Organization, and the staff at the Chinese Embassy and the Brazilian Embassy in Washington, DC, for background information on issues related to global pharmaceutical partnerships. I am also grateful to the FDA for directing me to useful information on the web sites.

In addition, my everlasting gratitude goes to my family for their unwavering support. My father's knowledge in plant-based medicine has sustained my life-long interest in medicine. My family's confidence in my ability is the driving force behind my love of writing. They are not only my best friends but also my source of intellectual inquiry. Their ideas have also broadened my analytical focus.

Lastly, without the inspiration of vulnerable, excluded people in the globe, this book would never have come into existence. My fieldwork with them has taught me the valuable lesson that all stakeholders can, and should, work together if we truly want to make a difference in global health. Global health through multi-level, multi-sector partnership is the 'tao' of sustainable development.

1
Global Health Partnerships: An Introduction

The need for innovative pharmaceutical solutions for global health has never been greater than it is today, because of the serious challenges brought about by the increase of epidemics and pandemics and the old persistent, health problems facing humanity. Given the magnitude and formidable nature of the challenges in global health, most have realized that no single stakeholder can act alone. Among the many solutions proposed, global health partnerships have increased their momentum and visibility since the beginning of the 2000s. Some of these partnerships, especially those aiming for life-saving pharmaceuticals, have brought about measurable success and have provided immediate and critical relief to a large number of people affected by neglected diseases or chronic illnesses. Thus, the importance of partnerships in the timely provision of effective pharmaceuticals for those infected and affected by intractable health problems has been recognized. On a grander scale, many are asking, "what kinds of partnerships do we need to bring about a useful solution to the increasing demand for effective and affordable pharmaceuticals in the world?" This book aims to answer this question by proposing the restoring of the balance in the supply and demand/need chain through the use of *a planting strategy*. In specific, this writing analyzes the comparative advantages of major stakeholders and proposes a possible partnership between large multinational pharmaceutical companies and the stakeholders in the BRICA countries, namely, Brazil, Russia, India, China, and Africa (South Africa in particular) as a model for solving the problem of improving global health.

Global health challenges

The state of global health has received a large amount of attention since the inception of the AIDS epidemic, mainly because of the social, economic, and population consequences. An increasing number of epidemics and pandemics have affected populations both in developed and developing countries. The world has witnessed the scourge of HIV, SARS, and recently the Avian Flu, as well as the persistence of intractable chronic illnesses.

In developing countries, old problems and neglected problems exist side by side. In the developing world, communicable diseases are the major health challenge. These include lower respiratory tract infections, HIV/AIDS, infections at birth, diarrheal disease, malaria, TB, chronic obstructive pulmonary disease, and measles. According to US Centers of Disease Control (CDC) (2005), approximately 5 to 10 percent of all children under five years of age in developing countries are infected with pneumonia each year and the mortality is approximately 2 million. Pneumonia is a leading cause of death in this age group. And about 1 percent of the pneumonia cases result in sequelae (such as bronchiectasis), a risk factor of recurrent respiratory infections. In China, for example, one estimate shows that in 1997 about 26 percent of deaths were related to respiratory problems (Hertsgaard, 1997). On HIV and AIDS, according to UNAIDS (2006), about 90 percent of people with HIV live in developing countries. About two-thirds (63 percent) of all adults and children with HIV globally live in sub-Saharan Africa, concentrated mainly in southern Africa. In 2006, almost three-quarters (72 percent) of all adult and child deaths due to AIDS occurred in that region. On malaria, according to the World Health Organization (WHO, 2007c), about 40 percent of the world's population, mainly the world's poorest, are at risk of malaria and more than 500 million people become severely ill with malaria every year. Most malaria cases and deaths are concentrated in sub-Saharan Africa. Despite the lack of attention to heart attacks in developing countries, heart attacks rank third, after HIV/AIDS and lower respiratory diseases, as one of the leading causes of deaths in those countries (WHO, 2007b, "Cardiovascular diseases"). According to WHO, about 17.5 million people died from cardiovascular disease in 2005, accounting for 30 percent of all global deaths, among which 7.6 million were due to heart attacks and 5.7 million were due to stroke. And most of these deaths occurred in low- and middle-income countries (LMIC). It is predicted that if there is no effective control strategy, by 2015 about 20 million people will die from cardiovascular disease every year (ibid.). On infection and mortality at birth, about 8 million infants, of the 125 million newborns, die every year before reaching one year of age and most of the deaths occur in the least developed and developing countries in Africa, Asia, Mexico, and South

America. The major causes of death are asphyxia, sepsis, pneumonia, and premature birth (Vidyasagar, 2002). On tuberculosis (TB), WHO estimates that about 2 billion people, or one-third of the world's total population, are infected with TB bacilli, the microbes that cause TB; and in 2005, 1.6 million people died from TB, which is about 4400 deaths a day. Half of the TB-related deaths occur in Asia (WHO, 2007d, "Stop TB partnership"). TB affects mainly the poor and mainly the young adults in resource poor countries (WHO, 2007d). Although the highest rates per capita occur in Africa (28 percent of all TB cases), half of all new cases are in six Asian Countries (WHO, 2007d).

In addition, the neglected diseases, which have been overlooked by the developed world in terms of investment in research and the development of effective therapeutics, continue to pose major threats to population health. According to WHO (2007a), more than 1 billion, or one-sixth of the world's population, suffer from one or more neglected diseases (NTDs). The NTDs often mentioned include Buruli ulcer, cholera, cysticercosis, dracunculiasis (Guinea-worm disease), foodborne trematode infections (such as fascioliasis), hydatidosis, leishmaniasis, lymphatic filariasis, onchocerciasis, schistosomiasis, soil-transmitted helminthiasis, trachoma and trypanosomiasis. A number of these diseases and also dengue fever are vector-borne. Most of the populations affected by NTDs are the resource-poor and most vulnerable in tropical and subtropical areas of the developing world. Some diseases cause serious and long-lasting morbidity, such as trachoma. Others, such as malaria, are acute infections that could lead to serious outcomes, including mortality (WHO, 2007a, "Control of neglected tropical diseases"). African trypanosomiasis, sleeping sickness, can be fatal. Leishmaniasis, which is usually fatal if the infected are not treated, is prevalent in 88 developing countries around the world and the Indian sub-continent has seen most of the new cases of infection. Chagas disease, endemic in Central and South America, affects more than 18 million people, with an estimated mortality of more than 50,000 people annually.

Trachoma, an eye infection caused by Chlamydia trachomatis, is the most common preventable cause of blindness and ranks second, after cataract, as the most common cause of blindness. The disease is endemic in 48 countries in Latin America, Africa, the Middle East, Asia, and Australasia. The affected are mainly poor, rural populations with little access to modern sanitary systems. According to one estimate, trachoma has caused approximately 15 percent of the world's blindness (Mecaskey, Knirsch, Kumaresan and Cook, 2003; Thylefors, Negrel, Pararajasegaram and Dadzie, 1995). In another estimate by WHO, about 6 million people are blind due to trachoma and an additional 146 million people have active forms of the disease. The economic cost resulting from trachoma morbidity is estimated to be around US $2.9 billion per year in lost workforce productivity (see Medical Ecology, 2007).

In another example, schistosomiasis, a parasitic disease caused by several species of flatworm, is also prevalent in the developing world. Despite its low mortality, schistosomiasis can cause debilitation and liver and intestinal damage. It is endemic in 74 tropical developing countries in Asia, Africa, and South America, and is a major vector for the transmission is freshwater snails, which contain the parasite. It was estimated that approximately 200 million in these populations are already infected and another 600 million people are at risk of becoming infected (Microbiologybytes, 2007, "Shistomiasis").

Developed countries are not free of population health concerns, either. According to the World Health Organization (WHO, 2004), the major causes of illness and death in developed countries are heart attacks, stroke, lung and tracheal bronchial cancer, lower respiratory tract infections, chronic obstructive pulmonary disease, colon and rectal cancer, diabetes, self-inflicted injuries, hypertensive heart disease, and stomach cancer. For example, in the United States, one in every five deaths is attributed to coronary heart disease (CHD) and it is a leading cause of death (American Heart Association, 2007a, "Heart attack and angina statistics"). In the European Union (EU), cardiovascular diseases (CVD) cause more than 19 million deaths. CVD causes nearly 42 percent of all deaths in the EU. CVD is the main cause of death in women in every European country and is the main cause of death in men in all European countries except France and San Marino (American Heart Association, 2007b, "International cardiovascular disease statistics"). CVD also reduces life-expectancy by a third in those suffering from the condition (European Cardiovascular Disease Statistics, 2005). In Canada, it is estimated that every seven minutes, a Canadian dies of heart disease and stroke. CVD has caused more deaths than other diseases. In a 2000 statistic, about 34 percent of male deaths and 36 percent of female deaths were attributed to CVD. In Canada, the economic cost due to CVD is about $18.4 billion annually (American Heart Association, 2007b; see also 2004 QuickFacts).

Another example is lung cancer. According to the American Lung Association, lung and tracheal bronchial cancer is a leading cause of death for both men and women in the United States and between 1979 and 2003, lung cancer accounted for a 60 percent increase (American Lung Association, 2006, "Lung cancer fact sheet"). A similar phenomenon is observed in some European countries (see Cancer Research UK, 2007; Borras et al., 2000, "Pattern of smoking initiation in Catalonia (Spain) from 1948 to 1992"). Diabetes is a particularly serious health problem in the United States, affecting especially the ethnic minorities. According to the American Diabetes Association (2007), approximately 20.8 million children and adults in the United States, or 7 percent of the population, are affected by diabetes. And it was also estimated that the total annual economic cost of diabetes in 2002 was $132 billion, accounting for one out of every ten health care dollars spent in the United States. Lifestyle issues, imbalance of nutrition, and social determinants of health are considered to be the major causes of these health problems in the developed world. Most recent pharmaceutical innovations are designed specifically to target these problems. Furthermore, the developed world is also affected by some communicable diseases, such as HIV/AIDS, MDR (multiple drug resistant) TB or MRSA (Methicillin-resistant Staphylococcus aureus), but these problems account for a small percentage of overall health care problems.

The health challenges facing both the developing and developed world today bring about serious implications for the sustainable development of the global community. First of all, health problems have incurred economic cost, which comprises health costs, illness costs, and productivity loss due to absenteeism. For example, in the United States, according to the Commonwealth Fund survey, an estimated 18 million Americans between the ages of 19 and 64 who have a disability or chronic disease are not working because of health reasons (Davis, Collins, Doty, Ho and Holmgren, August, 2005). In addition, about 29 percent of those employed full- or part-time reported having health problems, defined as being of fair or poor health status, or having a chronic condition such as cancer, diabetes, arthritis, or heart attack/heart disease, or a disability (ibid.). The same survey pointed out that even using the minimum wage to calculate lost work time, American workers' health problems cost the nation about $185 billion each year in economic output (ibid.).

In the global picture, SARS was a major financial disaster for the affected countries, mainly in East Asia. According to an estimate by *Far Eastern Economic Review* (2003, pp. 12–17), during the spread of SARS in April of 2003, SARS cost $2.2 billion for China; $1.7 billion for Hong Kong; $400 million for Indonesia; $2 billion for South Korea, $660 million for Malaysia; $270 million for the Philippines, $950 million for Singapore; $820 million for Taiwan; $490 million for Thailand; $15 million for Vietnam; $1.1 billion for Japan. The affected countries found themselves facing the loss of tourism, lost businesses, and delayed transportation. In the early stage of the SARS epidemic, Hong Kong's tourism industry almost lost its pulse. For example, the Cathay Pacific Airways, having to cut 37 percent of its weekly capacity, had witnessed SARS as the worst crisis in the carrier's history. Dragon Airways had to reduce 44 percent of its normal capacity. The hotel industry saw its occupancy falling to single figures. The renowned Hotel Mandarin Oriental faced a booking rate of below 10 percent. According to the Hong Kong Tourism Board, visitors to Hong Kong decreased by 10.4 percent in the second half of March (EMSNow, 18 April 2003).

For the SARS epidemic, various estimates by such investment groups as Merrill Lynch, Goldman Sachs, JP Morgan, Lehman Brothers, Morgan Stanley, ING Financial Markets, BNP Paribas Peregrine, Standard & Poors, and IDEAGlobal showed a direct financial loss ranging from an average of $10.6 billion to $16 billion by the Asian Development Bank (see EMSNow, 18 April 2003; *New York Times*, 1 May 2003). When factoring in both the direct and indirect financial loss, BioEnterprise Asia made a forecast of a higher estimate of $50 billion loss for the region and $150 billion for the global community. In total, Asia was estimated to have lost more than 0.6 percent of GDP that year.

Another example of the dire consequences of global health challenges is the economic impact of malaria in Africa. The impact is considered one of the major obstacles to Africa's sustainable development. For the near term, the cost of malaria includes direct and indirect costs. According to Roll Back Malaria Initiative (2001), the direct costs of malaria include personal and public expenditures on both prevention of and intervention in the disease. Personal costs include individuals' spending on insecticide treated mosquito nets (ITNs), doctors' fees, anti-malarial drugs, transport to health facilities, caretaking of the patient and in-patient care fees. The public sector also has to contribute to spending on health care infrastructure (facilities, equipment, personnel, and treatment), publicly managed vector control, education, and research. The indirect costs of malaria include productivity or income loss (cost of lost workdays or absenteeism from formal employment and total of unpaid home-based work) due to malaria morbidity. Malaria-induced mortality also discounts future earnings potential. In one estimate, the disease may account for as much as 40 percent of public health expenditure, 30 to 50 percent of inpatient admissions, and up to 50 percent of outpatient visits. In another estimate, malaria accounts for a "growth penalty" of up to 1.3 percent per year in some African countries. It is believed that in the long term, malaria contributes to substantial GDP differences between malaria-endemic countries and malaria-free countries (facts cited in Roll Back Malaria Initiative, 2001).

Besides the loss of tangible capital, global ill-health has also incurred calculable costs on human and community capital and the implications of this impact are even more negative than the tangible financial loss. First, health crises have weakened social and community integrity. For example, the spread of HIV in the developing world has led to much shorter life expectancies in HIV-prevalent countries, a large disabled adult population, and HIV-infected and affected children that need care. It has contributed to a vicious cycle of social degeneration and fragmentation. Women and men of productive age are disabled by the epidemic, which drives them into a deeper poverty cycle. Women who have lost their husbands or livelihoods due to HIV have to engage in other means, such as prostitution, to survive, which leads to an even faster rate of transmission of HIV among the population. Children orphaned by the disease face heightened health risks too. They are either HIV-infected themselves or are left with diminished access to socioeconomic resources to survive. HIV-related death has also caused a shortage of teachers, which places an even heavier burden on the community. In this context, children are facing even scarcer opportunities to improve their life chances.

In addition to HIV, malaria is another case in point in terms of how global health challenges have aggravated the disintegration of community capital. It was noted that malaria has also affected children's schooling and social development because of absenteeism and permanent neurological and other damage in severe cases (Roll Back Malaria Initiative, 2001). The fact that malaria does not discriminate means that it has also infected teachers, doctors, and nurses. But the most serious impact has been on poor children, who are at the highest risk of malaria infection and mortality. In this case, the deficiency of human capital and community capital has a two-way interaction with financial losses. Malaria risks in endemic areas might deter business investment, which further diminishes the locals' means and capacity to fight against the disease. This lost capacity feeds back to the downward spiral of underdevelopment by bringing about an even more negative impact on local economies and development. For example, malaria has deterred tourism because travelers are reluctant to visit malaria-endemic areas. Regional and global investors do not want to incur additional human resources or environmental costs in malaria-endemic countries. Lost economic opportunities are translated into deepening poverty and dependency. Poverty has reduced the locals' ability to administer vector control and contributes to difficulty in obtaining timely care for the infected individuals (see related discussions in Roll Back Malaria, 2001).

The malaria epidemic is not a unique case. A similar implication of human capital loss is also observed in the case of trachoma. It is estimated that trachoma accounts for about US $2.9 billion in lost productivity every year (International Trachoma Initiative, 2005). In addition to financial costs, trachoma has long-term human capital loss. Trachoma causes blindness among adults in the prime of their productive years and women are three times more likely to be at risk than men. This means that it effects men's and women's ability to support their families. Yet the effects are particularly negative on women. It is noted that when a mother can no longer perform vital activities for her household, an older daughter leaves school to perform the mother's duties, thus depriving the daughter of access to a formal education and related life opportunities. This can lead to an intergenerational transfer of poverty for women, creating a vicious cycle of women's economic dependency.

Conversely, the elimination of wide-spread diseases has also contributed to substantial economic gains. For example, it was noted that elimination of onchocerciasis (river blindness) would deliver an economic rate of return of 17 percent (Porter, 1998). In the case of malaria, both Billiton and Exxon Mobile have learned firsthand the importance of addressing health care for their employees at risk of malaria. The success in their prevention and intervention effort has translated into significant and tangible economic and productivity gains.

A population's health problems have political and global implications as well. For example, the public demand for governments to take concrete actions to address the affordable health care issue is given a prominent place in a number of countries, especially in the United States and China. This issue is a top concern for the presidential candidates in the United States in 2008. By the same token, this issue has also been recognized as a top priority for Chinese leaders in the Seventeenth People's Congress, adjourned in the fall of 2007. Citizens in the United States and China have found that one of the most formidable challenges in their lives is that of health care and they are looking to their governments to meet this challenge. In both cases, a lack of action in responding to the public need would seriously affect the political capital of the government.

Health challenges have also posed a threat to global security. The chain reactions set off by some recent health events and epidemics have made the global community realize that when health problems travel beyond national borders, the whole world has to pay. The cases of TB, HIV, SARS, and the Avian Flu have all illustrated that global health challenges have the potential of becoming the worst terrorism confronting humanity. This explains why public health officials in the United States, Europe, and Canada were alarmed when an Atlantic lawyer, Andrew Speaker, infected with XDR TB (Extensively Drug-Resistant Tuberculosis, a drug-resistant form of TB) had traveled to Canada and Europe without following the advice of his doctors (see CNN, 31 May 2007). It prompted the US government to issue a health quarantine, the first since 1963, because of the concern that he might have exposed fellow passengers to TB risks on two international flights (National Public Radio, June 2007). Public health concern was not unfounded because, according to the Centers of Disease Prevention and Control, in the United States in a five-year survey (2000–04) of a worldwide sample, XDR TB had increased from 5 percent of MDR TB cases in 2000 to 6.5 percent in 2004, except in South Korea. This survey also shows that in the industrialized nations in this survey, XDR TB had increased from 3 percent of MDR TB cases in 2000 to 11 percent in 2004. The security threat of TB is evidenced by the fact that according to CDC, about one-third of the world's population is infected with the bacteria that causes TB, and each year approximately 9 million people become ill with the disease, among whom 2 million will die. In addition, TB control is facing a severe challenge because it has developed resistance to existing treatments and travels easily across national borders (Centers of Disease Prevention and Control, 2006).

The example of Africa illustrates the worst case scenario in relation to the implications of health challenges to sustainable development. Throughout history, Africa has been a major commodity market, rich in oil, metals, cocoa, and a number of agricultural products. These industries are labor-intensive and require high volumes of human labor input. If Africa were free of infectious diseases, its economic potential would be immeasurable and its populace would enjoy a much higher living standard than it is today. Most of the diseases affecting Africa are the ones that effect physical strengths. This is evidenced in the impact of HIV, malaria, river blindness, and sleeping sickness on the health of African laborers. The prevalence of these diseases have severely affected African participation in labor-intensive economies.

The consequences of health challenges in Africa have forced the private sector to take a proactive approach to dealing with these challenges. The involvement of BHP Billiton's malaria project is a relevant case in point. It shows that health challenges could bring about serious consequences to the private sector's bottom line. When the private sector tackles the challenges head-on, it tends to generate multiplicative effects on sustainable development.

When BHP Billiton started its operations in Mozambique, it found that malaria was one of its worst enemies. Malaria is endemic in the areas where the Mozal aluminum smelter was built. BHP Billiton, with market capitalization valued in 2007 at US$156.5 billion, is the world's largest diversified resources company with more than 35,000 employees in more than 100 operations in 30 countries. It is a known leader in commodity businesses, including aluminum, energy coal and metallurgical coal, copper, ferro-alloys, iron ore, and titanium minerals, and it has substantial interests in oil, gas, liquefied natural gas, nickel, diamonds, and silver. In 1999, BHP Billiton's Mozal smelter recorded more than 6000 cases of malaria, 13 fatalities, and falling productivity through absenteeism and sickness. Malaria became a major concern to the business because of the threats to the construction timelines and the future of the smelter, which cost more than US$ 2 billion investment. Facing the threat of malaria to its workforce, BHP Billington took effective action to tackle malaria (Forbes, 2007, "BHP Billiton"; The Metropolitan Corporate Counsel, June, 2004). BHP Billiton applied its business competencies strategicallyand has successfully reduced malaria infection among its workforce through the Mozal Development Trust (ibid.). The program has led to the reduction by 50 percent of cases of malaria in the Mozal workforce and the infection rates among children have declined by 40 percent.

It is obvious that in both developed and developing countries, diseases and illnesses have increased an already large burden on health systems and governments' fiscal programs. Global health problems have affected global sustainable economic development, peace, stability, and security. And they have become a challenge to every global stakeholder.

Solutions: types and components

It is obvious that global health challenges require innovative solutions. According to Wang and Nantulya (2008), global health solutions can be modeled in a solution framework. In this framework, solutions are categorized into several different types: downstream solutions, upstream solutions, and top-stream solutions.

A downstream solution provides immediate relief for the diseases and scarcity of basic needs (such as medicine, food, water, and temporary shelter). An upstream solution generates a global platform for horizontal and vertical integration in resolving technical aspects of the problems, such as development projects integrated with government policies, or global policies on technology transfer, intellectual property rights, and resource sharing. An example of an upstream solution is the African Comprehensive HIV/AIDS Partnerships (ACHAP) or Merck/Gates/ Botswana Partnership for HIV/AIDS (International Federation of Pharmaceutical Manufacturers and Associations, September 2006). Established in 2000 (and extended to 2009) by the Government of Botswana, the Merck Company Foundation, Merck and Co., Inc., and the Bill & Melinda Gates Foundation, ACHAP presented a comprehensive approach to HIV/AIDS prevention, care, treatment, and support to enhance Botswana's response to the HIV/AIDS epidemic. In addition to the total of $100 million donations from the Merck Company Foundation and the Gates Foundation, Merck has also donated its anti-retroviral (ARV) medicines to Botswana's national ARV treatment program, to the partnership. Strategic priorities include ARV program support, expansion of HIV testing capacity, increasing post-treatment services, as well as empowering the HIV/AIDS infected and affected. This partnership has achieved measurable results. For example, by December 2005, around 50,000 patients of the 56,500 patients enrolled in the program were receiving medication with more than 1000 new enrollments in the program each month (International Federation of Pharmaceutical Manufacturers & Associations. September 2006). The partnership was instrumental in constructing 32 regional treatment centers. It has also helped develop laboratory capacity for blood testing and monitoring as well as using information technology to track patient adherence. The partnership also offers HIV/AIDS clinical care training to all health care professionals in Botswana. To date, more than 3200 health care workers have received hands-on clinical training from HIV/AIDS experts. It has also conducted education related to HIV awareness and de-stigmatization for nearly 5000 teachers in primary and secondary schools (International Federation of Pharmaceutical Manufacturers and Associations. September 2006). It was noted that the strength of the partnership lies in its full integration with government strategy and its ability to capitalize on unique cross-sector expertise in support of public policy goals. An upstream solution targets the root causes of global health and development, such as poverty, gender, a lack of education and community capital. An example of an upstream solution is the Millennium Development Goals. It is important to know that these different types of solutions are interconnected. Providing downstream solutions without addressing the root causes tends to limit the effectiveness of sustainable development. In essence, long-term solutions focus on sustainable community and human capital building.

Given the urgency in providing immediate relief for the aforementioned global health challenges, this book will focus on downstream and upstream solutions in the provision of pharmaceuticals both by the traditional large pharmaceutical companies (pharmas) in the developed world and by those in the emerging powers of Brazil, Russia, India, Chinam and Africa or BRICA. The critical components in a downstream solution are the provision and pricing of pharmaceuticals, population needs, supply chain management, public health infrastructure, regulation, and finance (some of these elements are mentioned by Fan, Liu, Bhattacharyya, and Hu, 5 November 2007). On this list, the issue of balance in the provision of pharmaceuticals in the supply and demands/needs chain takes up a prominent place in discussions of global health partnerships.

Major issues in global pharmaceutical provision

On the supply side, multinational pharmaceutical companies have been the major suppliers of biomedicine for several decades. Their profit profile is one of the highest when compared to other industries; however, in the meantime, their global positions are facing increasing challenges. These challenges include the constant need for innovation, the expense and risks associated with research and development (R&D), competition, increasing regulatory barriers, quality control and the fight against counterfeits, its role in rapid response to global health crises, and its ability to meet the need of excluded populations.

Optimistic forecasts of the pharmaceutical sector's bottom line mainly derive from the increasing health needs of the populations in both the developing and developed worlds. According to one estimate, the rate of growth for 2006 in the global pharmaceutical market was 7.0 percent, totaling US$643 billion at constant exchange rates (Business Monitor, 2006). The largest market is in the United States, but the fastest rates of increase are observed in the emerging markets such as China, Russia, South Korea, and Mexico, growing at a total of 81 percent (Herper and Kang, 22 March 2006). It has been predicted that most growth in future years is expected to come from the emerging market because the markets in developed countries are maturing and reaching their ceiling in pharmaceutical sale (ibid.).

In this picture, it is forecast that 60 percent of revenue growth for large pharmaceutical companies is likely to come from biologic products, with a 13 percent growth rate to 2010, compared to 0.9 percent for small molecule products (PhRMA MedDevice, 2007, "Pharmaceutical statistics"), although the top-ten selling drugs will still be small molecule drugs. It is worth noting that the small molecule drugs paved the way for pharmaceutical growth at the turn of the twentieth century (Herper and Kang, 22 March 2006). The key driver of growth is likely to be innovations in oncologics that account for 20.5 percent global growth in that therapeutic class (Intercontinental Marketing Services (IMS), 20 March 2007, "IMS health reports global pharmaceutical market grew 7.0 percent in 2006, to $643 billion"). By 2007, the globally top-selling drugs are the treatments for chronic diseases prevalent in developed societies, such as the cholesterol pill Lipitor by Pfizer, which remains the best-selling drug in the world for the fifth year in a row, with annual sales of $12.9 billion, more than twice as much as its closest competitors.

In addition, certain types of drugs are growing at a fast pace. The biotechnology sector has grown by 17 percent to $53 billion (Herper and Kang, 22 March 2006). Three anemia treatments, two from Amgen and one from Johnson and Johnson, that have made the top-10 list were produced by the biotechnology sector. The sales of generics are growing at a fast rate and have posed strong competition to the brands drugs. It was noticed that in 2005, generics accounted for only 9.7 percent of the market in value terms, but are likely to reach over 15 percent penetration by 2010. A major driver is the expiration of a large number of leading blockbuster drugs between 2006 and 2010 (*Business Monitor*, 2006). The global movement demanding affordable medicine is another driver for the growth of the generics market. This movement is experiencing a strong momentum in the United States and China particularly.

The center of pharmaceutical development remains in the United States. It was noted that for the 265 drugs widely circulated on global pharmaceutical market between 1970 and 1992, the United States was the leading producer, followed by Japan, the United Kingdom, Germany, and Switzerland. Valued at more than US$250 billion in 2006, or 48 percent of the global market, the United States remains the largest pharmaceutical market in the world (*Business Monitor*, 2006). Most of the large pharmaceutical companies are based in the Untied States, where most of the new pharmaceutical innovations are introduced. By 1997, the US held 92 patents of the 100 most commonly prescribed drugs (Schweitzer, 1997). Despite some recent criticisms about the Federal Food and Drug Agency, the United States is still considered to have the most comprehensive and strictest regulatory framework in the world. The growth rate of pharmaceutical sales in 2006 is about 8.3 percent in the United States, an increase over the previous year mainly because of an increase in prescribing volume in the implementation of the Medicare Part D program. The rate of growth is likely to be about 4 to 5 percent from 2007 to 2012 (*Business Monitor*, 2006).

In the global context, the increase in global pharmaceutical revenues has to do with the general increase in health care spending globally in an effort to address the increase of global health challenges. It was pointed out that health care spending grows at a rate faster than the overall economy. In the early 2000s, the United States already consumed 14 percent of its gross domestic product (GDP) on health care, followed by Switzerland and Germany, which spent more than 10 percent of GDP on health care. Britain plans to spend more than 9 percent of GDP on health care beyond 2008 (Maynard and Bloor, 2003; see also Organization for Economic Cooperation and Development, 2002, *OECD Health Data 2002*).

This rate of health care spending is likely to increase worldwide, and in industrialized countries in particular. In 2006, the United States spents 16 percent of GDP on health care, and this rate is expected to grow to 17.5 percent by 2010 (*Business Monitor*, 2006). In France, the rate increased from 8.5 percent in 1990 to 9.3 percent in 2000, and to about 10 percent in the mid-2000s. A similar rate is observed in Germany and Canada (BDI Initiative, 2001). Japan has increased its health spending from about 5.9 percent to 7.6 percent from 1990 to 2000 (ibid.). This rate is likely to increase because of the aging population.

In this context, pharmaceutical spending has also experienced a sizable increase. For example, in the 1990s, the total pharmaceutical spending in 1990 made up about: 8 percent of total health spending in the United States and Sweden; 11 percent of health care costs in the United Kingdom; 17 percent in France, and over 21 percent in Germany (Gross, Ratner, Perez and Glavin, Spring, 1994). Between the early 1990s and 2000, the rate of pharmaceutical spending was increasing at a rate of 10 percent in the United States, while other industrialized countries experienced a smaller rate of increase. In France, despite a slower growth rate, the pharmaceutical markets account for about 20 percent of the health care market (Maynard and Bloor, 2003). In terms of total volume, US prescription drug spending had doubled from an estimated $105 billion in 1999 to $212 billion in 2004 (Health Insurance Association of America, 2000). Also, US per capita expenditure on drugs was US $1,069 in 2006, about twice the amount of the rest of the world (PharmaDevice, 2008, "Pharmaceutical statistics").

The increasing US demand for pharmaceuticals sets the tone for the business growth of the large pharmaceutical companies. This can be explained by a number of factors. First, the belief in innovative and high-tech medicine is deeply ingrained in American culture. The pharmaceutical sector has been effective in promoting and diffusing new products for adoption. Second, the population in the United States is "graying." The baby boomers, who are an influential demographic group in terms of political support and economic consumption, are aging and demanding a healthy lifestyle during the aging process. Third, and most importantly, chronic health problems are increasing. In the United States, about 125 million Americans, or one-third of US populations, have one or more chronic conditions (e.g., congestive heart failure, diabetes). Chronic diseases account for 75 percent of all health care expenditures (PhRMA MedDevice, 2007). Take asthma as an example, about 5.7 percent of the US population has asthma and the prevalence of asthma has increased between 1980 and 2000 in a steady rate, but children under the age of five have seen a 2.5 increase (*Morbidity and Mortality Weekly Report*, 1998). Asthma-related mortality has increased by nearly two times since 1980, totaling more than 5000 per year and costing an estimated $11.3 billion (National Institutes of Health, 1999).

A major factor that determines the competitiveness of the industry is its long-term strategy, especially in research and development. These days, pharmaceutical research and development to meet global needs is a formidable challenge to the industry. The challenge lies in how it can generate innovative products that address health issues facing the different demographic groups in the globe, so that it can maintain not only a high-profit margin but also sustain its growth momentum in global health.

Pharmaceutical research and development

Pharmaceutical R&D is considered to be a high-stake enterprise, but the rewards can be significant. That the process of finding a drug that offers the best cure for a health condition is risky is widely recognized by the industry as well as its critics. The risk factors are the amount of time required to develop a new, effective, and safe drug, possible large initial investment, the regulatory environment, and uncertainty of the results. The amount of time required for a drug to reach the market is closely related to the lengthy drug development and approval process. Here, the model in the United States will be used as a reference point. To begin with, estimates for the time required to develop a drug range from 10 to 16 years. The major reason for the lengthy time frame is that drug development usually follows a well-regulated protocol and elaborate process (see DiMasi, May 2001, "New drug development in the United States from 1963 to 1999"). It is noted that drug discovery derives from two approaches: either the conventional method of the "happenstance approach" or a more focused, biomedical research approach (Schweitzer, 1997). Both approaches commence with basic research.

The goal of basic research is to understand the causes of a given health problem and to identify possible compounds as drug candidates. The significance of basic research has also been better recognized because it can shorten the time for drug development; for example, basic research has resulted in increasing understanding of molecular mechanisms in cancer has led to more targeted drugs (Gibbs, 17 March 2000). During the process of basic research, screening techniques are used to discover the pharmacological action and therapeutic potential (desired change in the biological system) of a particular compound. The initial tests, usually using computer modeling, aim to isolate cell cultures and tissues, enzymes, and cloned receptor sites. If a beneficial potential is detected, related compounds, each being a structural modification of the original, are tested to find out which one produces the highest level of desired therapeutic effects and least toxicity and side-effects. At this stage, thousands of substances may be synthesized and tested.

The successful chemical compound, or new molecular entity (NME), goes on to biological testing on animals. Efficacy and safety tests are then administered on animals. The goal of animal trials is to determine the toxicity level of the drug and this trial continues even when the drug candidate has advanced to other stages of clinical trial. During the preclinical stage, the drug sponsor applies for Investigational New Drug (IND) to the Food and Drug Administration (FDA). After FDA gives its authorization to proceed with the next stages of the process, clinical trials begin. During clinical evaluation Phase I, the drug is tested on healthy human volunteers. The Phase I study, which takes six to nine months with the participation of 20 to 100 healthy volunteers, aims to monitor the safety level of the drug in humans by examining how the drug is absorbed, metabolized, and excreted, along with information on the duration of its action in the human system. During clinical evaluation Phase II, controlled studies of the drug are administered to a large number of patients. The goal of the Phase II studies, which take six months to three years, is to determine efficacy, or the therapeutic effects of the drug on the patients who actually suffer from the condition that the drug is supposed to treat. During clinical evaluation Phase III, more information is collected on efficacy and safety and method of administration. Phase III study, which lasts one to four years, expands the drug trial to include an even larger pool of study subjects, usually several hundred to thousands of volunteer patients who are the intended beneficiaries of the drug. The process is usually administered by practicing physicians. The goal of Phase III studies is to examine reliability, generalizability of efficacy, and incidence of adverse reactions through a randomized, double-blind trial.

After successful completion of these trials, the drug sponsor seeks FDA marketing approval by submitting a New Drug Application (NDA), which usually contains all the information documented during the clinical evaluation process. The information includes the chemical makeup and manufacturing process, pharmacology and toxicity of the compound, human pharmacokinetics, results of the clinical trials, and proposed labeling. It can also include information documented outside the United States as well as external studies related to the drug (Lipsky and Sharp, 2001, p. 366). Based on the information in the NDA, the FDA conducts an independent review and makes its recommendations.

The length of the review was a major concern for approving life-saving drugs, especially those for HIV patients. As a result, the Prescription Drug User Fee Act of 1992 (PDUFA), which enables the FDA to charge user fees from pharmaceutical companies to expedite the review process, shortens the review process. The US Food and Drug Administration, or FDA, is mandated to review a standard drug application within 12 months and a priority application within six months. Applications for "me-too" drugs are considered standard, while those representing new innovations are priority applications. The FDA can request additional information when it needs to (Walters, 1992). The FDA makes the decision of approving or rejecting the application on the basis of the reviews, and explanations for rejection are provided. The FDA is also likely to request additional information to make the application acceptable. Tentative approval recommendation is possible, when a minor issue can be corrected before final approval. In the United States, the drug cannot be marketed without FDA approval.

Even after the drug is approved and allowed on the market, clinical evaluation Phase IV, or post-marketing studies, continues to monitor the therapeutic effects of the drug during general use of the drugs administered by physician practitioners (see US Food and Drug Administration, 2007, "Frequently asked questions"). For applications conditionally approved, FDA might request the drug sponsor to conduct

Phase IV studies in a different population or to conduct special monitoring in a high-risk population. In some cases, Phase IV studies might be conducted by the sponsor to monitor long-term effects or to support marketing purposes. Phase IV studies are important to confirm reliability, that is, efficacy of the drug in diverse populations. In this process, FDA's reporting system, Medwatch, continues to track serious adverse events. After the drug is approved, the manufacturer is required to report side-effects for the first three years after approval, especially serious and unexpected adverse reactions (see Lipsky and Sharp, 2001).

The drug development and approval process in the United States is regarded as the most comprehensive and is widely used as a model by other countries that have the regulatory capacity. Overall, the goal of the FDA approval process is to meet safety, efficacy, and quality standards (US Food and Drug Administration, 2008, "FDA").

Increasingly, the decision process leading to the development of a new idea into a drug is more than scientific consideration, however. It was noted that these days, it is a collective company decision involving more than biologists or chemists. The decision often involves clinicians, the manufacturing group, and marketing experts. After an idea is generated and assessed by the scientific unit of a company, a project is proposed. The criteria used to assess the project are chemical and biological feasibility, clinical feasibility, approximate estimates of the clinical cost of the project, estimates of development cost, and prospects of FDA approval. The key concerns are usually costs and expected returns, the likelihood of FDA approval, resource constraints within the company, competition, liability concerns. The liability concern is not insignificant. An estimate showed that out of 85,694 different federal product liability cases filed between 1974 and 1986, 13.5 percent were about pharmaceuticals and health products, regulatory restrictions and changes affecting cost estimates or FDA approval (The Parliamentary Office of Science and Technology, June 2005).

Other factors entering into the decision on inventing a new drug include: needs assessment of the socioeconomic characteristics of patients, potential of health insurance coverage, for example, Medicare, HMOs or other third-party payers. The ability of the patients to pay is an important consideration for large pharmaceutical companies, which makes the pharmaceutical producers more likely to address the needs of the populations in the developed world. It was pointed out that this also explains why a large percentage of new pharmaceutical R&D has been devoted to the diseases of organ systems affecting older Americans (Pharmaceutical Manufacturers Association, 1989). On the other hand, what explains the industry's behaviour is the initial large investment in developing a drug. It has been noted that the amount of investment required for inventing a new drug has been increasing. The estimates of costs vary and estimates of developing a drug include $200 million, $370.7 million, $640 million, or $802 million (see the Parliamentary Office of Science and Technology, June 2005; see also DiMasi, Hansen and Grabowski, 2003; Pharmaceutical Research and Manufacturers Association, 2003).

Among these estimates, the most cited figure derives from a study conducted by the Tufts Center for the Study of Drug Development (2007). They argued that the cost of developing a drug could reach $802 million (ibid.). In comparison, another study in 2006 showed that the average cost of developing a new biotechnology product is about $1.2 billion (ibid.).

A study by the consulting firm Bain & Company reported that the cost of discovering, developing, and launching (which factored in marketing and other business expenses) a new drug (along with the prospective drugs that fail) rose over a five-year period to nearly $1.7 billion in 2003 (Bain & Co. press release, 8 December 2003). These high estimates were refuted by consumer advocacy groups, however. Public Citizen, a vocal critic of the pharmaceutical industry, suggests that the actual cost is under $200 million, and about 29 percent of the cost is spent on FDA-required clinical trials (Public Citizen, 2002a, "Pharmaceuticals rank as most profitable industry, again"). The rate of increase of pharmaceutical R&D is also large over the years. In one estimate, between 1995 and 1999 R&D cost per new drug was only 186.6 million (fda.gov/cder/rdmt/pstable.htm) (Anslem Ministries, 2007). And in 1990, the cost was US$259 million (Schweitzer, 1997). In another estimate, the increase was 55 percent for the five years from 1995 to 2000 (Bain & Company press release (December 8, 2003).

It is not clear on what basis these estimates are generated. They might include a wide range of things. For example, they might include the training and education of personnel involved in basic research, clinical trials, the manufacturing process consisting of fixed-capital investment for pharmaceutical manufacturing equipment and facilities, in addition to the working capital required to pay salaries, buying raw materials and payments for other items require direct cash expenditure. Some estimates might include the handling of depreciation, interest, profits, and income taxes. And it is believed that these estimates also contain opportunity cost, which is a major controversy in global pharmaceutical access issues.

The parties who fund pharmaceutical R&D include government, industry and medical charities. Although pharmaceutical companies are mainly responsible for bringing an innovative idea to a final product, participation from other sectors cannot be ignored (the Parliamentary Office of Science and Technology, June 2005). One study pointed out that most of the important new drugs introduced by the industry in the past 40 years were developed with some contribution from the public sector. In 1990s, in the United States, the federal government and industry each funded about 45 percent, or 9.9 billion of health R&D (Schweitzer, 1997). About 62 percent of National Institute of Health (NIH) funding and 53 percent of all federal health R&D funding went to colleges and universities (Schweitzer, 1997). It is believed that federal funding was instrumental in the discovery of new biomedical knowledge in recombinant DNA processes, monoclonal antibodies, and gene synthesis and splicing, which has played an increasingly important role in new drug discovery (US Congress OTA, 1993). It was pointed out that only five out of the 21 most influential drugs introduced between 1965 and 1992 were developed entirely by the private sector (Congressional Budget Office of Research and Development in the Pharmaceutical Industry," October 2006). Although the percentage of average R&D investment in relation to overall revenues remains a point of speculation and the numbers can vary widely depending on the source of the data, it is believed that on average, the pharmaceutical sector spends around 14 to 16 percent of its revenues on R&D (Schweitzer, 1997; see also Families USA (September 2005) "The Choice: Health Care for People or Drug Industry Profits").

In addition to mounting criticism from outsiders, what aggravates the industry's worries about the financial returns of the initial investment is the increasingly stringent regulatory environment. Due to their health impact and economic and political implications, the regulatory environment for pharmaceuticals has become more restricting and restrictions have become the center of debate among the stakeholders due to their political and economic implications. In all cases, the major authority for regulating pharmaceuticals is vested in governments. And the model of regulation in the United States is often regarded in the world as the normative standard. In the United States, the Food and Drug Administration is the body that regulates pharmaceuticals and they also enforce standards set by the United States Pharmacopoeia (Wikipedia, 2007b, "Pharmacology"). The Food and Drug Administration (FDA), in charge of creating guidelines for the approval and use of drugs, requires the drug sponsor to fulfill the criteria of efficacy and safety.

These criteria are upheld, presumably after an extensive clinical trial process (Nagle and Nagle, 2005). The safety and effectiveness of prescription drugs is generally regulated by the US Federal Prescription Drug Marketing agency.

In the European Union, the source of one-third of new drugs in the world, pharmaceutical regulation is enforced through a decentralized framework, EMEA (European Medicines Agency), which was known as The European Agency for the Evaluation of Medicinal Products prior to 2004. Its major functions are to enforce standards set by the *European Pharmacopoeia* to evaluate medicinal products. Funded by the European Union and the pharmaceutical industry, as well as by indirect subsidy from member states, EMEA was set up in 1995 as a collective undertaking of the EU to harmonize (but not to replace) the regulatory bodies in individual EU states. Its goal is to improve efficiency and savings for drug companies and eliminate trade barriers across EU states. Drawing on resources of National Competent Authorities (NCAs) of EU member states, EMEA evaluates medicinal products for human and veterinary use, such as biologics/TEPs and herbal medicinal products. The major responsibilities of EMEA are to protect and promote human and animal health, specifically through the coordination of the evaluation and monitoring of centrally authorized products and national referrals, to develop technical guidance and provide scientific advice to sponsors (Wikipedia, 2007a, "European Medicines Agency").

In Japan, the regulatory body is the Pharmaceuticals and Medical Devices Agency (PMDA), one of the 11 bureaus of the Ministry of Health, Labor and Welfare. Based on the Pharmaceuticals and Medical Devices Agency Law in December 2002, the PMDA was established in April 2004 and consists of 13 departments and one office (Japan Pharmaceutical Manufactures Association, 2006, "Pharmaceutical administration and regulations in Japan"). In general, the role of the PMDA is to provide consultations concerning the clinical trials of new drugs and medical devices, and to conduct approval reviews and surveys of the reliability of application data. Drug-related issues are handled by several offices. The Office of New Drug I provides clinical trial notifications and information about adverse drug reactions and conducts the reviews required for approval, re-examinations and re-evaluation of new anti-malignant neoplasm drugs, antibacterial agents, anti-HIV agents and related drugs. The Office of New Drug II confirms clinical trial notifications and adverse drug reactions and conducts the reviews required for approval, re-examinations and re-evaluation of new cardiovascular drugs, urological and anal drugs, reproductive system drugs, metabolic disease drugs (combination drugs only), in vivo diagnostics, and radiopharmaceuticals. The Office of New Drug III confirms clinical trial notifications and adverse drug reactions and conducts the reviews required for approval, re-examinations and re-evaluation of new gastrointestinal drugs, metabolic disease drugs (other than combination drugs), hormone products, dermatologic agents, central nervous system drugs, peripheral nervous system drugs, sensory organ drugs, respiratory tract drugs, anti-allergy drugs and narcotics. The Office of Biologics confirms clinical trial notifications and adverse drug reactions of biological products and cell- and tissue-derived drugs and medical devices, and performs the reviews required for approval, re-examination or re-evaluation. Reviews required for approval of generic biological products are also undertaken. The Office of OTC and Generics conducts the reviews required for the approval, export certification, and quality re-evaluations of generic prescription drugs, non-prescription drugs, quasi-drugs, and cosmetics. The Office of Compliance and Standards reviews the documentation included with applications for approval, re-examination, or re-evaluation of drugs and medical devices to assure that the data complies with GLP (Good Lab Practice), GCP (Good Clinical Practice), and GPMSP (Good Post-Marketing Surveillance Process) both ethically and scientifically to determine if the documents have been prepared appropriately and accurately, based on the study results in accordance with the Criteria for Reliability of Application Data. Cooperating with the Ministry of Health, Labor and Welfare, the Office of Safety undertakes primary collection and compilation of information related to the quality, efficacy and safety of drugs and medical devices, and conducts scientific analysis and examination of collected information. It also undertakes consultations and information dissemination work. The Pharmaceutical Affairs and Food Sanitation Council (PAFSC) serves as an advisory body to the Ministry of Health, Labor and Welfare, and reviews and discusses important pharmaceutical and food sanitation-related matters.

In general, there are four targets or "hurdles" of regulation: safety, efficacy, quality, and cost-effectiveness. In addition, regulation of pharmaceuticals can be divided into three categories: regulating patients' use, influencing doctors' prescription patterns, and controlling industry's drug development and pricing (see Maynard and Bloor, 1997). The pharmaceutical sector is not the only target of government regulation.

The requirement for efficacy, safety, and increasingly cost-effectiveness, is the norm for regulation. Efficacy and safety standards require that the experimental conditions produce evidence of effectiveness and acceptable levels of side-effect/toxicity profiles. Efficacy, the focus of marketing strategies, is determined by the results of clinical trials (Maynard and Bloor, 2003).

Since the public outrage against the FDA on the handling of Vioxx recall, the FDA has taken a cautious approach to drug approvals. The approval of Trexima, a joint project between Pozen and GSK, was a relevant case in point. In 2005, after the FDA rejected the application of MT100, a pain killer, an NDA application was filed to the FDA for Trexima, a migraine treatment combining sumatriptan and naproxen sodium, but it was not approved until two years later. Trexima is the first product designed to treat multiple mechanisms of migraine: inflammation and vasodilation. On 12 December 2006, the FDA requested additional data, citing that the response to FDA's earlier inquiry was insufficient. The FDA decision immediately led to a 10 percent decrease in Pozen's stock value on the capital market (FierceBiotech, 12 December 2006, "Pozen shares sink on new demand for data"). In January 2007, Pozen and GSK responded to the FDA's first approval letter, submitting additional safety data from clinical trials, data from GSK's database, and additional in-vitro preclinical data. On 8 June 2007, the FDA sent the first approval letter of the drug with a request for additional safety data (FierceBiotech, 8 June 2007a, "FDA decision on Trexima may trigger new studies"). On 2 August 2007, GSK announced a delay of the drug because of the need to examine genotoxicity seen in a preclinical study. Prior to the second approval, the FDA had requested that Pozen further address the Agency's concern about the detection of genotoxicity in the combination of naproxen sodium and sumatriptan from one preclinical in-vitro chromosomal aberration study, a standard genotoxicity test, and its implications. Yet the toxicity was not detected in the other three standard genotoxicity studies (Ames test, mouse lymphoma TK assay, in-vivo mouse micronucleus assay) for the combination. Even after the second approval, the companies had to agree to conduct a prospective study to evaluate the effects on blood pressure during chronic, intermittent treatment (FierceBiotech, 2 August 2007d, "Press release: FDA issues second approvable letter for Pozen, Inc. and GlaxoSmithKline's Trexima: Approval delayed").

A similar safety-first approach was taken by the FDA in the handling of a number of new drug applications. For example, FDA's questions led to the withdrawal of the application of a cancer therapy by GPC Biotech AG of Germany. In another case, the FDA asked for the delay of a proposed cure for male erectile dysfunction (ED) (see Fiercebiotech 30 August 2007e, "Safety concern force delay for Phase III ED trial").

The FDA's concerns about the hormone-refractory prostate cancer drug Satraplatin (or Orplatna), a member of the platinum family of compounds, were mainly about efficacy and safety (see FierceBiotech, July 2007b, "Press release: FDA needs more data on GPC Biotech cancer drug"). Platinum-based drugs are widely used in chemotherapy for different types of cancer, but they require intravenous administration. Satraplatin is an oral compound that can be administered by the patients themselves. On efficacy, the FDA Oncologic Drugs Advisory Committee (ODAC) requested additional patient survival data before the drug could be considered for approval by the FDA. That is, the FDA wanted to know if the subjects in the experimental trial had lived longer than having the placebo. The length of survival was 11.1 weeks in the experimental condition compared to 9.7 weeks in the placebo condition. The interim data had not shown significant difference between these two conditions in survival rates. The FDA has also raised issues with the pain measurements in the study (FierceBiotech (25 July 2007c) "GPC cancer drug voted down by FDA committee"; see also Reed, 20 July 2007, "Spectrum plunges on potential drug delay").

A similar safety concern voiced by the FDA led to Palatin Technologies, Inc. and King Pharmaceuticals to delay plans for the initiation of Phase III clinical trials with bremelanotide, a first in the class of melanocortin agonist drug candidates for the treatment of male erectile dysfunction. The FDA seriously questioned the benefit/risk ratio in support of the progression of the proposed program into Phase III studies for ED. After Phase I and II studies, the FDA questioned the overall efficacy results and the clinical benefit of this product in both the general and diabetic ED populations. The FDA's major concern was the possibility of elevated blood pressure in patients. Despite the fact that the FDA was not supportive of the proposed Phase 3 studies for ED with bremelanotide, it was open to proposals about using the drug as a second-line therapy in patients who do not respond to current first-line drugs, the approved PDE-5 inhibitors.

The comment by Richard Miller, the CEO of Pharmacyclics, on GPC's decision to withdraw its application for Satraplatin, a cancer therapy, reflects the trend in pharmaceutical regulation by the FDA of taking a cautious approach in enforcing drug approvals for new drugs for cancer and other major illnesses. Miller commented in the *Wall Street Journal* that the FDA has been making life too difficult for developers. According to him, only one therapy achieved accelerated approval in 2006 and none had made it through that process by 1 August 2007 (*Wall Street Journal*, 1 August 2007). This trend in the global framework is likely to continue because the monitoring framework of the FDA is usually emulated by the regulatory bodies of most other countries, such as EU members, Japan, and China.

This regulatory trend for better safety and efficacy was not new, however. Its momentum was jump-started by the 1962 amendments to the Federal Food, Drug and Cosmetic Act, which requires pharmaceutical companies to show drug effectiveness, in addition to the safety standard. Despite the complaint that this regulation had doubled the cost of new drugs, the industry had gained from ensuring quality control (see Grabowski and Vernon, 1990, for discussion of the cost of the 1962 regulation). The exception is that the FDA's new regulation allows earlier access to investigational drugs by patients with life-threatening or serious diseases.

Increasingly, in addition to safety and efficacy, price controls have become the focus of attention of the regulators and their significance is also likely to be elevated on the policy agenda due to the public's increasing demand for price control. The public's concern for pricing is felt by the industry too. An industry source believed that the largest challenge facing the industry is outsiders' perception of "high-prices," that the drugs are not worth paying (Interview with Adam Clark, 16 November 2007, "Commentary on supply chain management").

Some have argued against price controls and the most cited argument is the possible impact of price controls on pharmaceutical R&D. For example Lichtenberg reported that 38 percent of the 864 new chemical entities would have been lost in the global economy from 1982 to 2001 if the US government had implemented the proposed price control regime in 1980 (Lichtenberg, 2003; see also Giaccotto, Santerre, and Vernon, April 2005). Many are convinced that price control might discourage innovation and encourage imitation (US Congress Office of Technology Assessment, 1993).

In actuality, the regulation of price controls is already in place in most of the countries. Despite the lack of the appearance of price controls in the United States, price controls in a subtle form has been exercised through various mechanisms in the United States. The 1984 Hatch-Waxman Act allowing a larger freedom for generic regulation already creates a market environment for price competition. Representative Henry A. Waxman has also advocated for price controls through government controls or market forces (Blankenau, 1993). In practice, price controls in the United States are already carried out through collective bargaining leverage by the government's health programs, such as Medicare. In addition, the third-party payers have exercised control over pharmaceutical prices by introducing some form of comparative/competitive mechanisms (Schweitzer, 1997). For example, insurers provide different health plans about cost-sharing for services and prescriptions. The insurers can also use formularies, a limited range of selectors within a therapeutic class. Furthermore, they can resort to drug utilization review (DUR), a screening process for drugs based on a set of criteria, as a reference. Or the insurers can use a "managed care" approach (the mode by Health Maintenance Organizations and Preferred Provider Organizations) by bargaining for discounts for a bulk purchase. In fact, the insurers have played an increasing role in containing health care cost since the 1980s in the United States (Schweitzer, 1997). Other US mechanisms of price control include tiered pricing when pharmaceutical retailers receive substantial price discounts from the prices paid by nonaffiliated pharmacies and distributors. Tiered pricing is an application of the economic theory that price setting is inversely related to demand elasticity for a seller to maximize its profits. Demand is high for the pharmaceutical retailers so they can bargain for lower prices (Schweitzer, 1997). US patients have also exercised their options in choosing affordable medicine. For example, it was noted that only one-third of Americans with a health condition seek professional help. The rest of them either ignore it, use over-the-counter medicine (OTC), or complementary medicine. The use of complementary medicine has increased among Americans, as evidenced in a study published in the *Journal of the American Medical Association* (Eisenberg, Davis, Ettner, Appel, Wilkey, Van Rompay and Kessler, 2001). On OTC, it was predicted that the OTC market has been growing since 1992, with sales of $11.5 billion to $28 billion by 2010 (Industry Surveys, 1993). Use of mail order to obtain less expensive drugs has also doubled between 1992 and 1997 (Schweitzer, 1997).

Outside the United States, price controls are often practiced in blatant forms. In Europe, price controls are exercised on the demand and supply side. On the users' end, demand for drugs is influenced by user charges. Governments in EU countries also influence the physicians' prescribing behavior by providing feedback to their prescribing behavior, costs, and on their generic prescribing rates. Increasingly, governments also provide formularies, clinical guidelines, and financial incentives as a way to control the volume demand (Maynard and Bloor, 2003). This can also be seen as an indirect way of controlling pricing. On the supply side, most European governments are in a dominant position to bargain for drug discounts because most of them provide universal health care and they are able to negotiate for bulk purchase.

In some countries, such as Australia, regulators' focus on cost-effectiveness as a way to control prices on the supply side.

Most EU countries use therapeutic comparators and compare prices across EU markets (Ibid.). In Denmark, Greece, Finland, Ireland, Italy, the Netherlands, Portugal, and Sweden, regulators set ceiling prices for drugs on the basis of the prices of the same products in neighboring countries. In Belgium, France, and Italy, the price comparators are relative cost, prices in other EU countries, and economic weight in the total of the national economy. In Austria, France, and Spain, price considerations include volume-cost and other rebate schemes. In Spain and the United Kingdom, drug prices are determined to ensure that the rates for profit return are within a limited range.

Most EU countries use reference pricing and reimburse the average price within a therapeutic category to reduce price variation across markets. The effectiveness of this intervention is uncertain. Some believe that this intervention has decreased the role of market competition as a way of controlling price and that it may induce inflation in generic prices and reduced competition, as the prices are moving toward similar levels. It is pointed out that in Germany, Australia, the Netherlands, New Zealand, Sweden, Denmark, and Norway, which have practiced reference pricing for more than a decade, only short-term savings have been achieved (Maynard and Bloor, 2003; see also Ioannides-Demos, Ibrahim and McNeil, 2002). It was pointed out that price controls need to be exercised on both ends. That is, there needs the market competition, referencing, and profit control on the supply side and volume control on the demand side. In the United Kingdom, prices are regulated through a profit scheme. The U.K. Pharmaceutical Price Regulation Scheme (PPRS) allows pharmaceutical companies to set prices according to a band of profits. The pharmaceutical companies are free to set pharmaceutical prices as long as the profits return are in the range of 17 to 21 percent on historical capital, with 25 percent variation on either end of the distribution. If profit returns exceed this range, the company has to reimburse the National Health Service (NHS) or reduce profit range the following year. Conversely, if the profits are lower, the company can raise the drug prices. The criticism of this scheme is that this intervention is not efficient because it reduces costs and increases the rate of return (Maynard and Bloor, 2003; Maynard and Bloor, 1997, "Regulating the Pharmaceutical Industry").

The other element of control being tried experimentally by some industrialized countries is cost-effectiveness. As mentioned earlier, cost-effectiveness assessment has been used strategically by the public sector to control pharmaceutical prices. Australia's Pharmacy Benefits Scheme (PBS) and the UK's National Institute of Clinical Excellence (NICE) require companies to submit evidence of the cost-effectiveness (see Australia Government Department of Health and Aging, 2008; see also Maynard and Bloor, 1997, pp. 200–1). Similar measures have been considered or used in Finland, Portugal, the Netherlands, France, Spain, and Sweden. Outside Europe, Canada has also used a similar cost-effectiveness mechanism. Cost-effectiveness, leading to the volume control of inefficient drugs and enhanced health levels, can be a possible, but not necessarily the ultimate tool for price controls (Maynard and Bloor, 2003).

Outside Europe, most other countries have price control mechanisms. In China, price controls are determined by the government, which sets the prices for essential drugs by providing formularies for reimbursement (Wang, Zhang and Wang, 2007).

Beyond price controls, the other risk factor of pharmaceutical development is the uncertainty of results. Estimates vary about the chances of success in drug development. The pharmaceutical research and manufacturers of America, the PhRMA, estimates that only one out of every 10,000 potential medicines investigated by America's research-based pharmaceutical companies makes it through the research and development pipeline and is approved for patient use by the US FDA (The pharmaceutical research and manufacturers of America, 2007). Another estimate showed that only around one in 60,000 compounds tested by pharmaceutical laboratories would become "highly successful" when success was defined as the drug's global sale performance in excess of $100 million per year (Redwood, 1993). These statistics have been widely used to counter the "high-profitability" criticism voiced by the public. In another estimate, it was believed that only around three out of ten drugs brought to market were able to cover the developing costs after taxes because of the many other, unsuccessful, attempts. It was also argued that about 55 percent of industry profits come from around 10 percent of the drugs developed (Sherer, 1993).

Despite the risk factors, the rewards for pharmaceutical development are higher than in other businesses. This "winners-take-it-all" phenomenon has also provided ample ammunition for critics of the pharmaceutical sectors, who believe the "public-good" nature of medicine. Estimates of pharmaceutical profits vary because it is a major point of contention between the pharmaceutical companies and their critics. It is widely believed that the value of the sector has been increasing since the 1980s and the pharmaceutical industry is one of the most profitable businesses today (see the conclusion by the Parliamentary Office of Science and Technology, June 2005). A study by the United States Congressional Office of Technological Assessment (OTA) showed that between 1981 to 1983, the sector made about 14.3 percent profit over a drug's life cycle, higher than the normal 10 percent rate of return. When compared to other industries facing similar risks, the sector was said to earn a profit 2 to 3 percent higher than those sectors (US Congress Office of Technology Assessment, 1993). A recent estimate by *Fortune Magazine* showed that the profit margin for the sector was 15.7 percent in 2006, higher than most other businesses (US Congressional Budget Office, 17 April 2006). The "high-profitability" scenario would not be a problem if it fully satisfied the demands of all populations in the global community. The fact that there is a serious problem that the pharmaceutical problem has not bridged the gaps between supply and demand/need subjects the pharmaceutical industry to increasing criticism.

Global demand for pharmaceuticals

Global demand is determined by such factors as purchasing power, health system effectiveness, the price of alternatives, and cultural and population preferences, while need is determined by professional health assessment (see a similar idea in Schweitzer, 1997).

There are some common denominators underlying cross-country needs for pharmaceuticals, but there are also country-unique factors. The common denominator is the need for effective and affordable medicines to treat diseases and illnesses prevalent in a given country context. The differences lie in a country's ability to meet this need. The ability to meet with the need is determined by a wide range of factors, such as financing, regulation, pharmaceutical infrastructure, and the bargaining position of a government in the international system and/or its geopolitical importance.

In general, the global need for effective pharmaceuticals has been increasing because of the increase of diseases and diversification of disease profiles in both developed and developing countries. As mentioned earlier, there is a large difference in disease profiles between developed and developing countries and the largest challenges in demand are "access" and "equity." Access is a problem due to trade-related barriers. It was pointed out that despite an enormous global supply of pharmaceuticals, drugs are widely available in only 28 percent of countries. There are many two-way barriers for the poor in developing countries to access medicine. Most developing countries are net importers of pharmaceutical products. Many of these countries impose tariffs and non-tariff barriers (NTBs) on finished drugs, active pharmaceutical ingredients (APIs), and excipients (inactive substances that contain the active ingredients). Tariffs and non-tariff barriers contribute to the increase of pharmaceutical costs (Global Health Council, 30 October 2007, "Access to life saving medicines for the world's poorest: Tariff and non-tariff barriers").

The other barrier is "asymmetry," that is, the imbalance between supply and need. The need for pharmaceuticals in developing countries, which is especially urgent because of the large disease burden, has never been fulfilled. For a long time, pharmaceutical products have been produced primarily to meet the needs of developed countries. A study shows that most of the new drugs registered between 1975 and 1999 with the US and EU regulatory bodies target diseases of developed societies, such as cancer (8 percent), diseases of the central nervous system (15.1 percent), cardiovascular disease (12.8 percent), and non-infectious respiratory conditions (6.4 percent). Another survey by the Association of the British Pharmaceutical Industry (ABPI) in 2001 showed that these diseases also form the main focus of drug companies' research programs (The Parliamentary Office of Science and Technology, June 2005). Most of the drugs in the R&D pipelines of the top pharmaceutical companies showed a similar trend (FierceBiotech, 28 November 2007f, "The top 15 R&D budgets"). One estimate showed that only 10 percent of the world's medical research is devoted to conditions that account for 90 percent of the global disease burden, this is known as the 10/90 gap. The drugs for diseases prevalent in the developing world, such as TB, malaria, HIV/ AIDS, and "neglected diseases" (such as river blindness) are lacking, have serious side-effects, or encounter resistance (The Parliamentary Office of Science and Technology, June 2005). It was noted that few new drugs specifically treat diseases confined to developing countries. Prior to the mushrooming of global health partnerships for neglected diseases in early 2000s, one estimate showed that only 0.3 percent of all new drugs were targeted at malaria. And of 1393 chemical entities taken to market between 1975 and 1999, only 16 were for neglected diseases, malaria, and TB. It also showed that global pharmas were 13 times more likely to develop drugs to treat the central nervous system than other drugs for those diseases accounting for a third of the worldwide disease burden (The Parliamentary Office of Science and Technology, June 2005; see also Trouiller, Olliaro, Torreele, Orbinski, Laing and Ford 2002, p. 2189).

The other related issue with asymmetry is that there is not enough incentives to increase supply to meet the needs of neglected diseases (i.e., NTDs) that are treatable. According to World Health Organization, a large group of the NTDs – mainly helminthic infections – have effective, inexpensive drugs for their prevention and control. For example, treatment is available for leprosy, yaws, and trachoma. Large-scale and regular treatment is also possible for filariasis, onchocerciasis, schistosomiasis, and soil-transmitted nematode infections (World Health Organization, 2007a, "Control of neglected tropical diseases").

It is important to note that the access and equity issues are not unique to developing countries. These are also major concerns in the United States, where there is also an asymmetry between supply and need and between supply and demand. And this explains the increasing momentum of the "affordable medicine" mass movement occurring in the United States. Groups like the Public Citizen have refuted the pharmas' claim that they need to maintain profit incentives for pharmaceutical research. Public Citizen cites a study indicating that cutting drug prices by 40 percent for people with Medicare would have a minimal effect on profits due to increased demand, but would significantly improve access and equity (Public Citizen, 26 June 2002b, "Would lower prescription drug prices curb drug company research & revelopment?").

Criticism about the asymmetry between supply and need has sharpened globally. The recent confrontation between Thailand and a large global pharmaceutical company was just one of the many cases contested. In November 2006, Thailand issued a compulsory license to import and produce generic versions of the anti-AIDS drug Efavirenz because Thailand wanted more patients to be treated at a lower price. In late January 2007, the Thai Health Ministry announced the compulsory licensing of Kaletra, an advanced anti-AIDS drug, and Plavix, a treatment for heart disease, by invoking Article 51 of the 1992 Thai Patent Law to import or produce a generic version of the two drugs. The WHO director general, Dr Margaret Chan, who intended to generate a win-win solution, encouraged a dialogue and pointed out that the large pharmas should be part of the solution. Dr Chan's comment that there needs to be a balance between seeking affordable medicines and the need for incentives for innovation accurately illustrates the crux of the problem. Some NGOs pointed out that the discounted prices made by Abbott for Kaletra, $2200 a year, was still a 300 percent profit margin and that this price tag is still beyond the reach of most of the poor, needy patients in developing countries (Martin, 13 February 2007).

This incident between the Thai government and Abbott shows that there needs to be a major rethinking by the multinational pharmaceutical companies about their business strategy to address the challenge of the asymmetry in the global supply and demand/need chain. Given this challenge, the goal of the book is to present a different strategy for global pharmaceutical stakeholders by exploring a global health partnership model between the large pharmas and the countries that make up the BRICA countries.

In pursuing this goal, the following chapters will provide an analysis that leads to a presumable, a win-win solution. Chapter 2 analyzes the history, development, positions, and challenges of large multinational pharmaceutical companies, mainly those based in the developed countries. Chapter 3 examines the competitive positions of the pharmaceutical stakeholders in Brazil, Russia, India, China, and Africa. Chapter 4 proposes a "planting" strategy for global pharmaceutical stakeholders in a collaborative partnership. A planting strategy aims for a sustainable solution. In the end, when the business of global health becomes the business of every stakeholder, everyone gains.

2
The Modern Pharmaceutical Industry: History, Current Position and Challenges

The development of modern medicine experienced a major leap forward in the nineteenth century because of advances in science and, since then, the evolution of scientific knowledge has pushed forward the growth of the modern pharmaceutical industry (Gribbin and Hook, 2004). The progress in human understanding of bacteriology and related subjects had replaced traditional knowledge of epidemiology and chemistry (Wikipedia, 2007a, "History of medicine"). The hygiene theory advocated by Ignaz Semmelweis (1818–1865) in 1847 paved the way for the germ theory of disease. The germ theory was put into practice later when, in 1865, British surgeon Joseph Lister discovered the principles of antisepsis (ibid.). The discoveries made by Louis Pasteur that pinpointed microorganisms as a major cause of diseases gave birth to a major conceptual breakthrough in the making of therapeutics. Against this background, Pasteur's invention of a vaccine against rabies in 1880 led to the success of other vaccine development (see Seppa, 18 and 25 December 1999). Pasteur's experiments, which confirmed germ theory, had important implications for using scientific method in the making of medicine. This method was articulated in Pasteur's book, *An Introduction to the Study of Experimental Medicine* in 1865. Pasteur and Robert Koch, who discovered tubercle bacillus in 1882, cholera bacillus in 1883, and Koch's postulates, founded bacteriology (Wikipedia, 2007a). These discoveries have paved the foundation for most modern pharmaceutical inventions.

In addition, genetic knowledge was advanced by Charles Darwin's publication of *The Origin of Species* in 1859 and Gregor Mendel's publication of a book in 1865 on Mendel's laws. Mendel's publication earned him the reputation of being the father of genetics (Gribbin and Hook, 2004; see also Darwin, 2003). Health sciences experienced another leap forward with discovery of the structure of DNA through the use of different models by Watson and Crick in 1953. These combined discoveries made a major contribution to the discipline of molecular biology and modern genetics (Watson, 2001). One of the most important contributions is that they provided a methodical, systematic framework for drug discovery.

On the whole, discoveries in bacteriology, genetics, and biochemistry have greatly advanced the use of scientific method in producing pharmacological products.

Drug development

A drug is defined as "a *chemical* substance used in the treatment, cure, prevention, or diagnosis of disease or used to otherwise enhance physical or mental well-being" (Dictionary.com Unabridged, v 1.1, 2007). The pharmaceuticals are synonymous with drugs, both of which denote the substances that have *medicinal* properties. Drug use varies with the nature of the diseases and the desired effects (The American Heritage Science Dictionary, 2007). The difference between drugs and hormones is that hormones are synthesized in the body while drugs are introduced into the body from outside.

Drug development requires some understanding of pharmacology. Pharmacology studies the interaction of drugs with living organisms to induce a change in function (Rang, 2006). Pharmacology entails the study of drug composition and properties, interactions, toxicology, therapy, and medical applications and antipathogenic capabilities (Wikipedia, 2007c, "Pharmacology"). Drug making also requires understanding both the pharmacokinetic properties of a drug in terms of absorption channels, distribution, metabolism/breakdown process, and excretion, and pharmacodynamics, such as knowledge of the therapeutic index (the chemical's toxic effect on the body) (ibid.). This knowledge dictates the choice of analogues as drug candidates. After a candidate drug is chosen, drug companies then launch a process of drug development to determine safety, stability, efficacy, and forms of dispensing (Newton, Thorpe and Otter, 2004).

The epistemological interaction between pharmacology and other disciplines has also broadened the knowledge of drug making. The subdisciplines of pharmacology include *clinical pharmacology*, the understanding of the medication effects on humans; *neuropharmacology* and *psychopharmacology*, the study of the effects of medication on behavior and nervous system functioning; *pharmacogenetics*, the science of clinical testing of genetic variation giving rise to differential response to drugs; *pharmacogenomics*, the use of genomic technologies for new drug discovery and further characterization of older drugs; *pharmacoepidemiology*, the study of the effects of drugs at the population level; *toxicology*, the study of the effects of poisons; *posology*, the understanding of the dosing of medicines; and *pharmacognosy*, the science of the making of medicines from plants.

The pathway for drug development has undergone many changes since the nineteenth century but the goal has always been the same. That is, the drug development process aims to enhance efficacy (through the control of dosing and formulation) and safety (by controlling toxic levels and side-effects) (*Nature* Reviews Drug Discovery, July, 2006, "Editorial: Keeping sight of the goal"; see also Wikipedia, 2007b, "Pharmaceutical companies").

The inspiration for drug discovery relies either on knowledge of traditional ideas or "accidental" types of discoveries. The drug makers can isolate the active ingredient from traditional remedies or totally rely on chance for discovering the therapeutic effects of a drug (Schweitzer, 2006). The latter approach explains why only one out of 5000 potential candidate drugs will ever reach the open market (Newton, Thorpe and Otter, 2004). For example, the discovery of Viagra was fortuitous in the beginning stage of the process. In the late 1980s, some at Pfizer's laboratories in Sandwich, England, generated a hypothesis about the possible utility of a blocker against an enzyme called PDE5 to expand blood vessels and treat angina (Osterloh, June 2007). Later in the 1990s, following up on this hypothesis, a powerful and selective inhibitor of PDE5, known at the time as UK-92480, was developed. Early tests showed it had a moderate effect on the blood vessels of healthy volunteers, but its efficacy was short and it generated the side-effect of muscle aches. Coincidentally, in one of the studies, the drug had also generated the side-effect of increased erections for some subjects who received the treatment. While the scientists continued to pursue the possibility of using UK-92480 in combination with nitrates to treat angina, positive results for the drugs' potential in treating erectile dysfunction were being reported from the volunteers. Later, knowledge of the biochemical pathway related to erectile dysfunction directed drug development in a direction that aimed at amplifying the effects of the drug on the penal blood vessels. Clinical trials, which included those subjects with diabetes, helped further determine dosing levels to assure efficacy and safety. The 1997 application for approval of Viagra resulted from an accidental discovery that led to eight years of drug research and four years of pilot studies.

Beyond the serendipity-based approach, increasingly drug development has benefited from the advancement of molecular biology and biochemistry (Larson, 2005). Molecular analysis of the biochemical processes and properties of cells and their functions has revolutionized the pharmaceutical industry. Modern biotechnology makes it possible to understand the metabolic pathways causing a disease. Understanding the functions of receptors renders it possible to design chemicals that manipulate the metabolic pathways so that they achieve a desired effect on cell-surface receptors that could affect cell functions (Wikipedia, 2007b).

The history of large pharmaceutical companies

Scientific breakthroughs and legislative initiatives have paved the way for large, modern pharmaceutical companies. The discovery of effective cures, such as insulin and penicillin in the 1920s and 1930s, was not only instrumental in improving population health but has also created a unique economic sector. The large pharmaceutical companies have mainly originated from Switzerland, Germany, Italy, the United Kingdom, and the United States (Nelson, 1983). Legislative improvements that facilitate the growth of the industry include quality and safety control, appropriate labeling, and separation of prescription from nonprescription drugs. The advances in pharmaceutical-related sciences, such as in molecular biology, led to fruitful results in the 1950s and 1960s, which were considered the beginning of the gilded age in drug discovery. A large number of effective pharmaceuticals were invented and produced. These include the invention of the first oral contraceptives; blood-pressure drugs and heart medications; and psychiatric medications (MAO Inhibitors), chlorpromazine (Thorazine), Haldol (Haloperidol), the tranquilizers, and Valium (diazepam) (Wikipedia, 2007b). In the 1970s, cancer treatment became a major focus of drug development (ibid.).

The need for regulatory oversight over pharmaceutical safety heightened in the 1960s because of the occurrence of certain life-threatening incidents. The most serious was the use of Thalidomide, which was causing birth defects among many infants. In the 1970s, the industry began to expand and was on its way to becoming a mega-industry. In the mid-1980s, horizontal and vertical integration led to the emergence of large multinational pharmaceutical companies. Strategic partnerships were formed between large pharmaceutical companies and small biotechnology firms. Mergers and corporate buyouts among competitors also expedited this trend.

The high-growth scenario experienced a change in the 1980s. Increasingly, the industry was facing barriers in innovation, regulatory pressure, and the need to address global health challenges. There was an urgent need to create effective drugs for HIV/AIDS that could be accessed by a large number of the resource poor populations in developing countries. Despite the breakthrough in the invention of useful drugs for heart disease that became a major source of profit for pharmaceutical companies at the time, the world intensified their criticism of the industry. The AIDS crisis has also made the world pay attention to the pricing controversy in the pharmaceutical industry. In a related development, the need to contain health care cost in the United States has also attracted the public's attention to the affordability issue of pharmaceuticals.

In the 1990s, with the aid of advancements in science and technology, the industry was growing at a new level and continued the vertical and horizontal integration momentum by involving a larger number of partners in the drug development process. Its partners include research institutes in the public sector, such as the National Institutes of Health (NIH) in the United States, and academia, which started playing an increasing role in the basic research stage of drug development. The outlets for pharmaceutical sale have also increased. The emergence of internet pharmacy during this time has effected quality control, pricing and large pharmas' marketing strategies and could pose a threat to the bottom line of the business. On the other hand, in the United States, direct-to-consumer advertising on radio and TV gave the pharmaceutical companies greater access to influencing consumers directly because of a more liberal approach adopted by the US Food and Drugs Administration (FDA), as a result of new regulations in 1997 in the presentation of pharmaceutical risks. Drug development during this time became more methodical and systematic. The "hits" included the new antidepressants (the SSRIs), especially the Prozac (Fluoxetine), Viagra, and new AIDS drugs. In addition to competition from complementary medicine and nutritional supplements, the industry was also facing uncertainty about the safety of newer drugs. For example, the Vioxx controversy put tremendous pressure on the regulatory agencies and the industry to improve the drug development process.

The first decade of the new millennia witnessed increasing dynamic and aggressive expansion and continuous consolidation of the industry.

It is noted that the pharmaceutical sector, composed of more than 200 major pharmaceutical companies, is one of the most profitable industries (USA Today, 2002, "How to buy prescription drugs at over 50 percent off US price"). The proliferation of new and intractable diseases has rendered this industry even more opportunities than before. Advances in the sciences, especially in biotechnology and genetics, have produced major breakthroughs in the discovery and making of medicines, such as gene therapy or individualized medicine. In the United States, the industry has also become one of the most politically influential players, as evidenced by the employment of the largest troop of lobbyists on Capital Hill (Center of Public Integrity, 7 July, 2005). A report by the Center of Public Integrity showed that between 1998 and 2005, the pharmaceutical and health products industry spent more than $800 million in federal lobbying and campaign donations at both federal and state levels – which effort was considered to be the largest in the United States during that period. These developments have alerted their critics. Scrutiny and criticism of the industry, targeting such issues as manipulation of pricing, insensitivity to the needs of the developing world, inflating efficacy claims and disease mongering, and lack of innovation, has also intensified (ibid.). As critics are increasing their scrutiny, so linkages between the industry and regulator are exposed to the public. Nevertheless, throughout the history of pharmaceutical development, the regulatory bodies in developed markets have in general played a positive role.

Regulatory environment

As mentioned in Chapter 1, the regulatory bodies play a major role in overseeing the approval, manufacturing, sales and marketing, consumption, and surveillance of pharmaceuticals. Among all the regulatory bodies in the world, the FDA in the United States, a scientific, public health and regulatory agency, is a major operational model for other countries.

The FDA has undergone tremendous growth since 1862, when it was the Division of Chemistry with a single chemist in the US Department of Agriculture (Swann, 2007, "History of FDA"). These days, with a budget of $2.4 billion in 2008, the FDA is equipped with a staff of approximately 9100 employees, including chemists, pharmacologists, physicians, microbiologists, veterinarians, pharmacists, lawyers, and many others. About one-third of the agency's employees are stationed outside of the Washington, DC, area, operating in 150 field offices and laboratories, including five regional offices and 20 district offices (AAAS, 2008; Swann, 2007). The items under the charge of FDA encompass most food products (other than meat and poultry); human and animal drugs; therapeutic agents of biological origin; medical devices; radiation-emitting products for consumer, medical, and occupational use; cosmetics; and animal feed.

The transformation of FDA from a Bureau of Chemistry in 1901 to the guardian of American consumption of health-related products was due to a number of historic accidents, incidents, and landmark legislation. The 1906 passage of the Federal Food and Drugs Act increased the FDA's regulatory functions. The Bureau of Chemistry was changed to the Food, Drug, and Insecticide Administration in July 1927, when the agency focused its role on the regulation and transfer of non-regulatory research functions to other agencies in the department. FDA's current name derives from a change made in July 1930. In June 1940, the agency was transferred to the new Federal Security Agency, but was moved back again to the Department of Health, Education, and Welfare (HEW) in April 1953. The FDA became part of the Public Health Service within HEW in 1968, and then in May 1980, FDA was placed under the Department of Health and Human Services, when HEW was renamed after removing its education function.

The evolution of the FDA has to do with the role of federalism in harmonizing approaches to inconsistent and unsafe food and drug-making practices. Some states, such as Massachusetts, were more progressive or protective than others. The FDA's short-lived enforcement of the Vaccine Act of 1813 was the first federal law attempting to harmonize consumer protection and therapeutic substances. Before the FDA was able to assert its authority, the states had the most control over the production, sale, and transportation of food and drugs. Federal authority was limited mostly to imported foods and drugs. However, at the time, unethical and inauthentic practices, such as adulteration and misbranding of foods and drugs, were prevalent and aggravating in the late nineteenth century. Drug safety was of particular concern to the public when, at the time, even ethical companies engaged in making "unethical medicine," such as by diluting quinine-containing cinchona bark powder with such other ingredients as alum, or using clay to mask poor wheat flour (Swann, 2007). The unethical practices increased profits for these companies, but took a toll on the health of the public.

In 1867, the lack of enforcement against misbranding and adulteration by the federal agency, forced a change in the Division of Chemistry at the public's demand (Swann, 2007). The arrival of Harvey W. Wiley in Washington as chief chemist in 1883 heralded a major change in FDA's public role (*FDA Magazine*, 2006). Widely lauded as a pioneer consumer activist, Wiley W. Harvey, a Harvard graduate, pushed the agency to start taking an active role in protecting the safety of the public in the consumption of food and drugs. By first publishing the division's research in this area in a ten-part study, *Foods and Food Adulterants*, conducted from 1887 to 1902, Harvey raised his concern about the "poison squad" experiments, the ancient version of unsupervised "clinical trials," in which able-bodied volunteers consumed varying amounts of questionable food additives to determine their impact on health. To address this dangerous practice, Harvey, with the support of state chemists and food and drug inspectors, the General Federation of Women's Clubs, and national associations of physicians and pharmacists, tried to enforce a federal law to prohibit the adulteration and misbranding of food and drugs.

Since then, the US Food and Drug Administration has a large influence on the US economy. It is noted that the $1 trillion worth of products monitored by the FDA is at a cost to taxpayers of about $3 per person per year. In another estimate, the items under the charge of US FDA account for 25 cents of every dollar spent by consumers (Swann, 2007).

Major legislations on pharmaceuticals

There are several legislations that form the backbone of the regulatory framework for pharmaceuticals sold in the United States and some of these standards have been used by other countries. In the United States, the major legislative effort was the 1906s Food and Drugs Act, or the Wiley Act, signed by President Roosevelt (US Department of Health and Human Services, 2007, "The 1906 Food and Drugs Act and Its Enforcement"). This Act prohibited the interstate transport of unlawful food and drugs under penalty of seizure of the questionable products and/or prosecution of the responsible parties. The basis of the law rested on the regulation of product labeling rather than pre-market approval. Drugs, defined in accordance with the standards of strength, quality, and purity in the US Pharmacopoeia and the National Formulary, could not be sold in any other condition unless the specific variations from the applicable standards were plainly stated on the label (ibid.).

In the wake of a therapeutic disaster in 1937, which caused more than 100 casualties due to the use of the "claimed" wonder drug Elixir Sulfanilamide, the Food, Drug, and Cosmetic Act was passed in 1938. The new law brought cosmetics and medical devices under control, and it required that drugs be labeled with adequate directions for safe use. Moreover, it mandated pre-market approval of all new drugs, so that a manufacturer would have to prove to FDA that a drug was safe before it could be sold. This act irrefutably prohibited false therapeutic claims for drugs, although a separate law granted the Federal Trade Commission jurisdiction over drug advertising. The act also corrected abuses in food packaging and quality by mandating legally enforceable food standards. Tolerances for certain poisonous substances were addressed. The law formally authorized factory inspections, and it added injunctions to the enforcement tools at the agency's disposal (US Department of Health and Human Services, 2007).

Other important legislation includes: In 1951, Congress passed a law requiring the use of doctors' prescriptions to buy drugs and in 1961, a law dictating that drugs have to show efficacy in addition to the safety standard.

Several legislations passed in the 1980s and 1990s have a far-reaching impact on the process of clinical development and regulatory review of new therapeutics in the United States. For example, the Bayh-Dole and Stevenson-Wydler Act facilitated technology transfer between research institutions and industries, including the pharmaceutical makers (Franklin Pierce Law Center, 2008, "Overview of federal technology transfer"). This Act allows small businesses and non-profit organizations a statutory right to choose to retain title to inventions made during federally assisted research and development (R&D) so long as they were interested in patenting and attempting to commercialize those inventions. To be more specific, under this Act, the universities can patent discoveries from NIH-sponsored research, and then grant licenses to pharmaceutical companies. It was believed that this Act increased technology transfer from public-sector resources to private sector, inducing a major impetus for the growth of the biotechnology sector and the large pharmaceutical companies (US Government Technology Administration, 9 May 2002; see also Franklin Pierce Law Center, 2008). The Orphan Drug Act, signed into law on 4 January 1983, was another attempt to stimulate the research, development, and approval of products that treat rare diseases, defined as diseases affecting fewer than 200,000 Americans (FDA, 1983, "Orphan Drugs"). The mechanisms to support the act include: marketing exclusivity for the drug's sponsors after the orphan drug product is approved; tax incentives for clinical research undertaken by the sponsors; assistance from FDA's Office of Orphan Products Development to coordinate research study design by the sponsors; support from the Office of Orphan Products Development for sponsors to conduct open protocols, allowing patients to be added to ongoing studies; and availability of grant funding to defray costs of qualified clinical testing expenses incurred in connection with the development of orphan products. It is noted that since the passing of Orphan Drug Act, over 100 orphan drugs and biological products have been brought to market. In 1984, the US Congress passed the Hatch-Waxman Act, or the Drug Price Competition and Partner Term Restoration Act. This law has also facilitated the growth of the industry. This Act was revised in 2000, when cross-border pharmaceutical purchases were liberalized. In this revision, Americans could buy back FDA-approved drugs from Canada (Angell, 2004). This is an improvement of a 1987 law passed by the US Congress that illegalized cross-border purchases of prescriptions by American citizens other than the manufacturers. In 1992, came the Prescription Drug User Fee Act, authorizing drug companies to pay user fees for drug evaluations to the FDA.

The legislation of the Food and Drug Administration and Modernization Act of 1997 is designed to address an unmet medical need. It applies to the combination of a product and a claim seeking FDA approval (FDA, 1997, "Food And Drug Administration and Modernization Act Of 1997"). This act was designed for fast track approval and is independent of Priority Review and Accelerated Approval. The benefits of the Fast Track law include FDA input in the development process in the form of scheduled meetings; the option of submitting a New Drug Application in sections without having to sub-mit all components simultaneously; and the option of requesting evalu-ation of studies using surrogate endpoints. This Act also allows one clinical trial, instead of two. Under this legislation, pharmaceutical makers are not required to test the new drugs against the old ones, which opens the door for "me-too" drugs. This allows US Medicaid program to pay for off-label uses after decisions by three private organi-zations (Angell, 2004).

The new FDA regulations in 1997 aroused some criticism because they were thought to have liberalized requirements for the presentation of risks in the direct advertisements to pharmaceutical consumers (Angell, 2004). Instead of having to present a comprehensive list of risks, this legislation allows the companies to list only major risks and to refer viewers to a source of additional information. This act was believed to have contributed to the rise in drug sales. For example, the new antidepressants, or the SSRIs, such as Fluoxetine (Prozac), rapidly became bestsellers and were marketed for additional disorders (ibid., 2004).

Pressure from the public to lower medicines led to the opening up of the pharmaceutical market (American Medical Student Association, 13 April 2008, "Prescription drug importation: A short-term effort to reduce drug prices"). As mentioned earlier, in 2000, the US Congress passed legislation allowing the re-importation of pharmaceuticals on condition that there was assurance of safety from the Secretary of Health and Human Services, with the advice of the FDA.

Global regulatory framework

In the global context, one of the most important policy guides was the issuance by the World Medical Association of the 1964 Declaration of Helsinki (The World Medical Association, 2004, "Declaration of Helsinki"). This declaration sets standards for clinical evaluations by demand that informed consent be obtained from clinical trial subjects before enrollment in an experiment. Pharmaceutical companies were mandated to prove efficacy in clinical trials before they could market their drugs.

On the issue of intellectual property rights, in the 1970s the legislation GATT (the General Agreement on Tariffs and Trade) allowing for strong patents, to cover both the process of manufacture and the specific products, came into force on the global scene (Wikipedia, 2007b). In late 1990s, the World Trade Organization set out to harmonize protection of intellectual property rights for traded goods, including pharmaceuticals, through the enactment of TRIPS (Trade-Related Aspects of Intellectual Property Rights). This global trade regulation is instrumental in facilitating the large pharmaceutical companies to expand their global frontiers, with far-reaching implications on global health.

Pharmaceutical companies

The modern pharmaceutical industry would not exist were it not for some innovative nineteenth-century pioneers, who laid the foundations for the development of large multinationals today.

Eli Lilly.   One of these pioneers was Colonel Eli Lilly, the founder of Eli Lilly Pharmaceuticals. He started his career in 1854 as a 16-year-old intern in an Indiana apothecary shop, equipped with mortars, pestles, rows of gleaming glass flasks, and ceramic apothecary jars (Eli Lilly Company, 2007, "History"; Bioanalytical Systems Inc., 2007e, "The pharmaceutical industry: A history and calendar"). When Lilly himself opened his shop on 10 May 1876, his staff of three included a drug compounder, a bottler and finisher, and his 14-year-old son Josiah K. Lilly, Sr. In this traditional setting, herbs, roots, minerals, oils, and other materials were the sources of medicines.

Eli Lilly's new company in 1876 offered the so-called "ethical" medications, when other companies produced such medicines as were brewed and peddled by slick hucksters. These "ethical" medications were dispensed only on the advice of authentic physicians. His first products in herbal preparations, extracted from Bear's Foot, Black Haw, Cramp Bark, Hardhack, Life Root, Skullcap, Sea Wrack, Squaw Vine, Wahoo, and Wormseed, were reputed for their quality and the generosity and community spirit of the company's founder. The major product of the company was insulin, which Eli Lilly & Company co-developed with Canadian physician Frederick Banting in 1921. This discovery was based on observation by Banting and graduate student Charles Best in experiments showing that animal pancreas extractions were able to regulate sugar metabolism in diabetic dogs. Another improvement in insulin production was made in 1922, when Lilly scientists invented the iso-electric precipitation procedures to increase manufacturing yields and improve the purity, potency, and stability of insulin product. In 1923, Iletin was registered as the first commercial insulin from Eli Lilly and Company (Bioanalytical Systems Inc., 2007b, Eli Lilly and Company).

Merck.   The other early pioneer was Merck, one of the oldest chemical and pharmaceutical companies in the world. Merck and Company was founded in 1668 when Friedrich Jacob Merck, an apothecary, bought out the "Engel-Apotheke" in Darmstadt, Germany (see Merck and Company, 2002, "History"). After 1816, Merck began to manufacture bulk quantities of alkaloids, plant extracts and other chemicals and in 1888, Merck had started selling guaranteed pure reagents to the market.

Merck continued to expand in the turn of the nineteenth century (Bioanalytical Systems Inc., 2007d, "Merck and Company"). In 1891, Merck and Co., under George Merck who was grandson of Emanuel Merck, started increasing Merck's presence in the United States by presiding over the New York office. In 1902, Merck began to produce such fine chemicals as bismuths, iodides, and narcotics (including morphine and cocaine). Merck's mergers in 1927 with chemical producer PWR and in 1953 with pharmaceutical company Sharp & Dohme made the company focus on the business of pharmaceutical research. Since the 1970s, Merck has introduced Sinemet to treat Parkinson's disease;

Timoptic to treat glaucoma; Heptavax-B vaccine to treat hepatitis B; and Zocor and Mevacor to treat cholesterol. Zocor and Mevacor today control about 40 percent of the world market. In addition, the company produced the top-selling Vasotec for hypertension, Crixivan for AIDS treatment, and Propecia (for baldness) (ibid.). Today, Merck & Co., Inc. is a leading pharmaceutical producer with 70,000 employees in 120 countries and 31 factories worldwide and their products are sold in more than 200 countries (see Merck and Company, 2002).

Bayer.   Bayer started making its name in pharmaceutical history when the precursor of aspirin was invented (Bayer, 2007, "Bayer: Science for a better life"). The general partnership "Friedr. Bayer and company," founded on 1 August 1863 in Barmen, Germany, by dye salesman Friedrich Bayer (1825–1880) and master dyer Johann Friedrich Weskott (1821–1876) paved the way for a very successful pharmaceutical business. In 1881, Bayer was transformed into a joint stock company "Farbenfabriken vorm, Friedr. Bayer & Co." On 10 August 1897, Dr Felix Hoffmann, a chemist in Farbenfabriken vorm, part of Friedr. Bayer & Co., successfully acetylated salicylic acid into a chemically pure and stable form of acetylsalicylic acid (ASA) that could be used to relieve rheumatic pain; ASA is the active ingredient for aspirin. Introduced in 1899, aspirin is the best-known and most frequently used medicine in the world. In 1915, aspirin, the first drug in tablet form, was available without a prescription. The benefits of the drug far extended its original purpose. Today, its therapeutic effects include the possible prevention of heart attacks and colon cancer. Bayer also discovered polyurethane chemistry in the 1930s and developed the first broad-spectrum antimicrobial for treatment of fungal diseases in humans (Bioanalytical Systems Inc., 2007a, "Bayer corporation").

Bristol-Myers Squibb.   Bristol-Myers Squibb has become a dominant player in the sector after a merger with the Squibbs in 1989, one of largest single stock transfers in the history of the health care industry (Bristol-Myers Squibb, 2006, "A Brief History of Bristol-Myers Squibb"). The new company became the second largest in the pharmaceutical sector.

The company started out in 1887 when William McLaren Bristol and John Ripley Myers put their investment of $5000 into a failing drug manufacturing company named the Clinton Pharmaceutical Company, Clinton, New York. On 13 December 1887, the company was officially incorporated (ibid.). The initial $5000 investment has grown into a $12 billion diversified global health and personal care company with more than 47,000 employees worldwide and thousands of products marketed in more than 130 countries.

Bristol-Myers Squibb Worldwide Pharmaceuticals is reputable for therapies for cardiovascular, metabolic and infectious diseases, central nervous systems and dermatologic disorders, and cancer. The research arm of the company, the Bristol-Myers Squibb Pharmaceutical Research Institute, was established to engage in research in oncology, cardiovascular and metabolics, anti-infectives, neurosciences, immunology and inflammation, dermatology, and pain management (Bristol-Myers Squibb, 2006). The better known products include treatments for HIV and cancer. For example, in 1991 the company's Videx® (didanosine), or ddI, was second only to AZT as the most used medicine available for treating HIV infection. In the same year, the company's Cooperative Research and Development Agreement with the National Cancer Institute led to the development of a new compound, TAXOL® (paclitaxel). TAXOL, derived from the bark of the endangered Pacific Yew tree, was found to be effective in treating cancer. Since its launch in 1993, TAXOL has become one of the world's most widely used cancer treatments; ibid.).

Pfizer.   Pfizer, a leading player in the pharmaceutical industry, is always associated with penicillin as its most famous drug (Pfizer, 2008a, "About Pfizer"). Penicillin, discovered by bacteriologist Alexander Fleming in 1928, was not mass produced until Pfizer used the technique of deep-tank fermentation to produce penicillin in the 1940s. By 1944, Pfizer was the largest producer of penicillin in the world (Bioanalytical Systems Inc., 2007f, "Pfizer"). Today, Pfizer is widely known for its innovative new drugs. For example, Geodon® (ziprasidone hydrochloride) is a new antipsychotic for the treatment of schizophrenia; Relpax® (eletriptan HBr) was developed specifically for the treatment of migraines; Exubera® (insulin human [rDNA origin]) Inhalation Powder is the first diabetes treatment for adults with Type 1 and Type 2 diabetes that can be inhaled (ibid.). Beyond its pharmaceutical leadership, it is widely known for its participation in global health partnerships to improve health in developing countries, such as the Diflucan® Partnership Program, a member of the UN Global Compact, and its HIV/AIDS Health Literacy Grants Program.

Hoechst.   Hoechst AG is the world's largest chemical manufacturer with businesses in 120 nations around the globe and since the mid-1990s, most of its revenue, more than 75 percent, derives from foreign sale

(Hoechst, 2008, "Hoechst A.G."). Hoechst Marion Roussel is the pharmaceutical company of Hoechst AG and its major products include therapies for allergic, metabolic, and central nervous systems disorders and cardiovascular and infectious diseases (see Pfizer Inc., 2008b, "Pfizer Inc and Hoechst Marion Roussel to Co-Develop and Co-Promote Inhaled Insulin").

Hoechst Marion Roussel, with roots in its aniline dye factory in 1863 at Höchst am Main, Germany, introduced its first pharmaceutical product, Antipyrin, in 1883 as the world's first safe and effective synthetic painkiller and the first drug to leave the factory in a ready-dosaged and packaged form. Other important products included tuberculin (1892), diphtheria and tetanus antitoxins (1894 to 1897), and Novocain®, the first safe local anesthetic (1905). Its Salvarsan®, discovered in 1910, was the first effective treatment for syphilis and the inception of chemotherapy. A leader in research in diabetes, Hoechst helped produce the first insulin in Europe in 1923, and it also went on to introduce products to improve tolerability, such as crystalline insulin and the popular oral hypoglycemics Orinase® and DiaBeta®.

Hoechst's acquisitions of other companies have also expanded its business profiles. In 1995, Hoechst's acquisition of Marion Merrell Dow, which was known for the production of calcium supplementation, Os-Cal®, made of oyster shells, the Cardizem family of cardiovascular drugs, the non-sedating antihistamine Seldane, and Carafate, an anti-ulcer product. In 1997, Hoechst acquired Roussel Uclaf, which, created in 1929, had produced Hemostyl, an anti-anaemia product, and was one of France's most important pharmaceutical companies. Roussel Uclaf, which built its first fermentation plant in 1946, had developed such breakthrough antibiotic products as Cefotaxime, a third-generation cephalosporin (1981), and the macrolide antibiotic Roxithromycin (1987). By the 1990s, this French company held 10,000 patents worldwide (Bioanalytical Systems Inc., 2007c, Hoechst Marion Roussel).

Glaxo-Smith-Kline (GSK). Glaxo-Smith-Kline combines the history of a number of pharmaceutical leaders, such as Glaxo, Wellcome, Affymax (a leader in the field of combinatorial chemistry), and Smith-Beecham-Kline. Today, GSK has 7 percent of global market share and produces medicines that treat asthma, virus control, infections, mental health, diabetes, and digestive conditions. It is a major stakeholder in vaccines and cancer treatments (GSK, 2007, "Our company"). GSK's other products include over-the-counter (OTC) medicines, such as Gaviscon and

Panadol; dental products such as Aquafresh and Macleans; smoking control products Nicorette/Niquitin; and nutritional health care drinks such as Lucozade, Ribena and Horlicks.

The founding of Smith-Beecham-Kline could be traced back to the combination of three individual pharmaceutical pioneers in the nineteenth century. The founder of Beecham, a shepherd boy in the 1820s, started his pharmaceutical business based on his observation of the medicinal properties of the vegetation consumed by his sheep. His observation led to the production of "Beecham's Pills," which reached a million tablets each day by 1913. The company made its mark in the 1950s with the discovery of 6-APA, the form of the penicillin nucleus important in suppressing resistant strains of infectious disease.

In 1830, John K. Smith founded an apothecary shop in Philadelphia and delved into the drug wholesale business as a result of a partnership in 1865. The company, renamed Smith, Kline and French, after a merger with French Richards and Co., was Philadelphia's leading drug vendor, selling hundreds of products, including tonics, medicines, liniments, and perfumes. The company ventured into new medicines after the 1929 Wall Street crash. The company made its mark by developing Benzedrine for nasal congestion; Dexedrine for treating obesity; and Thorazine for mental illness. Its inventions of capsules that allow the release of medicine over an extended period of time together with Tagamet for treating peptic ulcers were among some of its well-known achievements. Tagamet was a blockbuster with sales reaching an all time high of $1 billion.

Today's SKB has derived from several mergers. The merger between Smith Kline Beckman in the United States and the Beecham Group in the United Kingdom in July 1989 created SmithKline Beecham, and its core products include prescription medicines, vaccines, consumer health care products, and the business of clinical testing in the world (Bioanalytical Systems Inc., 2007g, "SmithKline Beecham"). In 1995, Glaxo and Wellcome merged to form Glaxo Wellcome. Then, Glaxo Wellcome acquired California-based Affymax, a leader in the field of combinatorial chemistry. In 2001, GlaxoSmithKline was formed as a result of the merger of Glaxo Wellcome and SmithKline Beecham (ibid.).

Wyeth.   A company incorporated as "American Home Products" (AHP) in 1926 became Wyeth in 2002 (Fundinguniverse, 2008, "Wyeth"). American Home Products were associated with such popular products as Black Flag insecticides, Easy-Off oven cleaner, Woolite, and Chef

Boyardee, and familiar pharmaceuticals like Anacin, Advil, Dristan, Robitussin, and Dimetapp. A global operator, Wyeth develops and markets traditional pharmaceuticals, vaccines, and biotechnology products, such as over-the-counter (OTC) medications and nutritional supplements. Its clients spread to more than 140 countries, and it has manufacturing facilities on five continents. During the 1990s, the company started focusing on medicine and pharmaceuticals by selling off other businesses. In 2002, the company changed its name from American Home Products to Wyeth. In fact, AHP had already acquired Wyeth Chemical Company (now Wyeth Laboratories) in 1932.

Wyeth Laboratories, the core of today's Wyeth-Ayerst Pharmaceuticals that began in Philadelphia, Pennsylvania, was founded by brothers John and Frank Wyeth in a drug store in 1860. The brothers were pioneers in pharmaceutical supply chain management. John was a pioneer in preparing frequently prescribed compounds in advance, and later, they published a catalog listing their line of drug preparations, elixirs, and tonics. A counterpart, Ayerst, McKenna & Harrison, Ltd., established in 1925 in Montreal, Canada, became the first commercially operated biological laboratory in Canada when the company was trying to produce a biologically tested cod liver oil (Bioanalytical Systems Inc., 2007h, "Wyeth Ayerst"). After Wyeth in 1866 absorbed A. H. Robins, a former apothecary and manufacturing chemist shop in Richmond, Virginia, it acquired a broad line of prescription medications. Wyeth also included Lederle Laboratories, founded in New York in 1906 by Dr Ernst Lederle, a pioneer in the fight against disease among children, and was known for its invention of diphtheria antitoxin.

Wyeth made its name in developing the "compressed pill," or tablet. The first rotary tablet press was also invented by Wyeth in 1872. Other products include an infant formula patterned after mother's milk; the first orally active estrogen (which became the pioneer product for estrogen replacement therapy); the first penicillin tablets and oral suspensions; and development of a heat-stable, freeze-dried vaccine and the bifurcated needle used to deliver 200 million smallpox vaccinations per year.

These aforementioned companies were among some of the oldest pharmaceutical businesses that laid the foundations for today's larger pharmaceutical companies. In 2006, the top large pharmaceutical companies in terms of market share were: Pfizer (7.2 percent), GlaxoSmithKline (5.9 percent), Sanofi-Aventis (5.7 percent), Novartis (4.6 percent), Hoffmann-La Roche (4.2 percent), AstraZeneca (4.1 percent), Johnson & Johnson (3.7 percent), Merck & Co. (3.6 percent), Wyeth (2.5 percent), and Eli Lilly (2.4 percent). These top ten dominated global sales of pharmaceuticals in 2006. The fastest rate of growth was experienced by Hoffmann-La Roche with 21.8 percent, followed by Novartis' 18 percent, AstraZeneca's 10.5 percent, and GSK's 9.7 percent (Ebisch, March 2005, "Prescription for change"; see also Wood McKinzie Productview, March 2007). The top ten pharmas are followed by Bristol-Mers Squibb, Amgen, Abbott, Boehringer-Ingelheim, Takeda, Bayer Schering, Schring-Plough, Astellas Pharma, Daiichi-Sankyo, Novo Nordisk, Eisai, Merck KGaA, Solvay, Forest, and Akzo Nobel Wood (ibid.). Their growth is determined by their global strategy, especially in R&D.

Large pharmas and R&D

The increase of R&D in the pharmaceutical sector is considered an industry priority (see European Commission, 2007, "The 2007 EU industrial R&D investment scoreboard"). In a report by the European Commission, pharmaceuticals and biotechnology have overtaken other businesses and have become the top R&D investing sector. On the whole, this sector has shown an increase of 15.9 percent of R&D, or a total of more than US$98732.9 million (or 70523.5 million euros) investment in R&D. The largest increase was 24.3 percent by Merck, followed by AztraZeneca (about 15.5 percent), Roche (about 15.5 percent), Johnson & Johnson (about 12.9 percent), and GlaxoSmithKline (over 10 percent). The pharmaceutical companies that had the largest R&D budget in 2006 are Pfizer, Johnson, GSK, Sanofi-Aventis, Roche, Novartis, Merck, AstraZeneca, Amgen, Bayer, Eli Lilly, Wyeth, Bristol-Myers Squibb, Abbott, and Schering-Plough. Pfizer took the lead in its increase in R&D not just among drug developers but among all industries (see also FierceBiotech, 2007a, "The top 15 R&D Market").

Company profiles in R&D

Pfizer.   R&D investment reflects the business strategy pursued by the largest pharmas in the world and they share very similar trends. Pfizer, based in the United States, has a 2006 pipeline budget of $8.34 billion (€5.76B) (Pfizer, 2008c, "Pfizer pipeline – new medicine in development"). In 2007, Pfizer, who lost Torcetrapib in late 2006, causing a laying off 10,000 workers, tried to boost its profile by hiring a new R&D chief for its worldwide operations and has moved its investment in the biotech sector to reduce competition in the generic business. This move is said to threaten the company's profits level (ibid.). A pipeline update by the end of December 2007 shows that the company has 47 Phase II drugs, 11 Phase III drugs including CP-945598 for Obesity; Apixaban for

Venous Thromboembolism prevention; Zithromax/Chloroquine for Malaria; CP-675206 for Melanoma; Axitinib for Thyroid Cancer; Axitinib for Pancreatic Cancer; Sutent for Breast Cancer; Sutent for Colorectal Cancer and Lung Cancer; Maraviroc for HIV in Treatment of Naïve Patients; Lyrica for Epilepsy Monotherapy; Generalized Anxiety Disorder (US); Geodon for Bipolar Relapse Prevention, and 14 biologics in its pipeline. Thirteen projects, including Lasofoxifene for Osteoporosis, Maraviroc for HIV Treatment of experienced patients, and Dalbavancin for Skin and Skin Structure Infections, were abandoned in 2007.

Johnson & Johnson. Based in the United States, Johnson & Johnson is also a leader in R&D with a 2006 pipeline budget of $7.9 billion (€5.40B) (Johnson & Johnson, 2007, "Innovations"). In 2007, despite the controversy surrounding anemia drug safety, Johnson & Johnson had several late-stage drugs that are important to the company's future, these include Telaprevir, two HIV drugs, Golimumab co-developed with Schering-Plough and Rivaroxaban. The mid-term prospect is believed to be promising when 18 to 21 new drugs will be filed or approved over the next three years, five of which are expected by the end of 2007, including Concerta for Adult ADHD, Remicade for Pediatric Ulcerative Colitis and UC colectomy avoidance, Ceftobiprole for Complicated Skin and Skin Structure Infections, Doribax for Nosocomial Pneumonia, and TMC125 for NNRTI HIV/AIDS treatment of experienced patients.

GSK. Following Johnson & Johnson in R&D investment ranking, GlaxoSmithKline, based in the United Kingdom, has a 2006 pipeline budget of $7.51 billion (€5.13B) (GSK, 2008, "Research and development").

GSK is facing short-term challenges, which might effect its stock performance and its competitiveness. This issue was reported to the public when safety concerns were raised about Avandia, a blockbuster diabetes drug and when several big GSK drugs, including Wellbutrin XL, Coreg IR, and Zofran, are facing generic competition. It was noticed that GSK's R&D competitiveness is still in the lead given the fact that it has 33 drugs in Phase III development, which is three times as many as Pfizer (GSK, 2008). In addition, the company will possibly launch as many as 25 new drugs in the next two years and increase marketing of the new drugs of Alli, Cervarix and Tykreb.

GSK's drugs pending approval include Avandia + simvastatin for Type 2 diabetes; Hycamtin for small cell lung cancer and second-line therapy (oral formulation); Globorix for diphtheria, tetanus, pertussis, hepatitis

B, Haemophilus influenzae Type b disease, and Infanrix-IPV/Kinrix for diphtheria, tetanus, pertussis and poliomyelitis prophylaxis; a cure in Pandemic influenza prophylaxis; Gepirone ER for major depressive disorder (once-daily); Lamictal XR for epilepsy; ReQuip XR for Restless legs syndrome; and Trexima for migraine.

Roche. Based in Switzerland, Roche has a 2006 pipeline budget of $5.99 billion (€4.09) (Roche Pharmaceuticals, 2008, "Innovative R&D"). The R&D plan reflects its changing business plans. In 2007, Roche increased its R&D spending and restructured its research work into five arenas of molecular mechanisms: oncology, virology, inflammation, metabolism, and the central nervous system. It has also planned a number of acquisitions. The company's progress in cancer and diabetes research is worth noticing because the company has 33 oncology drugs and five diabetes drugs in clinical trial stage. There are nine additional indications for its blockbuster cancer drug Avastin in Phase III and three more are pending approval. With 40 drugs in Phase III, 32 in Phase II, and 34 in Phase I, the company has a promising position in R&D. For Roche, its drugs pending approval include Xeloda for oral fluoropyrimidine metastatic colorectal cancer (the first line) combo, oral fluoropyrimidine metastatic colorectal cancer (second line) combo; Avastin for renal cell carcinoma, metastatic colorectal cancer (first line) combo oxaliplatin, metastic breast cancer (1st line) combo taxol; and Nicorandil (Sigmart) for acute heart failure.

Novartis. Novartis, a global health stakeholder, has a 2006 pipeline budget of $5.94 billion (€4.06B) (FierceBiotech, 28 November 2007f, "Novartis"). Novartis has experienced success and setbacks in drug development since 2006. In 2007, the FDA approval of Aclasta/Reclastin in the United States and European Union for Aclasta/Reclast is likely to generate $1.2 billion in sales by 2011. The FDA has also approved Tekturna, a potential blockbuster drug for hypertension. Yet safety concerns were raised about the painkiller Prexige, which got a "not approvable" letter. The FDA made a similar decision on the diabetes drug Galvus.

In addition, Novartis continued its niche in vaccines development in 2007, paying Intercell €270 million to license more than ten early and pre-clinical development programs. Also a leader in R&D, Novartis currently has 50 of its 138 projects in Phase II or Phase III. The drugs that anticipate filings in 2008 include QAB149 for COPD; LBH589 for solid tumors; AGO178 for depression; Tifacogin for CAP; MFF258 for

COPD/asthma; RAD001 for solid tumors; Tobramycin for Cystic Fibrosis; and Tekturna for hypertension.

Merck. Based in the United States, Merck had a 2006 pipeline budget of $5.3 billion (€3.62) (FierceBiotech, 28 November 2007e, "Merck – Top 15 R&Ds"). Merck is hoping to gain a potential of a $15 billion market with its cholesterol drug Anacetrapib, a CETP inhibitor, designed to increase good cholesterol and decrease bad cholesterol. Merck's long-term prospects bode well, with several promising drugs. In 2007, Merck received FDA approval of the HIV drug Isentress. The billion-dollar acquisition of Ariad's late-clinical trial cancer drug AP23573 for metastatic sarcomas is said to add ammunition to the company's cancer drug pipelines. Merck's other drugs pending approval are MK-0518 (Raltegravir) for HIV and MK-0517 for chemotherapy-induced nausea and vomiting (approvable). Merck's obesity drug Taranabant, which is in Phase III, expects FDA approval in 2008. This drug could pose a challenge to Sanofi-Aventis's drug Acomplia. Merck has also filed an NDA for Cordaptive (a cholesterol drug that combines a known ingredient with a new one that reduces the risk of flushing).

AstraZeneca. AstraZeneca, based in the United Kingdom, had a 2006 pipeline budget of $4.32 billion (€2.95B), and is taking an aggressive strategy in R&D by spinning off its research institute as a separate company supported by venture capital (FierceBiotech, 28 February 2008a, "AstraZeneca may shake up R&D with spin-off").

Facing serious generic competition to 11 of its drugs (three in the near future and eight in the next eight years), AstraZeneca has aroused concerns from the investment bank Dresdner Kleinwort, which expressed the view that AstraZeneca is likely to be the worst-performing pharma company in upcoming years. This might explain its eagerness to sell off its research institute. A possible source of confidence might be gained from the anticipated approvals of Crestor, an atherosclerosis treatment; Nexium for NSAID GI side-effects – symptom resolution; Nexium for NSAID GI side-effects – ulcer healing; Seroquel for bipolar maintenance; FluMist for Influenza virus; and Symbicort for COPD.

Amgen. Amgen, the world's largest biotechnology company and based in the United States, had a 2006 pipeline budget of $3.73 billion (€2.55) (FierceBiotech, 28 November 2007c, "Amgen – Top 15 R&D"). Amgen has experienced some setbacks and hopes. Safety issues surrounding Amgen's anemia drug, the most profitable for the company, have caused some concerns about the future of the biotech sector in general. Nevertheless, the company's R&D seems to be moving ahead with several promising drugs, such as Denosumab, a fully-human monoclonal antibody testing for a number of indications, including bone loss induced by hormone, postmenopausal osteoporosis, bone metastases, and prevention of cancer-related bone damage; Cinacalcet HCl for cardiovascular disease in patients with secondary hyperparathyroidism and chronic kidney disease undergoing maintenance dialysis. Other drugs include Panitumumab for first- and second-line colorectal cancer; AMG531, an autoimmune blood disorder drug that treats immune thrombocytopenic purpura, an autoimmune bleeding disorder; and Darbepoetin alfa for cardiovascular disease in patients with chronic kidney disease and Type 2 diabetes.

Bayer.   Bayer, based in Germany, had a 2006 pipeline budget of $3.58 billion (€2.45), is planning to expand its biotech sector (FierceBiotech, 28 November 2007c). Since 2007, its plans also consist in aggressively expanding its biotech products, especially in cardiology, hematology, and oncology. Bayer's R&D profile is considered to be in good shape (ibid.). In addition to eight projects submitted for marketing authorization in 2007, Bayer has 14 projects in Phase I, 17 projects in Phase II and 19 projects in Phase III. Promising projects include Rivaroxaban, a potential blockbuster anti-clotting therapy pending for approval by the FDA and European Union, that showed more efficacy than Sanofi-Aventis' Lovenox in a Phase III trial. Other drugs pending for approval include Fosrenol for CKD; rThrombin for bleeding control; Rivaroxaban for VTE prevention; Menostar transdermal for VMS; E2/LNG for HRT (Japan); Magnevist MRA for MRA; Primovist for MRI; Avelon for PID/ new indications (EU).

Eli Lilly.   Based in the United States, Eli Lilly had a 2006 pipeline budget of $3.47 billion (€2.37B) (FierceBiotech, 28 November 2007d, "Eli Lilly – Top 15 R&D"). Lilly is said to face some challenges to its business growth due to the lack of innovative drugs capable of becoming blockbusters and the upcoming expiration of several of its brands. The company banked on Prasrugel, an anti-clotting drug to treat acute coronary syndrome to take on the blockbuster Plavix. Although Prasugrel has outperformed Plavix in reducing the number of heart attacks and other significant events, it has aroused some safety concerns due to an increasing number of bleeding incidents. Despite Lilly's high hopes, cardiac experts question its efficacy (Martinez and Goldstein, 6 December 2007,

"Big Pharma Faces Grim Prognosis"). Lilly's Phase III drugs include Enzastaurin for non-Hodgkin's lymphoma, Arzoxifene for osteoporosis & prevention of breast cancer, and inhaled insulin. Lilly's revenue is also likely to be affected by the upcoming patent expirations, which could potentially reduce 60 percent of Lilly's revenue.

Wyeth.   Based in the United States, Wyeth had 2006 pipeline budget of $3.44 billion (€2.35 billion). Like Amgen and Lilly, Wyeth faced some challenges in 2007 but it also named a new leader to face these challenges. Some of these challenges included that three of its leading drug candidates are delayed in the approval process; the FDA gave a non-approval letter for Bifeprunox, an antipsychotic for the treatment of schizophrenia; HCV-796, a Phase II hepatitis C drug candidate showed adverse events experienced by two patients. Pristiq received an approvable letter from the FDA, but there has been a delay in the launch of this drug for major depressive disorders. The silver lining of these challenges is that Wyeth's development of a new drug for Alzheimer disorder has brought about some hopes for the company. Other drugs also hold some promises, such as the Phase III drugs Lybrel, for continuous contraception; Pristiq for vasomotor symptoms of menopause; and Torisel for renal cell carcinoma III.

Bristol-Myers Squibb.   Based in the United States, Bristol-Myers Squibb had a 2006 pipeline budget of $3.39 billion €2.32 (FierceBiotech, 28 November 2008c, "Bristol-Myers Squibb – Top 15 R&D Budgets"). Bristol-Myers Squibb's R&D has shown some promises after heavy investment. Its melanoma drug Ipilimumab, co-developed with Medarex, is expected to be approved; Apixaban, a blood clot therapy, resulting from a $1 billion deal with Pfizer, is expected to become a successor for Coumadin. Bristol-Myers Squibb has also experienced some challenges, however. It is believed that BMS has withdrawn its plan to obtain FDA approval for Vinflunine, which for a while was an important part of BMS's strategy for gastric cancer, transitional cell carcinoma of the urothelial tract, bladder cancer, bladder neoplasms, transitional cell carcinoma, and metastasis. Other drugs that might hold some promise include the Phase III drugs Ixabepilone for breast cancer and metastic breast cancer; Ipilimumab for melanoma; Belatacept for renal transplant, kidney transplantation, chronic kidney failure; Saxagliptin for Type 2 diabetes mellitus, Type 2 diabetes; Apixaban for atrial fibrillation, deep vein thrombosis, pulmonary embolism, atrial flutter, venous thrombosis, and pulmonary embolism.

Abbott.   Based in the United States, Abbott had a 2006 pipeline budget of $2.5 billion (€1.71 billion) (FierceBiotech,15 November 2008b, "Abbott – Top 15 R&D Budgets"). In 2007, Abbott planned to follow up on its blockbuster anti-TNF drug Humira by running Phase III trials for additional indications. Although this is a conservative strategy, it ensures some consolidation of its existing market in this area. Several of its compounds are promising. These include Adalimumab (Humira) for rheumatoid arthritis, Crohn's disease, psoriatic arthritis, Ankylosing Spondulitis, juvenile RA, ulcerative colitis, uveitis, giant cell arteritis; Levosimendan for congestive heart failure, acute heart failure, cardiogenic shock, septic shock; ABT-335 androsuvastatin calcium for hypercholesterolemia and dyslipidemia; Atrasentan for cancer and prostatic neoplasms; and Pricalcitol for chronic renal insufficiency.

Schering-Plough.   Schering-Plough, based in the United States, had a 2006 pipeline budget of $2.14 billion (€1.65B) and has experienced a turnaround in its R&D progress under the new leadership of Fred Hassan (FierceBiotech, 28 November 2007b, "Schering-Plough – Top 15 R&D Budgets"). Schering-Plough is considered to be one of the most competitive pipelines in the pharmaceutical sector. Its $14.4 billion acquisition of Azko Nobel's Organon made the drug one of the five late-stage drugs in the company's drug repertoire. Other good news includes that its application for Asenapine, a tablet for schizophrenia and bipolar disorder, was approved by the FDA. Despite the expiration of Claritin, Schering-Plough, like other large pharmas, has also tried to preserve its market share of this drug by getting FDA approval for its Claritin/Singulair2 for treating seasonal allergic rhinitis. In addition, Asmanex for asthma and pediatric asthma is pending approval in Japan and in the United States. Also, Nasonex for allergic rhinitis is pending approval in Japan and Noxafil is pending approval in the United States for serious fungal infections.

Overall, R&D spending by the large pharmas does not necessarily translate into innovation. It is noted that although Pfizer invests the most in R&D, it is uncertain of the result of this spending. In contrast, Schering-Plough, for instance, is regarded as having the most promising pipeline despite having the smallest R&D budget among the top 15. It is also important not to underestimate Pfizer's investment in the biotech sector. It is quite possible that this investment might reap rewards when the biotechnology is mature enough to deliver downstream products. This investment might be a long-term strategy rather than a short-term calculation (see related discussions in Martino, 2007, "Comments on top-15 R&D budget").

Large pharmas' profit profile

The large pharmaceutical companies are at the apex of their development history, but they are also facing grave challenges in maintaining their current profit levels. As mentioned in Chapter 1, the pharmaceutical sector is a highly profitable industry (see Dobson, 2001; see also Public Citizen Report, 23 July 2001). In 2006, global spending on prescription drugs had increased, even as growth slowed somewhat in Europe and North America. Sales of prescription medicines worldwide rose 7 percent to $602 billion (IMS Reports, 17 February 2004, "11.5 Percent Dollar Growth in '03 U.S. Prescription Sales"). The leading profit makers remain those who have global presence. The leader in pharmaceutical sales in 2006 was Pfizer with $45,083 million, followed by GSK's $37,034 million; Sanofi-Aventis' $35,638 million; Novartis' $28,880 million; Hoffmann–LaRoache's $26,596 million; AstraZeneca's $25,741 million; Johnson & Johnson's $23,267 million; Merck's $22,636 million; Wyeth's $15,683 million; and Eli Lilly's $14,814 million (Ibid.).

Country-wide, the United States still accounts for most of the sales, about $252 billion in total, an increase of 5.7 percent in 2005 (IMS Reports, 2004). In 2004, the United States comprised about 45 percent of the pharmaceutical market worldwide, while Europe made up about 25 percent. In 2004, US sales grew to $235.4 billion, a growth rate of 8.3 percent compared with an 11.5 percent growth rate in the period from 2002 to 2003 (Trombetta, 1 September 2005). It is worth noting that in a slow-growth economy, US profit growth in this sector remains stable even when other industries have seen slower or no growth (IMS Reports, 2004).

As mentioned earlier, most of the multinationals derive pharmaceutical profits from sales in the markets of developed countries. In addition to Pfizer's cholesterol pill Lipidor, the blood thinner Plavix from Bristol-Myers Squibb and Sanofi-Aventis; the heartburn pill Nexium from AstraZeneca; and Advair, the asthma inhaler from GlaxoSmithKline are among the top-selling drugs (Herper and Kang, 22 March 2006). In 2007, Pfizer's Lipidor remains the top-selling drug of all prescription medicines, followed by AstraZeneca's Nexium. Nexium's sales totaled $5.2 billion (£2.7 billion) and was the world's second-biggest prescription medicine (Pagnamenta, 12 February, 2008).

The growth areas in pharmaceuticals reflect the convergence of several factors. It was noted by Murray Aitken, IMS senior vice-president of Corporate Strategy, that pharmaceutical growth is moving from mature markets to emerging ones and from primary care classes to biotech and specialist-driven therapies. It was also noted that oncology and autoimmune products have opportunities for growth because they respond to unmet patient needs (IMS, 2007a, "IMS Health Reports Global Pharmaceutical Market Grew 7.0 Percent in 2006, to $643 Billion").

A report by the IMS showed that market and profit trends have reflected population demand and needs, and these trends are likely to continue. Representing largely the industry's viewpoint, the IMS conclusion is based mainly on data gathered from 29,000 data suppliers at 225,000 supplier sites in 100 countries through monitoring 75 percent of prescription drug sales in over 100 countries, and 90 percent of US prescription drug sales, and by tracking more than 1 million products from more than 3000 active drug manufacturers (Gagnon and Lexchin, 3 January 2008). According to this report, most of the 2006 growth, about 62 percent, derives from specialist-driven products, which almost doubled the 35 percent share in 2000 (IMS, 2007). Generics and over-the-counter medicines continue to pose a challenge to a number of primary care classes, including proton pump inhibitors (PPIs), antihistamines, platelet aggregation inhibitors, and antidepressants (ibid.). The growth is slower for these primary care drugs and this might reflect the momentum of generics because of their price competitiveness.

The momentum of generics in 2006 was also confirmed in other reports (such as Visiongain, May 2006). In 2005, world generics sales totaled more than US$45 billion, a 14 percent rate of growth over 2004 (ibid.). In 2006, generics continued to be strong and accounted for more than half of the volume of pharmaceutical products sold in seven key world markets, including the United States, Canada, France, Germany, Italy, Spain, and the United Kingdom (IMS, 2007a). This trend is also likely to continue into the next decade (see Visiongain, May 2006). In an estimate by the *Wall Street Journal*, generics sold by top drug makers are likely to exceed $67 billion in annual US sales between 2007 and 2012, as more than three dozen drugs are losing their patents (Martinez and Goldstein, 2007). For example, Pfizer's patent on Lipitor, which ranks as the most successful drug ever invented, expires as early as 2010. Merck will also lose the patents of another three top-selling drugs: Fosamax for osteoporosis, Singulair for asthma, and Cozaar for controlling blood pressure. These three combined represent 44 percent of the company's 2007 revenue. In 2006, Merck had already lost its well-sold Zocor for controlling cholesterol (ibid.).

As mentioned earlier, major global health and demographic issues in the developed and developing countries have contributed to an increasing need for pharmaceuticals but there was an asymmetry in the R&D

of new drugs. For example, in 2006, most of the 31-plus new products launched in key markets were designed to address the health needs of the more affluent populations, such as cancer, cholesterol problems, diabetes, and so on. In this regard, the products that carried most expectation in 2006 were Gardasil®, the first vaccine to prevent cervical cancer; Januvia®, the first-in-class oral for Type II diabetes; and Sutent® for renal cancer (IMS, 2007a).

Of course, R&D drug development that caters to the affluent has paid off in the short term. In particular, drugs designed to contain high cholesterol problems, the top-ranked lipid regulators class, sold particularly well in developed markets and showed an increase of 7.5 percent over the previous year to $35.2 billion, despite patent loss of Simvastatin and Pravastatin in major markets. Other factors that drove up the sales volume include the entries of innovative generics such as Crestor® and Vytorin®, and the increasing demand from Medicare Part D patients in the United States (ibid.).

Given the high incidence of cancer in global populations, it is not surprising to see increasing sales of oncologics on the market (see Ozols, 1 January 2007). Those aimed at specific molecular targets are likely to sell well in the long run. The International Marketing Society (IMS) estimated that oncologics experienced an increase of 20.5 percent, reaching $34.6 billion in 2006 (IMS, 2007a). The sale of oncologics was the highest among the top ten therapeutic classes. Innovation in this class in 2006 resulted in an active program of R&D, leading to the development of 380 compounds. The targeted therapies have revolutionized cancer treatment, changing it from a life-threatening scenario to a chronic treatment-management program. The newer drugs are targeting specific molecules involved with cancerous growth (ibid.).

Other top-selling therapeutics were also designed to respond to population health needs in developed countries. Respiratory drugs sold well (Oversteegen, Rovini and Belsey, September 2007), ranking third among top therapy classes in 2006, and have experienced 10 percent growth in sales to a total of $24.6 billion, as prevalence of respiratory problems, such as allergies or influenzas, is rising. Autoimmune agents also experienced 20 percent growth in 2006 to $10.6 billion in sales. With the sale volume ranking the twelfth among leading classes, growth in autoimmune agents was driven by the increased use of anti-TNF agents such as Remicade® and Humira® and the expansion of approved indications for these products (IMS, 2007a).

Geographically, the share of profits does not necessarily reflect the direction of the growth momentum. On the one hand, North America, especially the United States, remains the center of action. North America accounted for 45 percent of global pharmaceutical sales, with an increase of 8.3 percent to $290 – a billion higher than the 5.4 percent in 2005. Canada experienced 7.6 percent growth. In comparison, pharmaceutical sales have slowed for three yeas in a row in the five major European markets (France, Germany, Italy, Spain and the United Kingdom), which, experiencing 4.4 percent growth to $123.2 billion, achieved less than 4.8 percent growth in 2005. The growth momentum is clearly with the emerging markets. For example, sales in Latin America grew 12.7 percent to $33.6 billion, while Asia Pacific (outside of Japan) and Africa grew 10.5 percent to $66 billion (ibid.).

On the US market, the increase in consumption is driven by a particular event. Namely, the growth in US prescription drug sales, which grew 8.3 percent to $274.9 billion in 2006, was mainly driven by the Medicare Part D prescription benefit (which extended the coverage to previously uninsured patients and provided more benefits to seniors) (DHHS, 29 September 2006). The plan has increased utilization of generics within new therapy classes, and the availability of new drugs for cancer and diabetes. In 2006, total US dispensed prescription volume grew at a rate of 4.6 percent rate, outpacing the 3.2 percent rate in 2005. It is forecast that US prescription sales growth is likely to remain in the range of 6 percent to 9 percent through 2010, as the Medicare Part D benefit is annualized and there is a need for more cost-effective medicine. It is believed that Medicare Part D has increased retail prescription volume by an estimated 1 to 2 percentage points and pharmaceutical sales by just under 1 percentage point. Clearly, Medicare Part D has directly contributed to strong pharmaceutical sales growth in 2006, as evidenced by the fact that more than 38 million Medicare beneficiaries had some form of prescription drug coverage by June 2006, according to Centers for Medicare & Medicaid Services (CMS) (see DHHS, 2006; IMS, 8 March 2007b, IMS Reports, "US Prescription Sales Jump 8.3 Percent in 2006, to $274.9 Billion").

Several components in the Medicare Part D plan have influenced pharmaceutical sales and will continue to affect the business strategy of the industry (Ibid.). First, the insurers are required to reimburse for all of the brands in six large, highly utilized classes, including antidepressants, antipsychotics, anti-convulsants, anti-retrovirals, anti-neoplastics, and immuno-suppressants. These classes made up about 20 percent of US pharmaceutical sales in 2006 (see the data from IMS, 2007b; and also DHHS, 2006). One related fact is that 17 percent of retail prescriptions in the United States were dispensed through the Medicare Part D program, and another is the need for savings and cost-effectiveness in Medicare Part D, which increases the demand for generics. The growing demand for generics is inevitable and will directly challenge the industry bottom line. It was noted that 15 of the top 20 products dispensed by Medicare Part D prescription volume were unbranded generic drugs. It was also noted that by the end of 2006, generics utilization, both branded and unbranded, through Medicare Part D already accounted for 63 percent of all dispensed prescriptions (IMS, 2007b). The largest increase was witnessed in generics of lipid regulators, antidepressants, and inhaled nasal steroids. What has contributed to the sharp increase in sales of unbranded generics was the $911 million worth consumption of Teva's Simvastatin, generic Zocor®; $902 million for Apotex's Clopidogrel, generic Plavix®; and $480 million for Greenstone's Sertraline, generic Zoloft®. Generics of Pravachol®, Flonase®, and Mobic®, would also affect the sale when the patents were expired (see the data from IMS, 2007b).

In this scenario of high demands for price cuts, product innovation is the key factor for the growth of the industry. Yet eagerness to roll out new innovations has been dampened by the FDA's cautious approach to approving drugs these days. This attitude is evidenced by the comparatively lower number of approvals in 2005 and 2006.

Nevertheless, this trend does not mean that the golden age of pharmaceutical growth is numbered. New potential lies in the sector's effectiveness in answering to the demands of the global population. As mentioned earlier, this agility in responding to population needs led to a handsome reward in 2005 and 2006, albeit only in developed markets. For example, in 2006, among the approved 18 new molecular entities (NMEs), four therapeutic biologics, and four vaccines, the largest profit potential (with blockbuster status of over $1 billion in global sales) was observed in Merck's ground-breaking cervical cancer vaccine Gardasil®; Merck's Januvia™ (the first of a new class of diabetes treatments); Genentech's Lucentis™ for macular degeneration; Pfizer's Sutent® for renal cell carcinoma; and Celgene's Revlimid® for transfusion-dependent anemia (IMS, 2007b). Merck's ground-breaking cervical cancer vaccine Gardasil® was the real story of pharmaceutical innovation. Similarly, the 2005 best-selling drugs also reflect population health issues. For example, the top-selling products among the 2005 drugs approved by the FDA included Pfizer's Lyrica® for epilepsy/pain; Sepracor's Lunesta® for insomnia; and Amylin/Lilly's Byetta® for diabetes (ibid.).

In 2006, the strongest growth was observed in the biotech sector. The search for new possibilities through biotechnology has led to a robust

20 percent growth to $40.3 billion. New products from this sector include Amgen's Aranesp®, experiencing a 42 percent increase and reaching $3.9 billion; Amgen's Enbrel® with a 12 percent increase to $3.1 billion; and Amgen's Neulasta® with a 28 percent increase to $2.9 billion. Oncologics showing strong growth are Rituxan® with an 18 percent increase to $2.1 billion; Avastin® with a 79 percent increase to $1.7 billion; and Herceptin® with an increase of 66 percent to $1.2 billion (facts cited from IMS, 2007b).

The unlimited possibilities in the biotech sector provide some hope for innovative pharmaceutical ideas. The approval of Sandoz's Omnitrope, a human growth hormone, by the US Food and Drug Administration in May 2006, through existing 505(b)2 pathway, was widely seen by the industry as a landmark decision for biotech products. Despite the uncertain prospects of the biotech sector as a whole, this development bodes well for other drugs in the pipelines because of the low barriers of entry and lack of regulation in this sector (see related discussions in IMS, 2007b). This explains why the industry has boosted its investment in the biotech sector. It was estimated that since 2005, large pharmas have spent $76 billion in buying up biotech firms (Mantone, 6 December 2007, "Big Pharma's Bitter Pill").

Despite the high hopes for biotech, it is questionable if it is the magic bullet that could possibly resolve all the problems facing the industry. The long-term outlook of the industry remains highly volatile. As IMS has pointed out, the pharmaceutical sector is likely to continue growing globally, but growth in developed societies will remain slow, with the United States leading at a growth rate of 6 percent to 9 percent through 2010 because of possible changes in the health care system after the 2008 presidential election. In addition, the expiration of some brands in 2006, estimated to be worth $14 billion of sales, and other brands' sales, worth $12 billion in 2007, in lipid regulators, antidepressants, platelet aggregation inhibitors, anti-emetics, and respiratory agents are expected to have had some impact on the industry.

Given the imbalance in supply and demand/need, the industry will be under increasing pressure from the outside to change its operation strategy.

Outsiders' perception of the pharmaceutical sector

In any discussion of the challenges facing the industry, it is important to address what outsiders perceive as the major strategy taken by the industry to maintain a robust growth level these days. These issues were summarized in a number of publications but the most comprehensive summary was offered by the former editor of the *New England Journal of Medicine*, Marcia Angell, in her 2004 book *The Truth about the Drug Companies*. Her criticism summarizes the concerns of the public about the growth strategy employed by the industry, that is, the failure to strike a balance between a high profits goal and its public heath obligations.

Problems with the cost of innovation

It is widely agreed that the pharmaceutical industry requires a high level of innovativeness and that the industry's efforts in generating certain innovative drugs has been quite successful in the 1990s. Yet increasingly, questions are raised as to who has really contributed to the innovativeness. It was pointed out that some of the basic research leading to eventual drug development has been carried out by universities and research institutions (see SciDeve, 2008; see also Wikipedia, 2007b; Angell, 2004). Angell pointed out that one-third of drugs marketed by the major pharmaceutical companies were licensed from universities or small biotech companies and these drugs were believed to be the most innovative ones (Angell, 2004; see also Lamberti, 2001). Some of the most innovative and effective drugs, such as Taxol, Epogen, and Gleevec, derived from NIH-funded or university research.

In the case of the discovery of AZT, an HIV treatment, it is believed that the scientist Samuel Broder, head of the National Cancer Institute in the United States, and his colleagues at the Duke University, had more to do with the discovery of the AIDS drug AZT than Burroughs Wellcome, the company that actually patented it.

Some questioned the innovativeness of the pharmaceutical sector because of the abundance of the "me-too" drugs on the market. It was pointed out that a large amount of resources were devoted to the development of a few drugs and that this redundancy could jeopardize the industry's ability to innovate. Angell reported that by 2004, there were six statins (Mevacor, Lipitor, Zocor, Pravachol, Lescol, and Crestor) on the market as lipid regulators and they are variants of Mevacor. In addition, it was noted that only 17 of the 78 drugs approved by the FDA in 2002 were regarded by the FDA as improvements over older drugs, with the rest being no more effective than the old ones. In another account, between 1998 and 2002, only 133 of 415 drugs approved, or 32 percent of the total, were new molecule drugs and only 14 percent were considered to be "truly innovative" (Angell, 2004). And, only 3 of the 7 innovative drugs approved in 2002 came from PhRMA members (ibid., 2004).

Critics of the pharmaceutical industry also voice their concern about the need to sustain a high level of innovation through pursuing a high-cost strategy. The cost of developing a drug is highly controversial and so far there is little knowledge about what the true cost is (see Public Citizen, 2001; Cptech, 2001, "Pharmaceutical industry R&D costs: Key findings about the Public Citizen Report"). One estimate in 2000 showed that the cost was no greater than $175 million after tax but another estimate by Public Citizen (2000) showed that the actual after-tax cost of developing a drug was less than $100 million (Angell, 2004). The $802 million estimated by the Tufts' Center was deemed by the industry's critics to be high, believing that this figure might be a pre-tax estimate that included the opportunity cost. Yet the industry counter-argued that this figure did not include the opportunity cost of capital and that in any case, including this opportunity cost is a usual practice in financing. The critics also pointed out that tax credits for the pharmaceutical companies could be as high as 50 percent when the tested drugs are orphan drugs, such as in the case of Retrovir, an AIDS drug (Angell, 2004). It was also pointed out that the tax rate for Pharmas was much lower between 1993 and 1996, 16.2 percent, compared to 27.3 percent for other major industries (see Public Citizen, 2001). The critics believed that if we took into account all the tax incentives that the industry has received, the actual after-tax estimate of the $802 million could be as low as $266 million (Angell, 2004).

In addition, when observing the phenomenon that a large amount of spending on R&D has produced few innovative drugs, the critics have also raised the issues of efficiency and effectiveness of pharmaceutical development (Angell, 2004), the latter of which has a direct impact on population health.

Effectiveness, validity and reliability

So far, the industry's efforts to generate effective cures for diseases, especially those in the developed societies, is a known achievement. Drugs like Prozac, Gleevec, statins, Viagra, Epogen, Taxol, and Prilosec are direct evidence of this effort. But questions were raised about the effectiveness of some heavily promoted drugs. It was pointed out that an NIH sponsored experiment, ALLHAT (Anti-hypertensive and Lipid-Lowering Treatment to Prevent Heart Attack Trial), involving 42,000 people and 600 clinics, which was also the largest experiment of this kind, showed that a generic diuretic pill, the least expensive of all the four drugs used in the experiment, was as effective as the other three drugs, Cardura by Pfizer, Zestril by AstraZeneca, and Prinivil by Merck.

The inexpensive old generic drug was also said to be better at preventing some of the complications of high blood pressure, especially heart disease and strokes (Angell, 2004). In another NIH study on prevention of adult-onset diabetes, it was found that diet and exercise was more effective than using a placebo or the drug metformin, the generic form of BMS's Glucophage). When examining these studies, the critics raised the same issue about the efficacy claims that had been made by the pharmaceutical industry.

In general, the critics raised issues concerning the industry's claims about pharmaceutical effectiveness in several areas. First, they point out that the potential of some new drugs tends to be overestimated, such as in the case l'Exubera, an insulin inhaler (*Le Monde*, 19 October 2007). The critics also questioned the practice of comparing a new drug with the placebo instead of comparing the new drug with an older drug when evaluating the effectiveness of the "me-too" drugs in clinical evaluations. There were also some concerns about the "make-believe" phenomenon, as evidenced by a number of cases or incidents (Angell, 2004). A survey showed that industry-sponsored research was nearly four times more likely to be favorable to the company's product as NIH-sponsored research (Bekelman, et al., 2006). In addition, the critics also said that negative results seemed to be suppressed (Angell, 2004). In another case, it was pointed out that Parke-Davis tried to promote Neurontin, an epilepsy drug, for off-label uses for other conditions by asking academics to endorse company-sponsored articles, or use medical liaisons to disseminate the article widely to practicing doctors (ibid.). These promotion efforts were believed to have led to Neurontin becoming a blockbuster with $2.7 billion sales in 2003 (ibid.).

The other example cited by the critics was the practice of using Phase IV surveillance studies to raise the drug's publicity and to influence doctors' drug choices and formulary recommendations, instead of improving drug effectiveness (Angell, 2004). It was also pointed out that some Phase IV studies were not published (Privitera, 2003). Phase IV are often contracted by CROs, using networks of private doctors in their offices and as a result, doctors are likely to prescribe the medicine tested (Angell, 2004). As a prominent example, Angell pointed out that the recommended use of estrogen and progesterone hormone replacement therapy to prevent heart disease was mainly based on industry-sponsored research and that this conclusion supporting the use of hormone replacement therapy has been refuted by NIH-sponsored research since the mid-2000s. New research has questioned the effectiveness of hormone replacement therapy in preventing heart disease in menopausal women. For example, the Women's Health Initiative (WHI) Hormone Program, jointly sponsored by the National Heart, Lung, and Blood Institute (NHLBI) and the National Cancer Institute (NCI), part of the National Institute of Health, found that this therapy increased the risks of breast cancer, heart disease, stroke, blood clots, and urinary incontinence (National Cancer Institute, 2007).

The point of contention was that instead of initiating innovative research, the industry tried to resort to business strategies to promote the efficacy claims of the new drugs. The critics believed that these strategies do not necessarily reflect the scientific validity or reliability of the new drugs in curing diseases (Goozner, 2004). The critics even questioned the pharmaceutical companies' contributions to the drug development process, or the clinical evaluations of a drug. The critics believed that the industry included that process as making up the entity of "innovativeness" (Angell, 2004). It was believed that this contribution to clinical evaluation is often used as the key evidence supporting the pharmaceutical companies' claim of the need to maintain a "high-price" scenario for drugs. Furthermore, the critics argued that even that claim was questionable because these days, the clinical trials were arranged through contract research organizations (CROs), which conducted about 80,000 clinical trials in the United States in 2001 and included 2.3 million human subjects (ibid.). It is the CROs that are responsible for conducting clinical trial evaluation of new drugs.

The question of maintaining the high profit scenario

The questions surrounding the "high-profit" scenario have tarnished the image of the large pharmaceutical companies. As mentioned in Chapter 1, the profits of pharmaceutical companies rank as one of the highest, with the average net return as a percentage of sales at more than 17 percent, higher than most other industries. Angell pointed out that in 2002, the total profits of $35.9 billion for the ten drug companies in the Fortune 500 were more than those for all the other 490 businesses combined of $33.7 billion (Angell, 2004; see also Newton, Thorpe and Otter, 2004).

Critics have raised more issues with the pharmas' strategies to maintain the "high-profit" scenario than just the high-profit scenario itself (see Angell, 2004). They believed that the pharmas have generated very creative strategies to maintain the profit at a high level. To begin with, it was noted that unlike most commodity prices, which charge the customers on the basis of manufacturing cost and market-driven profit margins, the prices of drugs are determined by what the pharmas perceive as the monetary value of the drugs, especially in the United States. In addition, Angell (2004) argued that drug prices in the United States reflected what the patients were willing to pay, not the R&D cost or the medical value of the medicine. Her argument implied that the prices would be much lower if they were based on the calculation of the R&D and manufacturing costs because the public sector has paid for some of the most innovative drugs, such as Taxol, Epogen, Procrit, and Neupogen. For example, in the case of Taxol, $10,000 to $20,000 was charged for a year's supply of Taxol when it first came on the market. This price was believed to be a 20-times' markup (ibid.). Another case was that of Claritin, Schering-Plough's top-selling drug. The price of Claritin was raised 13 times over five years, to a total increase of 50 percent, which was believed to have outpaced the rate of general inflation (ibid.).

The most mentioned practice to maintain the "high profit" scenario was the extension of the patent life of a drug (Goozner, 2004). The pharmas' efforts to extend patents was noted by their critics in a number of strategies. For example, the Hatch-Waxman Act provided up to five years of additional patent life for drugs experiencing long delays in coming to market because of clinical testing and approval (Angell, 2004). In addition, if a brand-name company sues a generic company for patent infringement, FDA approval of the generic drug would automatically be delayed for 30 months. Also, the company can extend the patent life of a brand by suing a generic company who intends to make copies of the brand that has just expired.

This strategy of extending patents through legal maneuvers is believed to have been widely practiced by pharmaceutical companies. It was noted that since the passing of Hatch-Waxman, the brand name companies routinely file not just one patent on their blockbusters, but a series of them that spreads through the life of the first one. The companies list any patents they want and use the legal option to get 30 months' extension. Another patent privilege was added when the Food and Drug Administration Modernization Act of 1997 allowed six months of extension of patent life if the drug is tested on children. It was noted that AstraZeneca has taken advantage of these rules and extended the patent life of Prilosec (Angell, 2004). Scherling-Plough has used similar tactics to extend the exclusive rights of Claritin and the same is true for Lilly's Prozac, and GSK's Paxil (ibid.).

Alternatively, the companies can use other strategies than litigation. For example, the owner of the branded drug will try to carve out a share in the generic market by introducing a generic version before the patent expires (Wikipedia, 2007b). Also, the company can introduce a "me-too" drug before a top-selling brand drug expires. This practice was noticed in the rolling out of the new heartburn drug Nexium to extend the life of Prilosec, which was a top-selling drug that grossed $6 billion in global sales for AstraZeneca; the campaign to market the replacement was believed to have cost half a billion US dollars (data cited from Angell, 2004). A similar practice was observed in the promotion of Clarinex over Claritin, which accounted for $2.7 billion of one-third of Shering-Plough's revenues (data cited ibid.). There is also the new "me-too" of Levitra and Cialis to compete with Viagra (data cited ibid.).

This need to maintain high profit through extending the market life of a blockbuster has created a competition among "me-too" drugs, such as in those lipid regulators. It was believed that Merck's Zocor, Pfizer's Lipitor, BMS's Pravachol, Novartis's Lescol, and AstraZeneca's Crestor were all variants of Merck's original's Mevacor (Angell, 2004). Similarly, GSK's Paxil and Pfizer's Zoloft are competitors of Lilly's Prozac, which accounted for 25 percent of Lilly's revenues before its patent expiration (data cited from Angell, 2004). Lilly then re-branded Prozac by naming it Prozac Sarafem for treating premenstrual dysphoric disorder (ibid.). The "me-too" drugs focus on high profitability and therefore they target certain conditions, such as: (1) chronic conditions affecting a larger number of people; (2) customers who can afford to pay; and (3) a highly elastic market (such as drugs for hypertension or cholesterol issues). In order to maintain the profit momentum of the first blockbuster, the industry has neither reduced the prices of the "me-too" drugs" nor expanded choices (ibid.).

According to the critics, another strategy to maintain the "high profit" scenario is to promote diseases over health. Or in Angell's (2004) words, the pharmaceutical companies "promote diseases to fit their drugs," instead of promoting cures for diseases. Some call this phenomenon "disease mongering" or overmedicalization (Moynihan and Cassels, 2005; PLOS Medicine, 2006, *A Collection of Articles on Disease Mongering*).

Critics of the industry also observed that overmedicalization has become a phenomenon in developed as well as prosperous developing societies, such as Taiwan, or the urban populations in China. In the United States, it was noted that in 1965 when Medicare was enacted, drugs were cheaper and Americans took much fewer prescription drugs (Angell, 2004).

Aggressive marketing

Related to the increasing consumption of pharmaceuticals in developed societies, especially in the United States, is the creative marketing efforts of the industry and this is also the major criticism directed against the industry. Critics argued that most pharmaceutical expenditure has been invested in boosting marketing, not on innovative R&D (see, for example, Angell, 2004).

Estimates of the marketing budget of large pharmas vary. A conservative estimate showed that about US$19 billion a year was spent on the promotion of drugs (Moynihan, 2003b, "Who pays for the pizza? Redefining the relationships between doctors and drug companie"). But Angell (2004) pointed out that the estimate should be higher and that the budget for marketing and administration actually is larger than that for R&D and the marketing expenditure has continued rising. For example, in 1990, R&D was 11 percent of total sales; 14 percent in 2000; 35 percent in 2001; and then about 15.9 percent in 2006. In comparison, it was suggested the marketing budget has been constantly higher (ibid.). For example, the marketing budget was estimated to be 36 percent of the sales revenue in 1990 (ibid.). In 2002, which was the focal point of Angell's analysis, an estimate showed that the pharmaceutical companies had sales totaling $217 billion with a profit margin of 17 percent, but they only spent 14 percent on R&D. In contrast, about 31 percent was spent on marketing and administration.

The venues for marketing drugs are several and in exception to the ill-regulated regions in developing countries, the United States is one of the most liberal systems in allowing pharmas access to various marketing channels. These channels include health care journals, direct advertising to the general public, physicians, other health care providers, legislators, and health events (such as professional conferences and continuing education).

Among all the targets, marketing to physicians has one of the most important impacts because physicians are on the front line of contact with patients. They are the primary decision makers for prescription drugs use. They make decisions not only for FDA-approved drug use but also for the off-label use. They are the key to boosting prescription drug sales. Often, the physicians' offices are where the field troops, the pharmaceutical sales people, are deployed (see Myers, 2007). Pharmaceutical sales personnel compose the core of the aggressive marketing effort and their size is by no means modest for any pharmaceutical company. It is believed that a medium-sized pharmaceutical company might have a sales force of 1000 representatives and the number can exceed tens of thousands of sales representatives for the largest companies. It was noted that by 2003, there were approximately 100,000 pharmaceutical sales reps in the United States interacting with more than 120,000 pharmaceutical prescribers (see Robinson, November 2003). It was also noted that these had doubled in the four years from 1999 to 2003, costing more than $5 billion on communication with physicians, and this statistic was believed to be a conservative estimate. One of the tools used by pharmaceutical companies to market drugs to physicians and health providers is the use of specialized health care marketing research companies to perform marketing research. One of the marketing tools is free drug samples. Angell (2004) reported that in 2001, drug companies sent 88,000 representatives to give doctors nearly $1 billion worth of "free samples."

In addition to physicians, the other marketing target are the third-party payers, such as private insurance or public health bodies (e.g., the NHS in the United Kingdom, Medicare in the United States), who decide which drugs to pay for, and restrict the drugs that can be prescribed through the use of formularies. The buying power of the third-party can be very large because they restrict the brands, types, and number of drugs that they will cover. Angell reported that large pharmas in the United States derived a large part of their revenues from employee-sponsored insurance and state-run Medicaid programs (Angell, 2004). Not only can the third party payers affect drug sales by including or excluding a particular drug from a formulary, they can affect sales by tiering or placing bureaucratic hurdles to prescribing certain drugs as well. The state Medicaid programs often try to save programs by asking for deep discounts for drugs. This is also true for the new Medicare Part D prescription plan in the United States.

The most controversial channel of marketing is direct-to-consumer (DTC) advertising. As mentioned earlier, liberation in the presentation of risks in advertisements of drugs in the 1997 legislation allows direct marketing of prescription drugs to consumers. It was noted that expenditures on DTC ads almost tripled between 1997 and 2001, increasing from 25 percent to 64 percent in total TV ads. It was pointed out that in 2001, the FDA had only 30 reviewers to review 34,000 DTC ads (Angell, 2004). The critics believed that DTC ads mislead consumers, making consumers pressure doctors to prescribe new, expensive, and often marginally helpful drugs, even when a more conservative option might be better and safer (see also US Department of Health and Human Services, August 1999, "FDA Guidance for Industry on Consumer-Directed Broadcast Advertisements").

The center of the controversy related to pharmaceutical marketing is not the size of the marketing budget or force, but the methods employed (see the results of a 2005 review by a special committee of the UK government in the EU context; European Public Health Alliance, 2008). Criticism in this area surrounds accusations and findings of influence on doctors and other health professionals with inappropriate methods; buying research support; biased information to health professionals (see No Free Lunch (2008); see also Kaufman, 6 May 2005); high-prevalence advertising in journals and conferences; political influence peddling (more than any other industry in the United States (Ismail, 7 July 2005); sponsorship of medical schools or nurse training; involvement in continuing educational events and playing a role in influencing the curriculum (Moynihan, 2003a).

Key evidence was illustrated in several cases with the role of sales reps in influencing physicians often being criticized. For example, drug reps give doctors free samples, educational grants, consulting fees, free attendance at medical conferences in resorts, lavish gifts, expensive dinners, vacations, junkets to luxurious settings, or cash rewards, which are actually frowned upon by the American Medical Association and compromise the ethical guidelines of the PhRMA (Angell, 2004). Another way to influence physicians is through health meetings. It was noted that the number of promotional meetings has increased dramatically from 120,000 in 1998 to 371,000 in 2004 (Hensley and Martinez, 15 July 2005). In 2000, the top ten pharmaceutical companies were spending just under US$1.9 billion on 314,000 such events (Quintiles Transnational, 2001; see also Gagnon and Lexchin, 2008). Some of these meetings are framed as continuing education events. For example, in 2001, drug companies paid over 60 percent of the costs of continuing medical education and contracted private medical education and communication companies (MECCs) to plan the meetings, prepare teaching materials, and produce speakers (Angell, 2004). MECCs often have some links, or are even owned by large advertising agencies (ibid.). They are the go-between for the drug companies and doctors to promote drugs.

Influence peddling

The leading controversy is what many perceive as political influence peddling (see The Center for Public Integrity, 2005).

First, the pharmaceutical and health products industry is the largest among all industries. For example, in 2005, the sector spent more than $675 million in federal lobbying in the United States (Center for Public Integrity, 2005). It was noted that the industry hired around 3000 lobbyists, more than a third of whom were former federal officials in the House, the Senate, the FDA, the Department of Health and Human

Services, and other executive branch offices. These lobbyists for the industry had worked for the Ways and Means Committee, Senate Judiciary Committee, Health, Education, Labor and Pensions Committees. According to Public Citizen, from 1997 to 2002, the industry spent "$478 million on lobbying" and the planned budget of lobbying seems to have increased from year to year (Angell, 2004, p. 198). Second, political influence peddling is carried out through generous campaign contributions. For example, in 1999–2000, drug companies gave 20 million in direct campaign contributions, 80 percent of which went to the Republicans, and another $65 million in "soft" money (ibid.). Third, according to Angell (2004), influence is practiced through the setup of "front groups" masquerading as grassroots organizations, such as Citizens for Better Medicare, which spent $65 million in 1999–2000 to fight against any form of drug price regulation. United Seniors Association, spending $18 million in the 2002 election, supported PhRMA's position. Fourth, critics said that the large pharmas had tried to influence the FDA. For example, the PDUFA (Prescription Drug User Fee Act) passed in 1992 allowed the FDA to charge the large pharmas user fees for drug evaluations, which had accounted for more than half of the FDA's budget with a total of more than $260 million in 2002 (ibid.). This presented an obvious conflict of interest issue. Under this act, the FDA, who takes money from the pharmas, is under legal mandates to approve drugs faster in the United States than in their counterparts in Europe. In one case, the FDA hearing records that "at 92 percent of the meetings at least one member had a financial conflict of interest," and "at 55 percent of meetings, half or more of the FDA advisers had conflicts of interest" (Cauchon, D. 25 September, 2000, "FDA advisors tied to industry"; Gribbin, 18 June 2001). These political endeavors were said to have contributed to some form of political favoritism (Goozner, 2004; Angell, 2004).

Inadequacy in meeting the needs of developing countries

A more global criticism of the pharmas is the ignoring of its social and humanitarian responsibilities in the global community. This criticism originates from the late 1990s, during the height of the AIDS epidemic. In 2003, South Africa's Competition Committee ruled that GSK and Boehringer Ingelheim had violated the country's Competition Act by charging high prices and refusing to license their patents for generics manufacturers in return for reasonable royalties (BBC, 10 December 2003, "AIDS activists say GlaxoSmithKline is to allow the manufacture of cheap generic drug versions in South Africa"). Under the pressure from human rights activists, both companies had to agree to grant licenses for generic production of anti-retroviral drugs. Yet initially, the large pharmas had threatened to sue the South African government. In return, the Clinton Administration, who represented the pharmaceutical interests, threatened trade sanctions. If it was not for the vocal support from civil society, the pharmas would have prevailed in their insistence on not providing life-saving medicines at a lower price. Today, despite the DOHA declaration and 30 August decision allowing compulsory licensing and parallel imports for resolving some public health challenges, poor countries still face major difficulties in invoking these measures for pharmaceutical access. And the critics see that the major hurdle comes from the immense influence of the pharmas on global health care politics.

Challenges facing the multinational pharmaceutical industry

The major challenges facing the multinational pharmaceutical companies are several. Some of the most mentioned challenges include innovation, increasing competition from generics, asymmetry in addressing population health needs and over-concentration in developed markets, quality control, and pressure from regulatory authorities for price control. Among all the challenges, the need for innovative R&D is widely regarded as the most formidable challenge facing the industry, but innovation also has a two-way interaction with other challenges. Innovation requires an astute understanding of population health issues, etiology, environment, social determinants, cultural practices, and genetic origins. In other words, it is a test of the imagination in finding the widest range of possibilities of solutions. When the pharmaceutical makers have innovative R&D, which assures an inexhaustible supply of effective pipelines, then other challenges will be minimized. Even critics of the industry praise the pharmaceutical industry for what it has accomplished since the nineteenth century. The invention of antibiotics, aspirin, penicillin, statins, and so on has significantly improved the population health, both in quantitative and qualitative terms. As Angell (2004), one of the most candid critics of the industry, bluntly put it, "the truth is that good drugs sell." Gleevec provided the most relevant case in point; Angell (2004) commented that Gleevec can sell itself even without a major marketing and promotional effort with information from credible professional journals and meetings. The same can be said about Lipitor and Zoloft.

The need for innovation has never been more urgent given the difficulty in finding truly new drugs, increasing scrutiny from regulatory authorities, and the imminent expiry of patents on major profitable drugs. It was noted that between 2002 and 2006, the industry brought 43 percent fewer new chemical-based drugs to market than in the last five years of the 1990s, despite their doubling of research and development spending (Centre of Public Integrity, 2005). The situation is even more troubling when considering the scenario in which the pharmas are losing patents for their high-profit drugs, as mentioned earlier. According to one estimate, it is predicted that $40 billion in US sales could be lost at the top ten pharma companies because of patent expiration of 19 blockbuster drugs by 2008 (Ebisch, 2005).

The issue of innovation has become problematic for the pharmas since the beginning of the 2000s. It was forecast between 2000 and 2004, only 32 of 314 drugs would be truly innovative: these drugs coming mainly from Pharmacia, Merck, BJS in 2000; Merck in 2001; none in 2002; and one each from Pharmacia, Wyeth, and Abbott in 2003, with the conspicuous absence of either Lilly or Schering-Plough (data from Angell, 2004). In one instance, in the third quarter of 2007, Novartis's profit return was below the estimate of analysis because of its loss of three patents of Zelnorm (colon problems), Lotrel (hypertension), and Lamisil (ringworm) (*Le Monde*, 2007). Similarly, in 2006, the loss of patent life by two of the most successful and largest brands – Zoloft and Zocor – has impacted the profit profiles of the pharmaceutical makers (IMS, 2007b). A similar negative consequence is likely to follow with the expiration of Norvasc® and Ambien® (ibid.).

It is predicted that 150 mid-sized new compounds will be needed by 2008 in the US alone to compensate for the profit gap (Ebisch, 2005). The pharmaceutical companies have no other option but to increase their investment in R&D. In this case, innovation is not a choice, but a survival requirement. A counter strategy has been suggested that while pharmaceutical companies today focus on blockbusters, in seven years' time they will have to focus on thousands of drugs to maintain their profit levels (ibid.).

Some also suggest that one way to get out of this dilemma is to use biotechnology to improve innovation, but the concern with biotechnology in drug development lies in its high cost and high uncertainty (see, for example, some related discussions in Griffiths, 2004). The large pharmas' alliance with the biotechnology sector has certainly widened possibilities for innovative new drugs, as biotechnology makes it possible to manipulate cells' genetic structure to produce specific proteins.

The biotech sector complements the large pharmas' expertise. The new knowledge gained in molecular biology in the 1970s allows a new method of synthesizing potential drugs that is not in the traditional pharmas' expertise. This alliance allows the large pharmas to benefit from the fruit of the R&D, while the small biotech companies gain financing, marketing, and management support from the large pharmas (Schweitzer, 1997). Some fruitful results have been observed in the development of biogenerics and many companies focus on erythropoe-itin because of the size of the market (see Griffiths, 2004). Yet overall, the future of biotech gaining a dominant position remains more a calculation than a reality.

Besides the uncertainty in biotechnology, some saw the competition from generics as a challenge to the pharmas (see Martinez and Goldstein, 2007; see also IMS, 2007). The impetus for the growth of generics derived from the Hatch-Waxman Act legislation in 1984, which helped increase the generics' share from 20 percent of prescriptions in 1984 to 50 percent in 2002 (Angell, 2004). As mentioned earlier, the patent expiration of some major drugs, which started in the early 2000s, pro-vides another impetus. This trend, beginning with the expiration of Lilly's Prozac and AstraZeneca's Prilosec for heartburn and amounting to $6 billion in 2001 for those companies, was believed to have an impact on the revenues of $35 billion in annual loss for large pharmas (ibid.). This trend continued when Bristol-Myers-Squibb's lost its most profitable drug Glucophage for diabetes, and Schering-Plough lost Claritin in 2002, the latter of which accounted for one-third of the company's revenues (ibid.).

The increasing momentum of the demand for generics added another impetus for the growth of generics. It was noted that the profits of such large pharmas as Pfizer (United States) and Novartis (Switzerland) were already affected by the increasing sale of generics (*Le Monde*, 2007). In 2007, Pfizer announced that its profits in the third quarter, US$761 mil-lion, were much lower than the profits in the third quarter of the previ-ous year of about US$2.8 billion. In this trend, the emergence of so-called "branded generics," which are priced between the brands and generics, could pose another challenge to the makers of brand drugs (related discussions from Angell, 2004).

Asymmetry in meeting population health needs

The major challenge to innovation is related to the asymmetry in producing effective drugs in global settings. As mentioned in Chapter 1, most of the drugs have been produced to meet the demand and needs of the populations in developed societies, especially drugs for such chronic illnesses as cardiovascular problems, hypertension, diabetes, obesity, and so on. There has been very little investment in producing cures for those diseases or illnesses facing developing countries. Some global attention to neglected diseases, such as malaria, TB, onchocercia-sis, and trachoma, in resource-poor countries is a fairly recent phenom-enon. The controversy surrounding the patents of AIDS drugs has revealed the extent of this asymmetry in drug development to meet global health needs. As mentioned in Chapter 1, the focal point of the criticism against the global pharmas was that most of the disease burden has been in developing countries, but more than 90 percent of the cures were made for the populations in developed societies. The criticism was not just about the high-profit or patent protection scenarios for the large pharmas, but was also about the lack of understanding of this asymmetry, which actually helped the spread of diseases and epidem-ics. The litigation against South Africa by 41 pharmaceutical companies in March of 2001 for South Africa's enacting the country's Medicines Act, which would allow compulsory licensing and parallel imports of cheap AIDS drugs, was a reality check for the world and pharmaceutical industries. This makes plain to the world that the unfortunate dilemma faced by drug making is about striking a balance between business reality and population health reality.

The worry about price control

Price control, a major challenge facing the industry, occurs as a result of failure to address such other challenges as population health needs and over-concentration in the markets in developed societies, along with short-sighted strategies to protect market share and inadequacy in inno-vativeness.

The possibility of price control in the United States is said to be a major concern for large pharmas because, as mentioned in Chapter 1, more than 45 percent of their profits derive from pharmaceutical sales there. Yet the United States is also the only country without pharmaceutical pricing regulation that allows the pharmas to set phar-maceutical prices. As mentioned in Chapter 1, other major industrial-ized countries or emerging powers, such a Australia, Canada, and most EU members (such as France, Germany, Italy, Japan, the Netherlands, Spain, Switzerland, and Sweden) have some form of price control. Most countries, such as Canada, use reference indicators, such as the median prices of the pharmaceuticals in other developed countries. The United Kingdom does not regulate the price, but puts a ceiling on the profits.

The concern for pharmaceutical prices in the United States is not unfounded. First, the US population is graying. Second, the prevalence of chronic health issues, such as hypertension, diabetes, cardiovascular problems, depression, and respiratory problems has increased demands for effective cures. It was noted that from 1960 to 1980, the sale of prescription drugs as a percentage of GDP in the United States was stable, but from 1980 to 2000 this figure had tripled. In 2002, the total was more than $200 billion a year, which includes consumer purchases at drug stores and mail order pharmacies and 25 percent markup for wholesalers, pharmacists, and other middlemen, and retailers (Angell, 2004; see also Center for Policy Alternatives, 2000, "Playing fair: State action to lower prescription drug prices"). In total, this figure accounted for about 50 percent of the global sales of $400 billion (Angell, 2004).

Price concern is most acute among the elderly in the United States as life expectancies have continued to increase (Long, 1994; see also Lichtenberg, 11, July 2007, "Yes, new drugs save lives"). Between 1991 and 2004 alone, US life expectancy increased by 2.33 years and as this trend continues, the need for prescriptions has also increased (ibid.). In 2003, it was pointed out, the average price of the 50 drugs most used by senior citizens was nearly $1500 for a year's supply and it was noted that in this scenario, an American who does not have any health coverage would have to spend $9000 from their own pockets per year (Angell, 2004). A report pointed out that an estimated one million Americans bought their medicines from Canadian drugstores in 2002, totaling a $700 million business, or over the Internet, despite the US Congress' legal ban (see Barry, April, 2003). In 2002, there were 140 Internet pharmacies in Canada, an increase from 10 percent in 1999. And the cross-border drug trade is believed to be growing. It would be no exaggeration to say that Canada is likely to become America's backdoor pharmacy if the drug prices continue to grow at their current pace.

In the United States, there are increasing demands from the public for legislation to enact some forms of drug price control through the requirement of cost-effectiveness and use of generics alternatives. This is said to have put new pressures on pharmaceutical manufacturers to consider those issues related to value, pharmaceutical pricing, and affordability (see related discussions in IMS, 2007b). This has also given rise to the "MacDonaldization" of pharmaceutical provision in the United States, exemplified by the affordable pharmaceutical plans offered by one of the largest retail pharmacies, Wal Mart.

In addition to private initiatives, the US government has also taken notice of the need for affordable pharmaceuticals. Against the background of an increasing demand for affordable medicine, the Medicare Part D Plan emerged. This plan had made certain promises to address the pharmaceutical price issues facing the American elderly.

The Medicare prescription drug benefit, or Medicare Part D Plan, passed by Congress and signed into law by the President, made several promises. First, on savings, it promised to save seniors an average of $1200 a year (US Department of Health and Human Services, 2006). In addition, it also promised savings on premiums, because the premiums for these plans will even be lower than the ones the seniors signed up to in 2007, and this lower rate is likely to benefit 83 percent of beneficiaries as some plans would have premiums of less than $20 a month. The other promise is the increase of choices and expansion of coverage. Beneficiaries are promised that they will have more plan options that offer enhanced coverage, including zero deductibles and coverage in the gap for both generics and preferred brand name drugs. Some plans have promised to increase the drugs on their formularies by 13 percent (Department of Health and Human Services, 2006).

In a sense, Medicare Part D is a subtle form of price control; the mechanism of price control being competition. The US government reported that during the 2007 bidding process, strong competitive pressure among providers had led to lower costs of coverage by 10 percent less than in 2006. It is clear this competitive factor has indirectly achieved certain price control effects.

Summary

The global pharmas are standing at a paradoxical cross-roads in seeing their future development. On the one hand, they have never enjoyed such heights of profit splendor in their development; on the other hand, they have never faced so much criticism of their business strategy. This criticism reflects the question of the values of medicine in two divergent realities, the business reality and the global health reality. On the one hand, the global pharmaceutical industry is a formidable sector of the economy that has also created other sub-economies. But, on the other hand, they have made important contributions to the saving of lives in the world. Outsiders, though, also believe that the industry's contribution has been handsomely rewarded by their innovations as well as by their aggressive business strategies.

However, outsiders/critics were also concerned about the consequences of these strategies and have taken actions to force the industry to address them. Critics in the United States have generated a long list of what they believe are major challenges from the industry to health care in the United States and the world. For example, they alleged that the pharmaceutical companies were "illegally overcharging Medicaid and Medicare, paying kickbacks to doctors, engaging in anti-competitive practices, colluding with generic companies to keep generic drugs off the market, illegally promoting drugs for unproved uses, engaging in misleading direct-to-consumer advertising, and...covering up evidence...." And these accusations can go on and on (Angell, 2004, p. 19).

The critics see these revelations as the coming of a perfect storm that could effect the positive development of the industry. The possible consequences could be decrease in innovative output, increase in measures of price controls, cross-border trade, state demand for drug discounts, and increasing demand to reform the current intellectual property rights regime (see related discussions in Martinez and Goldstein, 2007).

Some local governments in the United States have taken action to reduce pharmaceutical spending and this is likely to have an impact on the bottom line of the pharmaceutical sector. In 2003, the governors of Minnesota, Illinois, Iowa, and Wisconsin expressed that they intended to import cheaper medicines from Canada in order to save state budgets, and millions of US dollars for their citizens in the process (Harris, 23 October 2003, "Cheap drugs from Canada"). At the same time, the Illinois democratic governor, Rod R. Blagojevich, supported an online petition to persuade federal officials to allow drug imports. Governor Blagojevich said that millions of US dollars could have been saved from the US$340 million spent in 2002 on prescription drugs for 230,000 Illinois state employees and retirees if Illinois imported drugs from Canada (ibid.). By 2002, the Mayor of Springfield, Massachusetts, had offered city employees a health plan for purchasing their prescription drugs from a Canadian pharmacy and he believed that it would save $9 million of city expenditure. The city of Boston also planned to follow in the footsteps of Springfield, and these developments have also attracted interest from other states.

The measure taken by Maine aroused the most attention. Maine was the first state to pass the "Maine Rx" law, allowing the state to bargain with the pharmas for lower prices for the uninsured (see Pear, 25, December, 2002; see also Denning, 2003). The state threatened to cap the prices or exclude the drugs from the state's formularies. The phramas went to the Supreme Court in 2003, but the Supreme Court refused to review the matter and sent the case back to the lower courts. Maine's action, which reflected a realistic concern for the budgetary bottom line facing most of the state governments, was supported by 28 other states.

It was noted that the public had also expressed their discontent with the pharmas and their efforts have brought about some results (see the evidence in Angell, 2004). It was observed that the industry has faced a tidal wave of investigations and lawsuits, such as defrauding Medicare or Medicaid by billing for inflated prices, anti-competitive practices, and marketing drugs for unapproved uses. In addition, critics also high-lighted the fact that consumer and activist groups were gathering their ammunition to fight against high prices. For example, the Prescription Access Litigation Project, whose goal is to make prescription drug prices more affordable for consumers, has resorted to the use of class action litigation and public education to bring about changes. They have challenged illegal pricing tactics and deceptive marketing by drug companies, Pharmacy Benefit Managers, and other pharmaceutical industry players that fail to pass on savings to consumers or health plans (Prescription Access Litigation, 2007). In early 2002, the public backlash had forced eight companies to pay a total of $2.2 million in fines and settlements (Angell, 2004).

In the face of these criticisms, the global pharmas have provided their responses and their responses also reflect some truths about the business world in which they operate. They have continued to point out that the large pharmas operate in a market-driven framework, in which profit returns are the guiding principle of its operation. It is also true that they have to answer to their investors and maximize the value of their stocks and that their investors include a large number of citizens with pension plans vested in the global pharmas' development (see related arguments in Angell, 2004).

Given these criticisms and counter-criticisms, those who are concerned about population health raise the question: what is the solution then? Or is there a solution at all? Chapter 4 will provide an answer to this question by presenting a contrast between a planting strategy and a plucking strategy in global pharmaceutical development. First, though, Chapter 3 looks at the role of BRICA in the global provision of pharmaceuticals.

3
BRICA in Global Pharmaceutical Provision

The future of the global pharmaceutical supply and demand chain lies in the development potential of the BRICA countries. BRICA is the abbreviation of Brazil, Russia, India, China and Africa. To begin with, most discussions about the future of the pharmaceutical industry surround the BRIC countries, that is, Brazil, Russia, India and China. The pharmaceutical potential of BRIC lies in its market size, population informatics for prevalent diseases, especially neglected diseases, as well as traditional and plant medicine. However, as the outside world has gained more understanding of the health issues facing Africa, the African continent also constitutes immense potential to be part of the solution of global pharmaceutical supply and demand.

This chapter will present a detailed analysis of BRICA's role in the global supply and demand chain. In specific, the analysis will present an overview of the macro-economic and population health profiles of BRIC; development of BRIC's pharmaceutical market, such as crude materials, life saving generics, OTC, and herbal medicines; BRICA's participation in the global market, and BRIC's future role in pharmaceutical access and global health. In addition, this writing will focus on analysis of the advantages and disadvantages, competition, domestic and global market potential, and critical challenges facing BRIC in the global pharmaceutical marketplace. The potential of BRIC's local strengths, such as traditional medicines and raw materials will also be offered. In addition, it will analyze the potential of Africa as a pharmaceutical production hub and market.

BRICA: The emerging economic powers

The term "BRICA" originally derives, as we have noted, from the acronym BRIC (including Brazil, Russia, India, and China) and commonly denotes a high-growth block of the emerging markets, although some also believe that the more accurate acronym replacing BRIC should be CEMENT, or Countries in Emerging Markets Excluded by New Terminology (Johnson, 11 December 2006, "Emerging Markets: BRICs sceptics have their backs to the wall").

To begin with, the term "BRICA" was coined in Goldman Sachs' report in 2003 highlighting the economic potential of Brazil, Russia (and its neighboring countries in Eastern Europe), India, and China. At the time, these countries already encompassed 39 percent of the world's population, with a GDP of $15.435 trillion dollars, predicted to become four major economies by 2050. Between 2000 and 2005, the BRICs contributed about 28 percent of global growth in US dollar terms and 55 percent in Purchasing Power Parity (PPP) terms (Goldman Sachs, 1 December 2005, "How solid are the BRICs?"). The report made the forecast that by 2025, the four economies combined are likely to account for more than half of the total of the G6 economies (Goldman Sachs, October 2003, "Dreaming with BRICs: The path to 2050"). In this forecast, India's economy will surpass that of Japan's by 2032; China's will surpass that of the United States by 2041; India will be among the top three economies; and Russia would be ahead of Germany, France, Italy and the United Kingdom by 2033. It was suggested that BRICs' economies could be larger than the G6 economies by 2039 (ibid.). Among the four, India has received the most favorable long-term prediction. It was predicted that while the GDPs of all other major economies would slow down in their growth rates, India is likely to maintain a steady 5 percent growth rate in the next 50 years and will raise its US dollar income per capita in 2050 to 35 times current levels.

In comparison to later events, these predictions proved to be conservative. By 2005, the BRICs had witnessed an increase in domestic savings to US$240 billion and had become an increasingly important source of lending to relieve US deficit situations. The volume of foreign direct investment in BRICs has also increased to 15 percent of the global total, about three times the 2000 level. The second Goldman-Sachs report has also shown that BRICs have also increased their global investment to more than 3 percent, an increase of about six times since 2000 (Goldman Sachs, 2005). BRIC countries are now the most favored target of investment. On capital flow, BRICs held more than 30 percent of world reserves by 2005, with China taking the lead, followed by Russia, India, and Brazil (ibid.).

On their participation in global markets, the BRICs have also become a major consumer of raw material, energy, and oil (see related discussions in Goldman Sachs, 2005). The demand of BRICs for oil has been conspicuous, rising to 18 percent of global share in 2005. A similar dynamic has been observed in BRICs' market capitalization. Their stock markets have continued to climb to about 4 percent of the global total by 2005 and are moving at a much faster pace than predicted (ibid.). Brazilian, Russian and Indian indices had increased by 150 percent between 2003 and 2005. The volume of the stock market has increased by 4 times from 2003 to 2007 (*World Journal*, 11 March 2007, "From the gold BRIC four to the new diamond of eleven"). In 2006 alone, the growth rate of BRIC reached 67 percent while in comparison, the average index of the global markets grew by only 17 percent. In 2006, the gross value of the four capital markets had increased by 113 percent, three times the growth of the global total. In this picture, China's capital market had doubled and Russia has experienced about 70 percent growth in the value of its capital market. China was projected to overtake the United States by 2040, while India was predicted to overtake Japan by 2033 (Goldman Sachs, 2005). The momentum of India and China in the service and manufacturing sectors has been observed in the global market (ibid.).

The economic momentum of the BRICs has not seen any limits. The rate of growth of BRICs was so fast that in the early 2000s, IMF's forecast of the growth of BRIC was outperformed by 2007. The IMF originally predicted that the growth rates would be 5 percent for Russia, 4 percent for Brazil, 8 percent for China, 5–6 percent for India. China was racing at a rate of about 10–12 percent of GDP growth from 2005 to 2007 (see (Reuters, 28 March 2007, "Update1-Brazil revises 2006 GDP growth upward to 3.7 percent"). By the beginning of 2008, China had already overtaken Germany in terms of overall GDP. At the same time, India's growth rates were about 9–9.4 percent (Kumar, 31 May 2007, "India's GDP expanded at fastest pace in 18 years"). Even Brazil is predicted to have a steady rate of growth of 4.3 percent from 2008 to 2012 (*Economist*, 23 April 2008, "Country briefings: Brazil"). By the end of 2007, the economy of India was the twelfth largest in the world, with a GDP of US$1.25 trillion, according to Credit Swisse (*Economic Times*, 26 April 2007, "Mr Re gets India $1 trillion gang"). India is the third largest in terms of purchasing power parity and it is the second fastest growing major economy in the world, with a GDP growth rate of 9.4 percent for the fiscal year 2006–07 (Kumar, 2007). Despite its historical economic fluctuations, Brazil has also shown a growth rate of more than 5 percent since the beginning of the 2000s. The Goldman Sachs' report believed that Brazil's economy is likely to overtake Italy by 2025; France by 2031;

and the United Kingdom and Germany by 2036. Brazil is likely to maintain about 5.3 percent of growth rate by 2050. A sequel to the first Goldman Sachs report also forecast that the GDP per capita in the BRIC countries will also see significant improvements. For example, it is suggested that there will be a large increase of the middle class in BRIC nations. That is, the number of people with an annual income over a threshold of $3000, will double in number by 2007 and reach 800 million people within a decade. It also predicts that in 2025, the number of people in BRIC nations earning over $15,000 may reach over 200 million with a spill-over effect in the consumption of higher-priced or even luxury goods. This second report suggests that in a decade, China and India are likely to dominate the world economy (Goldman Sachs, 2005). The BRICs also grew rapidly in global trade. As a follow-up report by Goldman-Sachs showed, by 2005, BRIC's share of global trade increased to 15 percent, which doubles its level from 2001 (ibid.). The fact that the sub-prime financial crisis that surged in 2007 in the United States has generated a less significant impact on the BRICs countries is also favorable to the movement of capital into the BRIC economies (see *Finance Management Weekly,* Part III: Review of Goldman Sach's prediction, 16 Jan, 2008, "BRIC 4 and BRIC 11").

BRIC's economies have also shown unique strengths in economic growth. For example, Brazil has the strengths of natural resources and agricultural outputs (*Economist*, 2008; *World Journal*, 2007). Brazil's GDP per capita is also higher than most of the BRIC countries. In global ranking of GDP per capita, Brazil ranks 65th, compared to Russia at 59th, China at 86th and India at 118th (Wikipedia, 2007b, "BRIC"). Among the four nations, Brazil's economy is more diverse and its financial system is also more globally integrated. Its investment policies are more friendly to foreign investors than other BRICs. Its efforts in poverty reduction is also likely to contribute to social and economic stability (*Economist*, 2008; Wikipedia, 2007b; *Economist*, 12 April 2007, "Land of promise").

In comparison, China's major advantages are market size, high savings rate, high investment rates, a large labor force, human capital, and political will and agile public sector leadership. India's advantages are a vast highly skilled labor force, human capital, and market size. It was predicted that around 700 million Indians are likely to move into urban settings by 2050, which will have significant implications for demand for urban infrastructure, real estate, and services (Goldman Sachs, 2007, "India's rising growth potential"). It is also predicted that between 2007 and 2020, India's GDP per capita in US$ terms is likely to quadruple, and that the Indian economy will surpass the United States (in US$) by 2043 (ibid.; Wikipedia, 2007b). Russia's advantages are natural resources, rate of industrialization, and market size.

For a long time, the African continent has been largely eclipsed from the radar screen of global development analysis. Yet Goldman Sachs' report provided a glimpse of South Africa's economic potential. They believe that South Africa is likely to grow at 3.5 percent in the next 50 years and that despite its potential, it bears no comparison to the size of each of the BRIC countries. On the whole, South Africa is projected to have a GDP of US$1.2 billion in 50 years, much less than the projection of US$5.9 billion GDP for Russia, the smallest of the BRIC economies. The major advantages of South Africa are its natural resources and vast inexpensive labor, but the major disadvantages are the dwindling population due to the AIDS crisis, infrastructure deficiencies, and inflation (Goldman Sachs, 2003). Yet the Sachs report was conservative in evaluating both South Africa's and Africa's potential. In the global hunger for energy and raw materials, Africa's economic value would be greatly enhanced if proper investments were made in improving its political, social, and economic infrastructure.

Certainly, despite their strengths, these economies have their weaknesses that could change the forecast. For example, China is facing major challenges in inflation, rising labor costs, energy supply, environmental pollution, increasing unemployment, and social discontent. India is also facing a similar challenge. In addition, both countries need major bureaucratic reform to improve efficiency; and also need to bridge rural/urban gaps in almost every area of economic development. India has a major issue with inefficiency in energy use (Goldman Sachs, 2003). Brazil is vulnerable in areas of inflation, fewer tradable goods, high ratio of public and foreign debt, low savings–investment ratio, high wages, interest rates, high tax, and a large wealth gap (*World Journal*, 2007). Russia's major issue is shrinking population (see related discussions in Goldman Sachs, 2003). In addition, Russia is facing challenges in political instability, environmental degradation, and a lack of efficiency, modern infrastructure, and pro-investment policies (*World Journal*, 2007). Its over-reliance on profits from energy and oil sales for economic growth could also affect the long-term picture of its economic growth (see related discussions in Wikipedia, 2007). For now, in a scenario of high prices for oil, energy, and raw materials, Russia's economy outperforms other countries in the region but when the downturn comes, it will face major economic challenges if the government fails to increase its revenues from alternative economies.

Among the BRICA countries, most of the discussions focus on China, India, and Brazil. In particular, the term "Chindia" has been used to describe the dynamic of the two largest economies in these emerging markets. "China and India, by contrast, possess the weight and dynamism to transform the 21st-century global economy" (Engardio, 22 August 2005a, "A new world economy"). These two countries share similarities and differences in their paths toward becoming two of the most dynamic economies since the beginning of the 2000s. As mentioned earlier, the GDP growth rates for China and India have been higher than most other countries, at 9–12 percent. It is believed that both countries are able to continue to grow at higher than average rates in the global context (ibid.).

Economic prowess

Chindia

Chindia are moving up in their global economic ranking due to their economic transformation. As the Goldman Sachs report had pointed out, by mid-century, China, the United States, and India will be ranked as the top three economies in the world, and China and India could account for half of global output (Goldman-Sachs, 2005). For now, the economies of China and India are going through rapid upgrades and transformation. One report shows that China's competitive edge is shifting from low-cost workers to state-of-the-art manufacturing. India is a center of innovation and outsourcing (*Business Week*, 22 August 2005, "The rise of Chindia").

It is noted that India plays a pivotal role in the global innovation chain. The large high-tech companies, such as Motorola, Hewlett-Packard, Cisco Systems, and Google, have increasingly relied on their Indian talents for innovative products. India's strengths in computer graphic design are increasingly obvious and their products include car engines, forklifts, and aircraft wings for General Motors, and Boeing. It also has major expertise in research and development, as embodied in the companies of B2K, Office Tiger, and Iris. It is estimated that by 2010, such outsourcing work could quadruple to $56 billion per year (Engardio, 2005a). In addition to computer chip design and software, India has unique strengths in pharmaceutical production. India's talent pool and vast amount of labor provides a large competitive edge in production costs, which explains why they attract major foreign direct investment (FDI) (see related comments by University of Michigan management guru C. K. Prahalad in ibid.).

So far, China and India are not intense competitors in their economic development trajectories. In a number of areas, there is room for collaboration between these two economies. It is predicted that if China and India choose to complement each other, they are likely to take over the global technology industry (see the prediction of analyst Navi Radjou of Forrester Research Inc., in Engardio, 2005a). China has been a leader in mass manufacturing, but it has shown some potential in information technology, heavy industries, and other higher value economies (see Wang, Zhang, and Wang, 2007). In contrast India has demonstrated its competitiveness in the design, services, and precision industries. Both countries also share certain unique similarities in economic development. In addition to production, both countries have large human capital, consumer markets, savings, and potential for market capitalization (Engardio, 2005a). In particular, both countries have shown the largest potential in the consumer goods' market, especially in the demand for telecommunication, information technology, and electronic goods. For example China already has the world's largest number of cell-phone subscribers, about 350 million, likely to increase to about 600 million by 2009, and Chinese subscription to broadband is likely to be the largest in the world by the end of 2008. A similar phenomenon is observed in India. For example, in India, since 2000, the number of cell-phone subscribers has increased from 5.6 million to 55 million (ibid.).

The unique consumption culture and a pattern that demands the latest technologies and features of information technology in both countries is conducive to the sale of new products. For example, it was pointed out that this trend of demanding the newest, or most "chic," products in telecommunication bodes well for the sale of next-generation multimedia gizmos, networking equipment, and wireless Web services (see comments by Executive Vice-President Leon Husson of Philips Semiconductors in ibid.). This consumer culture also bodes well for the demand for other products, such as pharmaceuticals.

Among the major advantages of Chindia, the most frequently mentioned is the possession of human capital. Both countries have abundant high-skill labor as well as inexpensive low-skill labor. In one estimate, China and India graduate a combined half a million engineers and scientists a year, in contrast to 60,000 in the United States (see Engardio, 2005a). In an estimate by McKinsey Global Institute, the total number of young researchers in life sciences in both nations will rise by 35 percent to 1.6 million by 2008, in contrast to the decrease of 11 percent to 760,000 in the United States. The training of life sciences talent is critical in the development of biotech, pharmaceutical, and health care-related economic sectors. These sectors are among the fastest-growing industries in the global context (ibid.). This abundance in human capital increases the competitive advantages that India already has in the pharmaceutical sector. In terms of the increase in the size of the population, India is believed to have a larger advantage. It is pointed out that India has nearly 500 million people under the age of 19 and higher fertility rates and it is estimated that by mid-century, India will have 1.6 billion people and 220 million more workers than China. Given the one-child policy in China, China's competitiveness in low-skilled labor is likely to decrease. With the increasing economic openness and liberalization in India, India can easily supplant China's role of being the major provider of inexpensive labor in 4 decades (ibid.).

In addition to manufacturing, both India and China are attractive financial markets. Financial liberalization is especially important for China's participation in global financial markets. Despite its recent move toward financial liberalization and relaxation of currency control, China has a major issue of economic and financial investment inefficiency. In 2004 half of the GDP, about $850 billion were invested in crowded sectors with low returns, such as crude steel, vehicles, and office buildings; more than 20 percent of bank loans are insolvent; and two-thirds of China's 1300 listed companies don't earn a return on their investment capital, according to an estimate by Beijing National Accounting Institute President Chen Xiaoyue (Engardio, 2005a). In contrast, India fares much better in this regard. Its FDI is believed to be much more capital-efficient because it is better integrated in the global financial system; it is endowed with long-established Western legal institutions, and a modern stock market and banking system. According to an analysis by *Business Week* of Standard & Poor's Compustat data on 346 top listed companies in both nations, foreign investment in India reaped higher returns on equity and invested capital between 2000 and 2005. In one comparison, an Indian company posted a 16.7 percent return on capital in 2004, higher than the 12.8 percent return in China (*Business Week*, 2005). India's problem is a high national budget deficit ratio of about 10 percent of GDP in its public finances. In one case, India had to be bailed out by the International Monetary Fund in 1991, while in contrast China withstood the 1997 Asian financial crisis (Engardio, 22 August 2005b, "Crouching tigers, hidden dragons").

Chindia's economic potential is dependent on the control of other challenges, however. Both countries are facing major geopolitical,

political, environmental, social, infrastructural, and population health challenges. For example, India has fought three wars with Pakistan since 1947 and both countries have threatened to use nuclear power to deter each other (Natural Resources Defense Council, 2002), "Consequences of nuclear conflict between India and Pakistan"). Since the beginning of the People's Republic, China has been challenged with the independence issues of Taiwan and Tibet and that it is surrounded by some neighboring states that were historical rivals, such as India, Russia, Japan, and Vietnam. Both Chindia countries are also facing serious environmental problems. China is in the process of overtaking the United States as the country that releases the largest amount of carbon-dioxide, the culprit of global warming. China is becoming the most polluted country on earth. In its social milieu, both Chindia countries are facing very large wealth disparities, as well as a urban/rural gap. Both countries are also facing severe challenges in unemployment. It was pointed out that China and India need annual GDP growth of at least 8 percent just to relieve the unemployment pressure (Engardio, 2005b). According to India's Planning Commission, a growth rate less than 6.5 percent is likely to result in a sharp increase in unemployment of 70 million by 2012 (ibid.). India's info-tech services industry, the most promising sector, employs less than 1 million people, while there are 200 million Indians who subsist on $1 a day or less. It is quite doubtful that India's hope of relying on export manufacturing to relieve unemployment could be feasible (see related discussions in Engardio, 2005a).

Wealth gap and poverty is a major challenge facing both countries. Like the United States, China has a GINI coefficient of 4.7, indicating a very large wealth gap. A similar scenario is observed in India. In this regard, both countries are confronted with social discontent in the form of social protests and open confrontation with the government. Both India and China lack a safety net. China is facing a very severe disadvantage in this regard, given its graying population. It was pointed out by Engardio that China's working-age population will peak at 1 billion in 2015 and then shrink steadily (Engardio, 2005a). It remains an open question whether China's current system can fully provide retirement benefits to its graying population.

Infrastructure-wise, both countries face a large rural/urban gap in physical infrastructure, such as roads, bridges, transportation, and energy supply. In social infrastructure, both countries have certain deficiencies that would pose as barriers to their economic transformation. For example, both societies are struggling with the issues of corruption and government inefficiency (*World Journal*, 11 March 2007). In addition, both countries have not fully realized its innovation potential due to social and legal constraints. For example, China, despite its abundance of human capital, is weak in innovative output. Yet the constraint is more related to its systemic deficiency rather than human deficiency. It was pointed out that Microsoft's 180-engineer R&D lab in Beijing was one of the world's most productive sources of software innovation (Engardio, 2005a). The problems of a lack of innovation have more to do with a lack of a supportive policy platform, horizontal and vertical integration, and a lack of enforcement of intellectual property rights protection (see related discussions in Wang, Zhang and Wang, 2007; and also in Engardio, 2005a).

A major challenge facing both countries consists in health crises. Both countries are facing a number of health issues that could severely effect their economic growth potential. Both countries are facing a rising array of epidemics and pandemics, such as HIV, TB, hepatitis, and other infectious diseases and chronic illnesses that have increasing prevalence, morbidity, and mortality. Health disparities are a major challenge facing both countries when rising health care costs make it difficult for their populations to fend off these threatening diseases. In China, the combined threats of rising prevalence of infectious disease and chronic illness could become a financial burden on Chinese society. A UN estimate shows that the number of Chinese with HIV could hit 10 million by 2010. China also has one of the highest rates of TB in the world (see Wang, Zang and Wang, 2007), with around 200,000 Chinese dying annually of the disease; and a serious flu epidemic could kill millions. In addition to diseases brought about by a rapid change of lifestyle, the graying population in China also means an increasing need for health resources to address chronic illness and disease. It is estimated that by 2030, about 20 percent, or 300 million Chinese, will be over 60 years old, while at present only one in six Chinese workers has a pension plan, and just 5 percent have guaranteed medical benefits. In India, the health challenges facing the poor, which is the majority of the Indian population, are particularly serious. In a conservative estimate, at least 5 million Indian adults are infected with HIV, one of the world's highest rates outside sub-Saharan Africa. According to India's National Intelligence Council, this statistic could pass 20 million in 2010. Health crises could easily cancel out the gains in economic achievements (Engardio, 2005b).

Despite these challenges, the multinationals that use a complementing model of working with Chindia have benefited from the combined strengths of these two countries. One positive example is Motorola.

Motorola's hardware is assembled and partly designed in China, while its R&D center in Bangalore supplies about 40 percent of the software in its new phones (Engardio, 2005a). TATA is another example. TATA's success reflects an efficient use of a global supply and demand chain strategy in market segmentation. This integration strategy of expanding consumer bases, capitalizing on inexpensive R&D and professional talent, and agile supply chain management is likely to distinguish the companies that succeed from those who lose out in global competition (see related comments by Jim Hemerling, of the Shanghai Office of the Boston Consulting Group, in Engardio, 2005a).

Brazil

Among BRICA countries, Brazil's potential is often underestimated. In most cases, the world mainly evaluates Brazil on the basis of its tangible qualities. For example, Brazil is the fifth-largest country and takes up half of the area of South America. It is slightly larger than the 48 contiguous states of the United States. It is the fifth most populous country. Yet its development potential mainly lies in other, not so obvious, benefits of its social, cultural, political, and geographical diversity. First and foremost, its population is the most diverse on the American continents and is composed of almost every ethnic category, such as the indigenous, Africans, Europeans, and Asians. Miscegenation that has lasted for 500 years makes Brazil one of the most racially mixed countries in the world. It is estimated that one-third of Brazilians are racially mixed, a rate higher than that in North America (Strada, 2007, "Brazil faces global economic and environmental pressures"). The indigenous people, the inspiration of cultural diversity, ecological management, and pharmaceutical inventions, accounts for less than 1 percent of Brazil's 155 million inhabitants (The World Bank Group, 2007, "Brazil – Inequality and Economic Development").

The geography of Brazil is also an important factor conducive to its development. The size advantage provides Brazil with a diverse climate, ranging from tropical to semitropical, which helps produce abundant, diverse agricultural output. Its geographical location, bordering on nine of the continent's eleven nations in South America, is a point of convergence between the Caribbean, Central America, and South America. This also makes Brazil a gateway to other Latin American countries for regional or global trade. And the fact that Brazil is one of the largest democratic countries in the world with a more progressive social solidarity ideology than its counterparts in Latin America is also an obvious strength when compared to other developing countries. Brazilian

society has a universal health care system; a comprehensive pharmaceutical coverage plan for most of its populace; and it is making progress
in its policies on the indigenous development (see The World Bank
Group, 2007).

One major strength of the Brazilian economy is diversity. It is
embodied by a wide range of economies, such as mature manufacturing,
mining, agriculture, tourism, and so on . Technology, pharmaceuticals,
and services are also increasing in their share in Brazilian economies.
On the whole, Brazil is a net exporter, with the world's eighth largest
economy in terms of purchasing power; and the tenth largest economy
at market exchange rates. Similar to China and India, Brazilian economy is marked by extensive inequality (Department for International
Development Health Resource Centre, 2004, Brazil health briefing
paper.). The fact that Brazil has rich natural resources, a large land mass
and a much smaller population than China and India renders Brazil
with the largest potential for a more equitable and sustainable
development path, if it can fully capitalizes on its role in the new global
economies. Its social solidarity mechanisms and polices, which play a
critical role in stemming the prevalence of the HIV/AIDS epidemic, also
give Brazil a competitive advantage in its ranking among the BRICA
countries (The World Bank Group, 2007).

Africa

The largest individual potential for economic growth among BRICA
countries comes from South Africa, due to its possession of natural
resources, diversity, and human capital. According to Obiageli
Ezekwesili, "there are signs that Africa is on the brink of economic take-
off" (Norbrook, October–December, 2007, "Interview: Obiageli
Ezekwesili," p. 91). These signs include that, for more than a decade,
Africa's economic growth has been about 5 percent on average; the
business climate is improving; stability is gradually being restored to
most countries; and inflation is more manageable.

Certainly, the stability factor plays a major role in assessing Africa's
long-term development and this factor is affected, in turn, by the
region's social, political, and population health challenges. These challenges include: poverty and debt, capacity building (education and
human capital, infrastructure, and improving governance and management), effective macro-economic policies and sector strategies, attract-
ing foreign investment, effective and efficient use of its own resources,
diversification in long-term investment, and population health
(Norbrook, 2007).

The increase in geo-economic competition among the EU, the United States, China, and India is also beneficial to Africa because it gives Africa more bargaining power in terms of negotiating for better commodity prices, foreign assistance, foreign direct investment, and capacity building. In this regard, the entry of China into Africa's commodity market, which is believed to provide Africa with much needed cash, is part of the solution to infrastructure building. China's engagement with Africa has also forced other countries to re-engage with Africa, albeit it is not clear what form their engagement strategy will take. An old-style mercantilist strategy is definitely against the interest of Africa.

The potential of Africa had not been noticed until China and India accelerated their collaboration with the African countries in the mid-2000s. South Africa is a relevant case in point. Among the African countries, South Africa is considered a much coveted target by geo-economic rivals, especially China and India, because of South Africa's economic strengths and potential. With a total of US$240 billion in 2007, South Africa contributes 25 percent of the total African GDP and this equals up to four times the GDP of its southern African neighbors combined (Nhlapo, 21 January 2008). South Africa, twice the size of the state of Texas in the United States, also accounts for 40 percent of industrial output, 45 percent of mining, and 50 percent of Africa's total electricity capacity. South Africa's GDP growth of 5.3 percent in 2007 is above the 3.2 percent of global average. This growth is projected to continue at the rate of 5.4 percent in 2008 (ibid.). The capital market, with a value of US$580 billion, is the sixteenth largest in the world. Despite its high-inflation scenario and large wealth disparities, its economic outlooks are believed to be improving with increasing reserves, low-debt, efforts to manage inflation, trade surplus, and expanded tax base. Services and manufacturing activities account for 70 percent of the economy (ibid.). South Africa is also one of the top 20 destinations for foreign direct investment, including US$5 billion for 20 percent of shares in Standard Bank. Tourism has also contributed to economic growth. Various social and political improvement measures in national reconciliation, gender equity, and macro-economic stabilization (including the recent efforts in infrastructure building) are conducive for economic stability and growth. The emergence of a black middle class is also likely to be a positive sign for reducing the wealth gap. The major constraints facing South Africa are related to the lack of socioeconomic improvements of the 80 percent of socially excluded populations.

In particular, the major challenge to South Africa's sustainable economic development is the commitments to address health, education, community building, high unemployment (about 30 percent in 2007), chronic and extreme poverty, and rural/urban gaps in accessing resources and opportunities. In this regard, South Africa is facing a larger challenge than Brazil. However, the non-violent approach to the political transition from Apartheid to a true democracy, and the fact that the South African government is taking concrete steps to improve those problems brought about by long-term colonialism, bodes well for the economic prospects of South Africa. For example, the government has infused US$60 billion in infrastructure building that aims to improve the deficiencies. It has also encouraged a sector investment strategy, such as tourism, agriculture, chemicals, metals, capital goods, creative industries, clothes and textiles, durable consumer goods, education, and micro-financing. In the larger African context, with the newly revived attention to Africa from the EU and the United States due to the geo-economic rivalry brought about by China's and India's rapprochement with Africa, South Africa is well-positioned to be the springboard of the multinationals to other African countries. On the whole, Africa is likely to benefit from the jousting among major economic powers like United States, China, the EU, and India. If this benefit is properly reinvested in its capacity building, especially the improvement of human capital and political, social, health, and economic infrastructure, Africa's long-term growth potential is immeasurable.

BRICA's Pharmaceutical Industry

The future of pharmaceutical-related business in BRICA countries can be evaluated on the basis of demand and supply. On the whole, the rate of demand and supply of pharmaceuticals is increasing and the room for the increase is even greater in the years to come. Usually, the pharmaceutical industry in a given market is related to its historical conditions, government policies, economic conditions, and population health situations, and this is also true for the BRICA countries. It was noted that economic growth, stabilizing political structures, growing need to resolve prevalent diseases and illnesses, and increasing direct foreign investment in Brazil, Russia, India, China, and Africa (BRICA) have offered significant opportunities for pharmaceutical growth. Most of the research to date has focused on the potential of BRIC, not BRICA. For example, in one estimate, pharmaceutical sales across the BRIC economies grew by 22.3 percent in 2005, compared to single digit growth in the major markets of the United States, Europe, and Japan (Business Insights, August 2006, "Pharmaceutical growth opportunities in Brazil, Russia, India and China: Healthcare reform, market dynamics and key players"). The following section will offer a comprehensive discussion of the status of BRIC's pharmaceutical potential.

Brazil

Brazil has the largest population in Latin America and has one of the major pharmaceutical industries and markets in the globe (Kermani, October 2005, Contract Farma). Among the BRICAs, Brazil has the strongest competitive edge in pharmaceutical innovation, manufacturing, and quality control because of several apparent advantages in the Brazilian context. Compared to other BRICA countries, Brazil has the highest amount of political stability and least amount of social, interethnic, and religious strife. Despite the large wealth inequity, the guarantee of obligatory education and universal health care system reduces the impact of wealth inequity on socioeconomic reality. In addition to the rich endowment of natural resources (including oil), Brazil accounts for 35 percent of biodiversity in the world. So far, humanity has only gained 1 percent understanding of the ecological biodiversity in Brazil (Silva, 6 March 2007). Government supports the integration of knowledge of medicinal plants in its educational training and research agenda. The ANVISA (Agencia Nacional de Vigilancia Sanitaria) is also instrumental in approving natural medicines. The potential for pharmaceutical innovation in this area is immeasurable. Brazil has the necessary human capital in basic science and pharmaceutical development and has supportive infrastructure for supply chain efficiency. Brazil is also the most promising gateway through which to sell drugs in other developing countries.

Most outside observers have based their analysis of Brazil in terms of the obvious market factor. It has been noted that the potential of the Brazilian market for pharmaceuticals is not fully realized because by 2004, medical facilities were inaccessible to over 50 percent of the Brazilian population and historically, about one-third of the population have no pharmaceutical access (Global Information Inc., December 2004, "Strategic analysis of the Brazilian pharmaceutical markets").

On the supply side, the multinationals have a large presence in Brazil and amongst them are major pharmaceutical suppliers. A number of large multinational pharmaceutical companies have their manufacturing facilities and/or their regional headquarters or subsidiaries in Brazil, such as Pfizer, Aventis, Bayer, GSK, and Hoest, and they serve as a useful base for operating in the Mercosur trading bloc (comments by John Anderson of Rio de Janeiro's Pro-Cardiaco Hospital in GlaxoSmith-Kline's Brazilian operations in Kermani, 2005). The Mercosur trading bloc, that is, the Mercado Común del Sur (Common Market of the South) is an ambitious economic integration project that includes Argentina, Brazil, Paraguay, and Uruguay with various trade agreements with other South American countries. The Mercosur, comprising 64 percent of population and 60 percent of GDP in South America, is emerging as a major market force (ibid.; Ministry of External Relations, Brazil, 2005, "Frequently asked questions about regional integration and Mercosur"). In this geographical context, Brazil is well positioned to increase its pharmaceutical regional spread. By 2008, the region already took up 25 percent of global pharmaceutical sales and this figure is expected to grow to 30 percent within a year (see Research and Development, 2008, "Clinical trials in Latin America: Why Latin America").

On the demand side, the Brazilian pharmaceutical market has a potentially large consumer base due to its population trends, including the rate of growth, graying population, urbanization, and disease profiles. For example, between 1970 and 1991, the Brazilian population grew from 93.1 million to 146.8 million, an increase of nearly 58 percent (Lobato, 2000). In 2005, the total population increased to 186,831 million (UNESCO, 2005, "UIS statistics in brief"). About 85 percent of the Brazilian population now lives in urban areas. In addition to infectious diseases and poverty, the population is increasingly affected by a rise in chronic diseases, such as cardiovascular, respiratory and metabolic conditions (Lobato, 2000; Department for International Development Health Resource Centre, 2004; Segatto, 2005).

Macro-policy context

Public sector leadership has played an important role in the development of Brazil's pharmaceutical industry and will remain so in the years to come. The fact that the Brazilian Constitution guarantees access to health care as a fundamental right of citizens makes Brazil a unique case in pharmaceutical provision. Under the aegis of the universal health care mandate, Brazil is known for its strengths of access, coverage, and affordability. This system has few parallels in the region or even in the world besides Europe or Canada. It is one of the few systems that has worked arduously to improve health care access. For example, it provides large incentives for health professionals to work in rural areas where access used to be scarce. Despite the criticism of being a fragmented health system, Brazil does offer choice for populations who have different health needs.

On pharmaceutical-related issues, the government sees the pharmaceutical sector as a strategic growth sector and provides strong incentives for its development. This incentive in many cases also applies to the foreign pharmas who support the government's goal. The government itself is involved in pharmaceutical production and is responsible for producing 70 percent of basic medicines (Silva, 6 March 2008). Pharmaceuticals for the underprivileged are almost free of charge. Brazil's goal to provide affordable medicine has also fostered the growth of generics production, which now sees a 10 percent increase every year (ibid.). In this context, Brazil's pharmaceutical exports have doubled in a period of ten years (ibid.).

The government's role in health care is not without controversy. In conventional thinking, the macro-economic contexts and the Brazilian government's political ideology have a profound influence on its health care and pharmaceutical policies, and are deemed a challenge to multinational pharmaceutical companies because the government emphasizes affordability and equitable access and has taken an aggressive approach to ensuring pharmaceutical access for all Brazilians. The government's position is based on stipulations in Brazil's Constitution and in 1988, a new health system, the Sistema Único de Saúde (SUS – the Single Health System) was created to combine the functions of a number of health care institutions and hospitals under a single body of control for the first time. In 1990, Brazil's Congresso Naciónal (National Congress) passed additional legislation to provide the operational framework of the new system (Anon, 2005b, Ministério da Saúde; Medici, 2002). Despite its success, Brazil's health system is not without constraints. In Brazil, it was noted that around 50 million people have health insurance coverage and the remaining citizens rely on the public health system for their health care. In general, the urban populations have more access and better health care. On health spending, according to one estimate, in 2002, Brazil's health care spending as percentage of GDP was only 5.2 percent, behind Argentina (8.0 percent), Chile (6.0 percent), and Mexico (5.5 percent). Brazil's per capita spending on health care was estimated at $50 per annum, below the $500 recommended by the World Health Organization (Sandullo, 2003). This relatively small budget puts constraints on the government's ability to improve health care, and quality of care and efficiency issues are major concerns in this picture. Despite the government's will to increase access and affordability, its plans are often subject to the whims of macro-economic development.

Macro-economic changes have imposed constraints on the health system in Brazil. Political or economic instability, especially currency devaluation and inflation, often brings about uncertainty to health care reform in Brazil. For example, it has been noted that the financial problems that afflicted Brazil between 1999 and 2002 were a major barrier to reform of the system. The January 1999 devaluation of the Brazilian currency, the réal, forced the government to reduce public spending and impose emergency taxes to cut the national debt, about half of GDP. It was pointed out that at one point during August 2002, Brazil's currency lost 13 percent of its value (Anon, March 2005c, "Brazil's economy"; see also Anon, 5 August 2002, "Brazil's looming economic crisis"). The economic problems naturally had consequences for the funding of health care and this had implications for the pharmaceutical market (Kermani, 2005). As in other countries, pharmaceutical prices are rising rapidly after increasing gradually since 1994. A large number of Brazilians have to rely on government funding for pharmaceuticals, which inevitably makes the Brazilian government a large negotiator for health care and pharmaceutical provision. And this also makes it essential for the government to rely on cost-reduction measures to increase access. These measures include price controls for medicines and promoting the production and use of generics in the 1990s and early 2000s.

Brazil exercises price controls through its regulatory framework of ANVISA (Agencia Nacional de Vigilancia Sanitaria), which requires that companies need authorization to operate in Brazil and that their products are registered with ANVISA (Kermani, 2005). ANVISA also promotes the production of generics through an increase of approved applications (Anon, 2003a, "Generics take off in Brazil"). The Brazilian government has also required hospital doctors and patients to use the generics, which are only a fraction of the cost of their brand counterparts (Kermani, 2005). For example, in one estimate, the generic version of an anti-retroviral combination cocktail costs $3000 in Brazil, compared to $10,000 to $15,000 a year in the United States in the early 2000s (Bailey, 2003; Anon, 2001, "Brazil to break AIDS patent").

Despite complaints from the multinationals and lawsuit threats, the government's stringent pharmaceutical policies were the key to the success of containing the HIV/AIDS crisis in Brazil (Anon, 2005b; Bailey, 2003). Brazil's National STD/AIDS Program (NSAP) offers one of the few comprehensive programs in the world. This program makes AIDS treatments free for Brazilian citizens who obtain these drugs through the public health care system. This explains the success achieved in the decrease of the incidence of HIV/AIDS by 38 percent from 1995 to 1999 (Anon, 2000, "National AIDS drugs policy").

Brazil's aggressive maneuvers have been quite effective in bringing about price controls on pharmaceuticals. For example, it has made intelligent use of WTO's TRIPS provisions to allow compulsory licensing and parallel imports. In August 2001, for the first time in its history, Brazil's health minister threatened to take away Roche pharmaceutical's patent on the anti-AIDS drug Nelfinavir after six months of negotiations. The minister estimated that the price could be reduced by 40 percent if they were manufactured locally (Bailey, 2003). This aggressive approach toward price reduction has paid off for Brazil and between 1996 and 2000 drug prices produced within Brazil had decreased by 72.5 percent, while the prices of imported drugs were reduced on average by 9.6 percent during the same period (Anon, 2000). In May, 2007, Brazilian President Luiz Inácio Lula Da Silva announced a compulsory license on the AIDS drug Efavirenz owned by Merck.

These controversial threats were the Brazilian government's bargaining strategies to reduce drug prices through negotiation and have actually resulted in substantive price reduction. These policy moves, which might seem negative to the operation of the multinational pharmas, were actually positive for the long-term development of the pharmaceutical business because they promote competition, expand the market base, and create a sense of urgency among the multinationals to research on innovative drugs. Certainly, the short-term commercial implications on price controls were obvious. Net sales decreased from $5.7 billion in 2001 to $3.9 billion in 2002 (Oliveira, 2003, "Brazil: Market overview of drugs and pharmaceuticals"). This also made Mexico the leading pharmaceutical market in Latin America at the time.

However, it is important to note that the ultimate determinant of pharmaceutical growth is economic growth, in addition to government encouragement. With a steady growth, about 3.5 percent to 5 percent, and a more stabilized economic environment, the pharmaceutical sector has shown it has room to grow. By 2005, the major economic indicators showed an improved Brazilian economy, with a trade surplus of about $35 billion and inflation under control between 5 and 6 percent. This also led to a rebound in the pharmaceutical market. In one estimate by the IMS Health Report, in the 12-month period leading up to February 2005, sales through retail pharmacies rose by 19 percent, surpassing the 9 percent sales increase seen in Mexico and the 13 percent increase in Argentina. The increase also reflects population needs for therapeutics in cardiovascular, central nervous system (CNS), and alimentary/metabolism products (Anon, 2005a, "IMS Retail Drug Monitor: Pharma sales growth continues at 6 percent pace in 13 major markets").

The economic growth scenario has been conducive to growth for all stakeholders in the Brazilian market. Although the major pharmaceutical suppliers are still multinationals, there has been increasing participation from domestic pharmaceutical makers. For example, it was estimated that about 20 percent of the 370 established pharmaceutical companies in Brazil are multinationals, mainly European or US companies who control about 70 percent of the internal pharmaceutical market. And they play a critical role in sustaining the Brazilian economy. It was noted that, in 2003, Pfizer, Schering, Boehringer-Ingelheim, Bristol-Myers Squibb, Novartis, and Organon were ranked as the top 100 companies to work for in Brazil (Anon, 2003b, "Pfizer, Schering, Boehringer Ingelheim, Bristol Myers-Squibb, Novartis e Organon são empresas TOP 100, segundo o Guia Exame"). Despite occasional pull outs from the multinationals, such as Apotex's sale of its manufacturing facilities, most multinationals are aware of the long-term potential of the market (see the Apotex story in Research and Markets, 2007c, "The pharmaceutical market: Brazil 2007").

Yet given the increasing capacity of the domestic companies in producing generics, their knowledge about the epidemiology of locally prevalent diseases, and their resources in the indigenous pharmacopoeia, the multinationals would have to resort to a more innovative strategy with the locals to sustain growth.

Outlook and challenges

In the larger picture, multinationals and domestic pharmaceuticals in Brazil need to develop unique strategies and niches that could produce a win-win situation for both.

Multinationals.   Despite its large potential, the Brazilian market is heavily regulated. It was noted that market penetration could be challenging because of regulations and price sensitivity, and that multinational competition could be restricted in sectors where the local pharmas dominate, such as generics (Research and Markets, 2007c).

For the pharmaceutical companies who plan to stay in the Brazilian market for the long haul, a local strategy is needed that could complement their global strategy. This local strategy requires fulfillment of local needs. That is, the multinationals need a long-term strategy to gain better understanding of local market norms. This means that the multinationals need to understand the demand, health needs, volume, and trends of the local markets. In addition, the multinationals need to understand the Brazilian government's policy goals of equitable access, efficacy, low-cost, and choices in pharmaceutical provision. Brazil already has a competitive generics market, and therefore innovative pharmaceuticals that meet the local needs and price range should be the focus of this long-term strategy (Kermani, 2005).

The multinationals stand the best chance to profit from this market if they understand and respond to local needs; capitalize their own strength, and create a collaborative approach. This suggests that the multinationals need to understand the potential of Brazil being one of the largest and growing markets in the world. The fact that it is a major pharmaceutical industry in South America and the fact that it plays a critical role in global health provide Brazil's immeasurable potential in the growth of its pharmaceutical industry. In a heavily regulatory environment, the multinationals need to develop a comprehensive strategy so that they do not only focus on their strengths, and develop their own "niche" markets while remaining fully supportive of the government's policy goals in this area (see some of the related discussions in Kermani, 2005).

Niche markets for the multinationals are those innovative drugs that respond to local health issues, such as rare diseases or highly prevalent diseases and clinical research (see Research and Development, 2008).

Rare diseases are important sources of innovation in themselves because they contain crucial information to go on to develop therapeutics. On clinical trials, the Latin American region as a whole has experienced a rapid increase of the clinical trial business. Between 2003 and 2008, the region experienced around 1000 percent of growth in clinical trials (see Research and Development, 2008). Brazil has similar advantages to other countries in Latin America, including strong enrollment rates; good patient compliance; enrollment efficiencies because of patient concentration in large public hospitals in metropolitan areas; reliable, well-trained and eager investigators; strong doctor–patient relationships; ethnic diversity covering most of the world's populations; quality assurance through strong adherence to GCP-ICH norms; competitive costs; and market potential for the approved drugs (see ibid.). On a related issue, the multinational concern about intellectual property rights in clinical research has improved because Brazil joined the World Intellectual Property Organization and World Trade Organization (Kermani, 2005). Among these aforementioned advantages, Brazil's major advantage in clinical trial is its human capital, which is in abundant supply (ibid.). For example, the majority of the population live in urban areas, which provide easy access to the patients available for clinical trial. Despite some negative public attitudes against clinical trials, patient recruitment, inclusion, and retention is not a challenge in the clinical trial process (ibid.). Also, qualified clinical researchers, trained mainly in the United States and Europe, are able to follow international clinical trial guidelines. In addition, it was noted that the Brazilian regulatory environment is conducive to the growth of the clinical trial business. Brazil's regulations enforce International Ethical Principles embodied in the Declaration of Helsinki. Based on these principles, ANVISA stipulates the process of clinical trial approvals and drug importation licenses (see Anon, 2004, "ANVISA estudia reglas para ensayos clínicos con voluntaries. Estado de Minas").

In addition to developing niche markets, the multinationals need to engage in both vertical and horizontal integration with local producers and research institutions in Brazil. For example, the multinationals could form R&D, production, or marketing partnerships with local stakeholders to expand its local market share (see related discussion in Global Information Inc., December 2004). The Technology Innovation Bill approved in 2004 encouraged partnerships between universities and enterprises to develop innovative products. This bodes well for the multinationals. Some pharmaceutical companies are already moving in this direction by forming partnership with the universities or research institutions for R&D, marketing, and distribution, and some already see concrete results. For example, according to the World Intellectual Property Rights Organization, at the beginning of 2008, INOVA-UNICAMP, the Innovation Agency of the State University of Campinas signed a record nine licenses for use and technology transfer agreements with private companies. The agreements allow commercialization of 22 technologies in a period ranging from 10 to 15 years. It is noted that the number of patents transferred within the first six months of 2008 is three times the number of licensing agreements in the entire history of this university affiliate (see World Intellectual Property Rights Organization, 2008, "Brazilian university leads the way in patent licensing").

Brazilian pharmas.   The future of the pharmaceutical sector favors the local pharmas because of the encouragement from regulatory authorities. For example, the government is supporting the increase of capacity through R&D, mergers, and alliances to create a large degree of integration to compete with multinational subsidiaries (Research and Markets, 2007c). Since 85 percent of the raw materials for pharmaceutical production rely on importation, the depreciation of the US dollar helps reduce production cost. Recently, the rapid growth of GDP and foreign reserves is also conducive to the domestic pharmas (ibid.).

The growth of Brazil's domestic pharmas is fortuitous. The AIDS crisis has accidentally brought about an unexpected opportunity for Brazil's domestic pharmaceutical industry. In addressing the AIDS crisis, Brazil boosted its pharmaceutical capabilities in pursuing R&D projects on managing diseases related to HIV/AIDs. In 1999, around 47 percent of anti-retroviral medications were produced inside the country (92 percent from national laboratories and 7 percent from private companies) and 53 percent were purchased from multinational pharmaceutical companies (Anon, 2000).

Brazil's capacity in producing generics and biopharmaceutical industries is now the most sophisticated within Latin America. Its potential in the global generics market must no longer be underestimated. The potential of generic production in Brazil will continue to increase because it offers an immediate solution to the high-price pharmaceuticals problem prevalent in other countries. By lowering the prices and promoting their use among the public, the government has also stimulated demand for the generics. Brazil's success in generic production has electrified a global movement demanding better pharmaceutical access. The convergence of various population trends, such as the increasing prevalence of diseases and illnesses and the aging population, has further expanded the generics markets for Brazilian pharmas (Research and Markets, March 2006a, "The image of pharmaceutical industry in Brazil: Challenges and opportunities"). One successful example is the Laboratorio Cristalia, which has grown from a small company producing only one cloned anti-hyperactivity medication to a firm with 1200 workers with 150 drugs in the pipeline (CBS News, 23 September 2005, "Brazil's drug copying industry").

The local pharmas could also take advantage of their knowledge in health profiles of the diverse populations in Brazil, as well as their knowledge of the etiology of the diseases affecting the locals. The Brazilian populations of native Indian, European, Asian, and African ancestry resemble a microcosm of the genetic pool of the global populations and they are a valid sample of the global health profiles (Kermani, 2005). The knowledge of this genetic pool as well as the knowledge of the causes of their diseases could be the basis of development of effective diagnostics or therapeutics. In Brazil, it was noted that there is a high incidence of chronic and infectious diseases, which combine the health issues of both developed and developing countries. In this regard, Brazil's biotech R&D is expanding due to the knowledge and research capacity in this area (ibid.).

On the whole, there are several major challenges facing the pharmaceutical industry in Brazil. First, macro-economic instability could affect the growth of the industry. For example, inflation and currency devaluation could hurt the industry because, as mentioned earlier, over 85 percent of the raw materials for pharmaceuticals are imported (Global Information Inc., 2004). Conversely, when the réal, the Brazilian currency, is strong, depreciation of the US dollar could help the imports of raw materials and finished pharmaceuticals. A related issue is when the commodity markets fare well, as is the case for 2007 and 2008, Brazil's pharmaceutical industry reaps the rewards. In addition, the strong GDP scenario also bodes well for both the domestic and multinational pharmas. Second, the strong regulatory framework has positive as well as negative implications. In a positive sense, the encouragement of integration has boosted the competitive edge of the local pharmas, distributors, and chains. For example, the increasing market share of ProfPharma, which owns 28 percent of local distribution, is conducive to efficiency and cost control. Similarly, the regulatory moves toward price controls by CMD, a new regulatory body created in 2003, and ANVISA have helped push down drug prices and have increased competition. They have also increased demand and revenues. However, it was noted that these measures have also increased some cost to the industry and decreased efficiency due to bureaucratic procedures (see related discussions in Research and Markets, 2007c; Love, 4 May 2007, "Brazil puts patients before patents").

Russia

As in other BRICA countries, the most important determinants of Russia's pharmaceutical market are macro-economic growth and population health profiles.

Since its bounce back from the 1998 financial crisis, the macro-economic picture of Russia has never been more positive. The Russian financial crisis, also termed the "Rouble crisis," in 17 August 1998, was a chain reaction of the global recession of 1998, mainly as a result of the Asian financial crisis in July 1997. The recession led to a decrease in world commodity prices, such as raw materials. Russia, as a major producer of oil, natural gas, metals, and timber, which account for 80 percent of exports, was seriously affected. However, it was noted that the main cause of the recession was the default of tax payments by the energy and manufacturing industries. Russia's economic down-turn was reversed because of other international events, such as the growing demand for raw materials from India and China, and the increase of oil prices because of the US conflict in the Middle East. The increase in commodity prices due to these events has brought about new fortunes for the Russian economy (Wikipedia, 2007d, "Russian financial crisis"). In one estimate in 2006, Russians' disposable income rose at an inflation-adjusted rate of 8.7 percent, far exceeding the European or US growth rates (Langley, 25 September 2006, "Russia's pharmaceutical market gains appeal").

The macro-economic affluence and the government's health program is also reflected in the growth of the pharmaceutical market, which saw a robust sales growth of $9 billion in 2005, increasing by 35 percent from 2004 (according to pharmaceutical research and development company DSM in Moscow, see Langley, 2006). The expansion of the pharmaceutical sector continued in 2006, when Russia, together with China, Korea, Mexico, and Turkey, was ranked as one of the top-performing pharmaceutical markets on the global scene, and its double-digit rate of growth in both the state and commercial sectors has far exceeded the developed markets (Dance with Shadows Communication, 2 April 2006), "Pharma markets in China, Korea, Mexico, Russia & Turkey gather pace"). The Russian pharmaceuticals and healthcare market is expected to increase by 10.5 in 2007 (Research and Markets, 2007d, "The Russian pharmaceuticals & healthcare market is expected to increase by 10.5% in 2007").

Another factor that drives the growth in Russia's pharmaceutical market is the government's drug reimbursement program, which is part of the US$1 billion health care initiative. This program helped drive the consumption of drugs to an increase of nearly 74 percent in 2006 (RNCOS, 2007, "Russian pharma sector analysis"). The program is designed to answer increasing population health needs.

The population's health-related needs have driven the growth of the pharmaceutical markets and this growth momentum is likely to be long term. The fact that these factors have serious implications for Russia's social and economic growth has aroused a sense of urgency to resolve them head-on. These factors include the aging population, the prevalence of chronic health problems, and the prevalence of such infectious diseases as HIV/AIDS, TB, and STDs. In a prosperous economy, the increase of wealth has led to an increasing demand for better health care and for imported and expensive medicines (see related discussions in RNCOS, 2008). Health and socioeconomic factors have also led to the government's action to provide better coverage through the DLO obligatory health care program. In this picture, several trends in pharmaceutical sales were noted. These include that although drug sales decreased in volume terms, they increased in value terms; there has been growth in the demand for imported drugs in Russia and this trend is likely to continue; the markets favor drugs which are more expensive, but more effective than cheaper traditional drugs (ibid.). The need for pharmaceuticals is reflected in the increasing participation of pharmaceutical traders in Apteka in Moscow, which is the main international trade fair for pharmaceuticals and related products and raw materials in Russia and the CIS (Biztradeshows, 2008a, "Pharmaceutical industry"; Biztradeshows, 2008b, "Health industry"). It is believed that the largest growth is likely to derive from drugs for cancer, HIV, cardiovascular, and diabetic problems (RNCOS, 2008).

In this high-growth picture, the multinationals will continue to gain while the domestic pharmas are facing serious challenges, like their counterparts in China. It was noted that since the 1990s, imported medicine has been increasing at competitive prices, while the competitive edge of the domestic pharmas has been decreasing. Inflation has increased production costs, which makes local producers less competitive. There is also a lack of quality control of medicine made domestically and there has been an increase of fake drugs. This has led to a decrease in the demand for locally made medicine (PRAVDA, 23 January 2008, "Mafia dominates Russian pharmaceutical industry"). This lack of demand in turn has weakened the local pharmas' capacity to supply. For example, the local pharmas produced 272 brand names in 1992; 119 in 1995; and 98 in 1998. The local pharmas' strength since then has been in food supplements. For example, in 1998, local pharmas produced 43 percent of vitamins, 36.4 per cent of antibiotics, and 17 per cent of synthetic medicines (ibid.). The weakened local capacity provides an incentive for foreign pharmas to enter into the Russian market. Since the early 1990s, foreign presence in Russia's pharmaceutical sector has increased. It was noted that, according to the Institute of State Control of Medications, in 1994, there were 32 foreign pharmas from 18 countries; in 1995, there were 54 from 17 countries; in 1996, there were 80 companies from 19 countries; in 1997, 169 foreign pharmas from 31 countries; in 1998, there were 219 from 36 countries; in 1999, there were 168 companies from 30 countries in Russia (ibid.).

The scenario of increasing pharmaceutical investment was temporarily stopped because of the Russian financial crisis, however, when the growth momentum of foreign pharmas' presence in the Russian market was put on hold. Some have chosen to leave the market or suspend their businesses, which rendered some opportunities for local pharmas to regain their market share. For example, in July 2003 the Millhouse Capital's acquiring ICN Pharmaceuticals and Abramovich's acquisition of five companies, including "Oktyabr" (St Petersburg), "Leksredstva" (Kurks), "Polypharm" (Chelyabinsk), "Marbiopharm" (Yoshkor-Ola), "Tomskchempharm" (Tomsk), as well as 96 pharmacies countrywide, were evidence of this realignment (ibid.).

On the whole, the domestic pharmas are still in a challenging position because of the globalization-related factors. Although in February of 2004, Russian President Vladimir Putin openly stated the government's intention to support the domestic pharmaceutical industry, it is difficult to see how this support can be translated into an immediate gain after Russia's WTO membership.

The challenges facing the Russian pharmaceutical sectors are many and include size, market share, innovation, a need for updated regulatory and enforcement framework, deficient IPR protection regime, poor quality control standards, and a large percentage of counterfeit drugs (see related discussions in RNCOS, 2007). Among these problems, the lack of innovation and quality control is a most serious challenge facing local producers. It was noted that the Russian mode of pharmaceutical production is out of date, some 15 or even 20 years behind pharmaceutical production in the developed world (Research and Markets, May 2006b, "Russian Pharmaceutical Industry Trails West"). It is also noted there is a lax distinction between prescriptions and over-the-counter medicines. In one case, Viagra was found on the over-the-counter market and also in the counterfeits market (Research and Markets, 2007d, "The Russian pharmaceuticals & healthcare market is expected to increase by 10.5% in 2007").

The challenge facing the domestic producers is particularly large. It is critical that Russian pharmas develop their own niche markets and maintain traditional strongholds, such as antibiotics, nutritional supplements, and vaccines. For example, Biomed, a leading Russian pharma, produces 80 brand products but with a keen focus on vaccine production. The company at one time supplied more than half of the state's demand for whooping cough vaccine, diphtheria vaccine, and tetanus vaccine. The company has also made an attempt to develop genetically engineered vaccines against Hepatitis B. Despite its legal dispute with an Indian company, this model shows that in a competitive environment, Russian companies can meet the challenges by either seeking a niche market or by being part of the global supply and demand chain (see PRAVDA, 2008; see also *The Economist*, December 1998, "Keep taking the tablets: Russian pharmaceutical industry suffering in economic crisis").

India

Just like other BRIC countries, macro-economic growth is a major factor that explains the fast growth of the pharmaceutical industry in India. India's economic liberalization since the 1990s has led to the emergence of successful private enterprises on the domestic front and increasing integration into the global economy. Despite the many challenges facing Indian society, its social, cultural, and population profiles have provided unique opportunities for innovative enterprises. The omnipresent success of Tata in India as well as in the globe is the most obvious example of this economic momentum.

India's economic momentum has accelerated since the beginning of the 2000s. As mentioned earlier, by the end of 2007, the economy of India is the twelfth largest in the world, with a GDP of US$1.25 trillion, according to Credit Swisse (*Economic Times*, 2007), and its annual rate of GDP growth is about 8–10 percent. As in the cases of Brazil and China, fast GDP growth bodes well for the supply and demand of pharmaceuticals.

The economic expansion has also led to a growth in Indian pharmaceutical and of the health care market, which provides increased opportunities for the supply of pharmaceuticals in the public and private sectors. In a high economic growth scenario, and its increasing participation in global trade, the Indian pharmaceutical industry is going through rapid changes and is expected to grow at a very fast pace (Research and Markets, 2007b, "Indian pharmaceutical industry: Issues and opportunities"). In one estimate, the volume of the Indian pharmaceutical industry is likely to be about US$10 billion by the end of 2008; including US$3 billion of patented drugs by 2008, and about US$7.5 billion generic drugs (ibid.). Despite the controversies surrounding the changes in India's patent laws to conform to WTO requirements, this policy move has also forced its pharmaceutical sector to improve its competitiveness. It was noted that India's pharmaceutical industry has been growing at a rate of 9 per cent per year since the early 2000s and given the macro-economic strength, this momentum is unlikely to decrease.

Major advantages in India

The major advantage of India in pharmaceutical business is its long history and capacity in pharmaceutical manufacturing. To begin with, the regulatory framework in India provides a supportive environment for pharmaceutical growth. New policies formulated by the National Biotechnology Development Authorities have facilitated private-public partnerships for biotechnology firms. Similar to China, India also has an abundant supply of health care workers at all levels and at very low cost (Research and Markets, 2005b, "Indian pharmaceutical and health-care market annual review, 2005"). India also has established strengths in research, manufacturing, and outsourcing. To outsiders, the most obvious advantage is its market size. India is known to be one of the largest pharmaceutical markets in the world.

In addition, unlike Brazil and China that mainly export their pharmaceuticals to developing markets, Indian pharmaceutical companies have established a reputation in both developing countries and developed markets. It was noted that some Indian pharmaceutical companies, Ranbaxy, Dr Reddy's Labs, Wockhardt, Cipla, Nicholas Piramal, and Lupin, have done well in such developed markets as the United States and Europe (Research and Markets, 2007b). India has more than 100 US FDA-inspected facilities and has increased their exports of health care products to the United States (BBC, 20 April 2008, "Heparin contaminated on purpose").

In specific, Indian companies are being recognized for their strengths in formulations, bulk drugs, and generics. In one estimate, the industry ranks fourth globally in terms of volume, and in terms of value, it is ranked thirteenth (see Research and Markets, 2007b). Among these, the making of generics is most noticeable. Similar to China and Brazil, the Indian generics market is experiencing a rapid growth (ibid.). This sector will be the most important niche for Indian pharmaceutical companies for several reasons. First, there is a global need for low-cost medicine in both resource-rich as well as resource-poor countries. This phenomenon is also related to the increasing demand for universal and affordable health care in the world, including the United States. In this context, the increasing use of generics through the use of formularies, is inevitable. As mentioned in Chapter 2, this phenomenon is already occurring in the United States. Second, as mentioned before, several high-demand brands produced in the developed markets are losing their patent protection and this trend will give generics makers a large opportunity to capture the market for these off-patent brands. These generics are said to be worth over $40 billion or 15 percent of the total prescription market in the United States (ibid.). Third, India clearly has cost advantages in process research for generic drugs and value-added generics production, which accounts for 60 to 80 percent of total sales (ibid.). India's cost advantage lies in the lower cost of infrastructure facilities, and lower remuneration for Indian scientists than those for the scientists in developed countries.

Related to generics production are several strengths embodied in India's pharmaceutical production. For example, reverse engineering is a known strength for Indian companies. Reverse engineering requires the copying of the molecule needed to make a particular drug through developing a modified process. This modified process is usually highly cost-effective. Reverse engineering is much less expensive because it does not involve basic research or clinical trials. The other niche of Indian pharmas is the Abbreviated New Drug Application (ANDA) process, or the equivalency tests of generics in comparison to the product already in existence in the market (Research and Markets, 2007b).

Unlike China, which is still struggling with quality control issues, the quality of India pharmaceutical production is considered as being close to the standard of industrialized countries. It was noted that India has the highest number of manufacturing plants approved by the US FDA outside the United States (Pharmabiz, 2006, "Moving towards a quality culture"). It was also noted that this sector has witnessed a change of participation between the multinationals and Indian pharmaceutical companies. The reverse engineering industry that was dominated by the multinationals is now led by India's local players. This sector is able to produce about 300 entities (Research and Markets, 2007b). The generics-related expertise by Indian companies has reduced the cost of production and has actually benefited global health. It makes India a major exporter of medicine for resource-poor countries.

Other areas that India has shown to have some potential in are the development of analogue, NDDS (Novel Drug Delivery Systems), research in biotechnology, clinical trials, outsourcing, development of high-value new chemical entities, bio-informatics, e-commerce, and research and development. On analogues, Indian companies are able to create new molecules by modifying an existing molecule, or a new one that has not been commercialized, after researching on international patent databases. Indian companies are also believed to have some strengths in NDDS. The discovery of a new drug delivery method could lead to a new patent or a license of exclusivity of three years in the United States (Research and Markets, 2007b).

The fact that biotechnology has offered a new possibility for drug discovery has also attracted the investment of Indian stakeholders in this sector. It has been noted that India is on the brink of a biotech revolution (see *Asia Times*, 19 June 2007, "India's blossoming biotech boom"). Revenues from this sector reached US$2 billion in 2006/7, an increase from $1 billion in 2004/5 and $1.5 billion in 2005/6 (ibid.). The sector is now growing at a rate of 30 to 35 percent per year, which is twice the global rate. The goal of the Indian biotech sector is $5 billion in revenues by the fiscal year 2010/11 (ibid.). The government's Department of Biotechnology projects annual sales to reach $25 billion by 2015 (ibid.).

The biotech sector allows the largest possibility of integration and collaboration between local and foreign pharmas as well as joint projects with research institutions. India's potential in this area is unlimited and has attracted attention from global pharmas because of its low labor and facility costs. For example, in 2007, US-based Biogen Idec, one of the pioneers of the biotech industry, set up an Indian subsidiary for strengthening R&D and integrating India into its global clinical development programs. Amgen, known as the world's biggest biotech company, has also made plans about setting up a clinical development center in India. Other global majors such as Genentech, Genzyme, Pall Life Sciences, Agilent Technologies' biotech division, and HistoGenetics have planned to increase their presence in the Indian market (see *Asia Times*, 2007). Overall, foreign investors have notably increased their presence in this sector in India. For example, it was observed that in 2004/5, about 20 privately owned drug discovery groups started to operate in India with the goal of creating innovative and patentable products (Research and Markets, 2005a, "Indian biotech industry").

Similar initiatives also came from India's domestic pharmas. For example, Biocon, India's largest biotech company, is collaborating with Deakin University in Australia for joint multidisciplinary research in the areas of biotechnology and biosciences. In specific, there could be joint development of a mammalian-cell bio-processing facility in Australia and research in metabolic diseases that Deakin will undertake for Biocon (Research and Markets, 2005a).

Forming partnerships with foreign pharmas, such as those from the United States and China, India's global market was estimated to be worth $91 billion by 2005 (Research and Markets, 2005a). Despite the often mentioned competition between India and China in this sector, India also has a higher advantage than China because of its language advantage and its integration and familiarity with the Western system. The fact that India has joined the World Trade Organization and has accepted certain terms of intellectual property rights required for the membership also helps India's pharmaceutical sector. The patent improvements are likely to increase foreign direct investment in this area, which creates a mutually beneficial situation for both the domestic and foreign pharmas. The global strategy developed by Indian companies is also a major competitive advantage for Indian companies. It was noted that Indian biotech companies are able to access capital investment, transfer knowledge, and expand overseas through setting up subsidiaries overseas (*Asia Times*, 2007). This strategy has been adopted by several major companies. For example, Hyderabad-based Shantha Biotechnics has an independent subsidiary, Shantha West, in San Diego in the United States, to develop human monoclonal antibodies. A similar arrangement was made by Dr Reddy's Laboratories, Transgene Biotek, and Bharat Serums and Vaccines to set up subsidiaries or research units in the United States to focus on early R&D (ibid.). This also allows Indian companies to improve their product commercialization capabilities and marketing in overseas markets.

The other niche market for the Indian pharmaceutical sector is its outsourcing business. India's comparative advantages in outsourcing, especially in information technology, have been globally recognized (Global Technology Forum, 9 January 2003, *"The Economist*: Indian software firms prosper due to outsourcing business"). Recently, the outsourcing advantages across the pharmaceutical value chain have also been noticed. These include opportunities in drug discovery research, preclinical research, clinical trial study design and management, clinical supplies management, manufacturing, packaging, distribution, and marketing and sales. It is widely expected that India's outsourcing market is likely to experience rapid growth if the stakeholders can take full advantage of the Indian research infrastructure, human capital, existing Western companies outsourcing models in general and clinical research in particular, regulatory support for research outsourcing, and beneficial partnerships and integration (see some of the discussions in Research and Markets, 2004, "BioMed Outsourcing Report – Drug Discovery Partnerships – The Indian Biopharmaceutical Outsourcing Sector"). Similar to Brazil, India possesses tremendous potential in clinical trials due to its low costs advantage, population diversity, research expertise, a large patient base, completion of clinical trials on time, improving infrastructure, and strong government support. It was noted that major pharmaceutical companies and Clinical Research Organizations (CROs) have a presence in clinical trials in India. The sector is expected to grow 36 percent between 2006 and 2011 with revenues worth US$546 million every year. It is also projected that by 2011 India is likely to conduct more than 15 percent of the total global clinical trials (Bharat Book Bureau, November 2007, "Booming Clinical Trials Market in India").

Challenges

The challenges facing India's pharmaceutical sector are innovative research and development, adjustment to the WTO's intellectual property rights environment, and global competitiveness.

Innovative research and development that leads to the discovery of new molecules is the major challenge in this picture. Despite the cost advantages that India has, only a small number of Indian pharmas, such as Ranbaxy & Dr Reddys, are active in this area. The percentage of research and development investment is much lower than that in industrialized countries. In one estimate, Indian companies spend 0.57 percent of their revenue on R&D expenditure, compared to an average of 12–18 percent spent by the multinational pharmas. India's investment is said to produce only 3 to 4 molecules a year. Most of India's R&D is supported by the public sector, while the private sector provides only 10 percent to 12 percent of R &D investment in drug development. This low investment ratio in R&D leads to a restricted ownership of patented drugs. It was noted that most drug patents are owned by the multinationals. The domestic companies' reliance on the profit from reverse engineering as its major competitive advantage has also reduced incentives to invest in basic research.

Even among the more competitive stakeholders, the R&D investment ratio in total revenue is low. For example, in 2004 the percentage of investment was 6 percent for Ranbaxy; 4 percent for Cipla; 4.4 percent for Dr Reddys Labs (DRL); 4 percent for Sun Pharma; 6.4 percent for Torrent Pharma; 1 percent for Lupin; 10.5 percent for Workhardt; 0.7 percent for Nicholas Piramal. On the whole, India's pharmaceutical industry's average investment in R&D was only 2 percent (see Datamonitor report, 2005, "India's growth prospects in pharma").

There are several reasons for low pharmaceutical R&D investment in India. The major reason is the lack of product patent protection prior to India's WTO commitment. This lack of protection was also deemed as the major deterrent for multinationals' entry in India. The other reason is the low profit margins for pharmaceutical sales. Like Brazil, the government has the authority to exercise price controls on pharmaceuticals. It was noted that in comparison to foreign markets, the profit margin of Indian companies, less than 6 percent pre-tax, is also much lower than those in developed markets that usually generate around 18 percent to 30 percent profit margins (Research and Markets, 2004).

Overall, in comparison, the Indian pharmas are much more agile than those in China, Brazil, and Russia because of India's integration and ties with Western pharmas, their business acumen, and their global vantage point. The trend of consolidation through mergers and acquisitions is likely to improve their competitiveness in the global environment.

In the WTO framework, there has been increasing partnership between the local and global pharmas, and the growth of the sector is likely to outpace that of developed countries. The key players are Aarti Drugs; Abbott India; Ajanta Pharma; Alembic; Astrazeneca Pharma; Aurobindo Pharma; Aventis Pharma; Cadila Health; Cipla; Dr Reddy; Elder Pharma; German Remedies; Glaxo Smith Kline; Ind Swift Lab; Ipca Laboratories; JB Chemical; Jagson Pharma; KDL Biotech; Kopran; Krebs Biochem; Lupin; Lyka Labs; Medicorp Tech; Merck; Natco Pharma; Nicholas Piramal; Novartis; Orchid Chemicals; Organon; Panacea Bio; Pfizer; Pharmacia; Ranbaxy; RPG Life Sciences; Shasun Chemicals; Siris Limited; Sterling Biotech; Strides Arcolab; Sun Pharma; Suven Life Sciences; Torrent Pharma; Unichem Lab; Wockhardt; Wyeth; and Zandu Pharma. On the whole, India's WTO membership has infused new dynamism into the pharmaceutical industry and both domestic and foreign pharmas are likely to gain. Despite some domestic opposition to the WTO's intellectual property rights requirement, the recent regulatory changes in patents are likely to increase India's competitiveness in global pharmaceutical provision. These changes are likely to increase global participation for the local pharmas and thus help obtain the funding that they need to strengthen their niche areas. For global pharmas, WTO helps them gain a foothold in India's market and this entry also leads to increased R&D for both the domestic and foreign pharmas. It is likely to be a win-win situation for both stakeholders.

China

The prospects for China's pharmaceutical industry are very positive when compared to the developed and other developing countries. Overall, growth of the pharmaceutical industry in China is determined by the larger social, economic, and population health factors. Among all the determinants for pharmaceutical growth, the macro-economic context has played, and will continue to play, an important role in the future development of China's pharmaceutical industry. China's economy is growing at an average of 10–12 percent since the beginning of its economic reform (*China Daily*, 24 January 2008, "GDP expands 11.4 percent, fastest in 13 years"). When measured in terms of exchange-rate terms, China's economy is the fourth largest in the world after the United States, Japan, and Germany, with a nominal GDP of US$3.42 trillion in 2007. As Chinese society has become more affluent, the demand for better health care, including more effective medicine, has also increased. Another factor that contributes to growth in the health care economy is the aging of China's population and a rapid increase of diseases. The wealth and rural/urban gap has also brought about different health problems for the population. The affluent section of population is effected by the chronic illnesses commonly seen in developed countries, such as hypertension, obesity, and cardiovascular diseases, while the poorest section of population is afflicted with malnutrition, respiratory problems, infectious diseases, and parasitic problems. The common threats facing both rural and urban populations are cancer, TB, hepatitis, imbalanced nutrition, diabetes, and HIV/AIDS. In this context, health care issues have become the most important concern for both the Chinese public and policy makers. For example, in an opinion poll in 2007, health care ranked top on the list of major social concerns for the Chinese public. About 64.83 percent of those surveyed believed that it is the major social issue facing China (*Sina News*, 19 December 2008, "Survey shows that health care is on the top of government's concerns"). In the context of an affluent environment, Chinese demand for better health care products, especially medicine, is increasing. A survey of 16 typical city hospitals showed that the usage of drugs increased by 32.23 percent in the first half of 2004 as compared with that of 2003 (Wikipedia, 2007c, "Pharmaceutical industry in China").

China's pharmaceutical industry

In comparison to the global average rate, China is experiencing a very high growth rate in its pharmaceutical market. It was noted that between 1978 and 2005, the average growth rate of China's pharmaceutical industry, about 16.1 percent, exceeded that in most other countries (*Genetic Engineering and Biotechnology News*, 2007). The fastest growth, with an average annual growth rate of 19.4 percent, was noted in the years between 2000 and 2005 (Dance with Shadows Information, 2006).

Various estimates provide very optimistic assessments of China's pharmaceutical market. For example, according to IMS Health, China's pharmaceutical market size was $11.7 billion in 2005 and reached $15 to 16 billion in 2007. Yet the estimate by Price Waterhouse Coopers showed that the total market for 2005 has actually reached 19.2 billion (see PriceWaterHouseCoopers, March, 2007). In 2007, China's market ranked second, next to Japan, in the Asian region and the ninth in the world. If this momentum continues, China will be the world's seventh largest pharmaceutical market by 2009 and the fifth largest market by 2010 (Dance with Shadows Communication, 2006).

It is projected that China's pharmaceutical market value is likely to reach US$120 billion and will become the world's second largest pharmaceutical market after the United States in 2020 (*Genetic Engineering and Biotechnology News*, 2007). Most of the pharmaceutical production and market in China is in the cities in the coastal provinces, mainly Zhejiang, Guangdong, Shanghai, Jiangsu, and Hebei. The so-called "growth poles" are in Eastern China, with Zhejiang in the center, and in South China, with Guangdong as the center of the action. Their output value combined accounted for 21 percent of the pharmaceutical industry of China between 1998 and 2003 (Wikipedia, 2007c).

History and development of foreign pharmas in China

Most large multinational pharmaceutical companies have their subsidiaries or joint-ventures in China. As of 2004 (three years after China's WTO entry), nearly all the global pharmaceutical companies had already entered into the Chinese market in one form or another. Foreign pharma's involvement in China can be traced back to their Chinese trade more than a hundred years ago. For example, Bayer of Germany, the inventor of aspirin, was in China as early as 1882. Hest, or Aventis, in partnership with 128 distribution agents in 1887, was known in China as a major medicine and dyeing provider. Eli Lilly and Company had its first overseas representative office in Shanghai in 1918. The China trade of ICI, or what is known as AstraZeneca now, began in Shanghai in 1898 (Wikipedia, 2007c).

Today, foreign pharmaceutical companies are present in almost every area of the pharmaceutical business in China, including production, marketing, distribution, and exporting. The most prominent stakeholders are those that have either entered the Chinese market early, have an effective interface with the local pharmas, or those who have catered to the needs of the Chinese market. For the early players, Novartis Beijing, the first foreign pharmaceutical company in China with partnership with Beijing Pharmaceutical group and Beijing Zizhu Pharmaceuticals in 1987, has invested in manufacturing in China patented drugs, generic drugs, eye protection drugs, and health products. Bristol-Myers Squibb is also an early player in the Chinese market. Eli Lilly, which was present in Shanghai in 1918 and restarted its operation in Shanghai in 1993, has a major facility in Suzhou, Jiangsu, and is close to Shanghai, the center of global commerce and trade in China. Lilly's main products are cipro, insulin, and erectile dysfunction drugs. Merck, which set up its first joint venture in China in 1994, focuses on antibiotics, prostate drugs, cardiovascular drugs, pain relievers, osteoporosis drugs, and vaccines that cater to the needs of the Chinese market. Boehringer Ingelheim, which started an operation in 1995 and moved into manufacturing by investing $25 million in Shanghai in 2002, has found its niche market in drugs for respiratory diseases and cardiovascular diseases. Boehringer Ingelheim has done very well with its niche market. Its subsidiary Shanghai Pharmaceuticals reported that, compared to the previous year, its revenues increased by 46 percent in 2007 to US$95 million and they are expected to grow to $327 million by 2012 (Bioportfolio, 2008, "Chinese pharmaceutical industry"; see also Biospace,1 April 2008, "Boehringer Ingelheim corporation profits from Sinopharm deal"; Boehringer Ingelheim, 2002, "Boehringer Ingelheim opens new production plant in China").

Some companies, like Bayer, see China as one of their core businesses and have developed a comprehensive strategy. For example, Bayer Greater China, Bayer's second largest single market in Asia, generates approximately one-quarter of Bayer's sales in China. Pfizer, with more than $500 million investment in China, matching the standard of Chinese Pharmacopeia, produces and markets more than 40 innovative drugs in China. The other example is AstraZeneca Pharmaceutical Company, which has its headquarters in Shanghai and 25 branch offices in major cities in China. Fully taking advantage of China's low-cost labor, in 2001 AstraZeneca invested $170 million to establish a manufacturing site in Wuxi, its largest in Asia, with major products Seroquel and Nexium. The workforce of AstraZeneca in China totals more than 3000 employees, including 800 representatives in 110 targeted cities working in various stages of the supply chain, such as manufacturing, sales, clinical research, and new product development (AstraZeneca, 2006, "AstraZeneca in China").

Similarly, GlaxoSmithKline, employing more than 2000 in China, markets drugs for HBV, asthmas, and infections in 60 cities. Other major foreign pharmas, such as Sanofi-Aventis, Abbott Laboratories, Johnson & Johnson, Roche, Schering-Plough, and Boehringer Ingelheim all have a major presence in China.

In terms of their China strategy, most foreign pharmas use a partnership approach, such as the joint venture of US$37 million Shanghai Corporation of Pharmaceutical Economic and Technical International Cooperation that was initiated on 5 August, 1994 by Schering-Plough Pharmaceutical Company with the Shanghai Pharmaceutical Industry (Group) Corporation. In 2007, more than 25 percent of products in the Chinese market were from Sino-foreign joint-venture products; 12 percent from imported products; and 63 percent from domestic makers (*Genetic Engineering and Biotechnology News*, 2007). Despite the high percentage of domestically produced drugs, approximately 40 out of 50 of the best-selling drugs in China were foreign-made (ibid.).

In terms of pharmaceutical sales and profit levels, in 2005 the volume of pharmaceutical sales grew by 25.78 percent to $55.8 billion (437.28 billion RMB) and the profit level was US$46.89 billion, an 18.63 percent increase over 2004. As mentioned earlier, China's pharmaceutical industry continued to expand in 2006. The industry has experienced a high-growth scenario, about 18 percent in 2006, with a profit level of 7.9 percent due to price controls. In terms of product types, Chemical synthetic medicines, traditional Chinese herbal medicines, biological products, and medical devices constituted 93 percent of the Chinese pharmaceutical market in 2007 (*Genetic Engineering and Biotechnology News*, 2007). The generics and OTCs are the niche areas for local pharmas, while innovative drugs came from the multinationals. On generics, the largest source of revenue in Chinese pharmaceutical sales derives from the sales of the non-branded generic industry (Wikipedia, 2007c). Generics production has been a key strength for China for decades. By 2005, about 95 percent of pharmaceuticals in the Chinese market were generics. On the OTC drugs, China's over-the-counter market (OTC) is experiencing a high-growth scenario and has become the fourth largest in the world. This trend has attracted attention from the large pharmas. For example, Merck started its OTC program in China in September 2003. Roche aims to grow its OTC drug sales in China by 50 percent by 2012 to reach 1.3 billion in 2008. For Roche, China is already its top ten markets. Both Novartis and Wyeth have plans to grow their OTC market in China (see Euromonitor, 2007a, "OTC health care in China"; see also Wikipedia, 2007c). In terms of sales outlets, hospital drug sales account for the major source of revenue for pharmaceutical manufacturers. In this picture, chemical synthetic drugs generated US$2.24 (RMB17.57) billion profits, accounting for 47.86 percent of the total profits. However, with China's entry into the WTO, competition has intensified and it was noted that 23 percent of Chinese companies experienced a total of $0.46 billion (RMB3.59 billion) loss in 2005, a US$24 million (0.19 billion RMB) increase over the previous year (*Genetic Engineering and Biotechnology News*, 2007). This competition is likely to filter out weak, domestic stakeholders from China's domestic pharmaceutical market.

Price controls

It is important for all the stakeholders to understand that price control mechanisms have always been a part of China's health care system and strong policy interventions to ensure access and affordability of pharmaceuticals will continue. For example, the government has always monitored the most often prescribed prices through the National Development and Reform Commission, which has launched 19 drug price reduction campaigns over the past decade. For example, in June 2004 the price of 400 antibiotics in 24 categories, including penicillin, was reduced by, on average, 35 percent, with a savings of US$42 million. In August 2006, the target of price reduction is the retail price of 99 types of anti-microbial drug associated with 2000 manufacturers in China. In this case, the prices were lowered by 30 percent, and have resulted in savings of RMB 4.3 billion ($550 million) to Chinese consumers (*Genetic Engineering and Biotechnology News*, 2007).

Manufacturing

Vertical and horizontal integration in manufacturing has become a trend to increase efficiency in the pharmaceutical industry. In 2007, there were around 3500 drug companies in China, which has seen a decrease from 5000 in 2004. Of all the manufacturers, 90 percent are still medium to small-sized and only about 250 manufacturers in China have revenues in excess of US$12.77 million (RMB100 million). About 36 percent of all China's pharmaceutical enterprises are state-owned. Another 35 percent are privately owned domestic enterprises and 29 percent are foreign-funded (Wikipedia, 2007c). The foreign pharmas, around 1700 in 2005, also have an important presence in China. As mentioned earlier, China's domestic companies account for more than 60–70 percent of the market while the foreign companies account for about 20–30 percent of the sale.

The local drug makers' competitiveness remains a challenge. Some of the most mentioned challenges facing the local producers include lack of investment in R&D, lack of integration and efficiency, small production scale, duplication and competition for a narrow range of generics, incomplete government incentives, a lack of collaboration between domestic research institutes and drug companies, outdated management structure, weak intellectual property rights capacity, and weak international trading competitiveness (see related discussions in Wang, Zhang and Wang, 2007; Worldwatch Institute, 6 May, 2006, "China's pharmaceutical industry lacks innovation, lags behind"; see also Research and Markets, 2007a). Their strengths lie in their stronghold in traditional Chinese medicine, local marketing and distribution knowledge, large concentration in generics and chemical production. Their fast acquisition of modern management models and business strategies and agile adaptation to international trading networks has also boosted their competitive advantages in China's domestic markets. Globally, they will continue to excel in areas where they already have a large market share, such as chemicals, but it will take them a long time to increase their share in innovative biomedicine. Their best bet for now is to increase collaboration with foreign pharmas in this area.

In specific, most of the Chinese domestic pharmas still concentrate on making generics and traditional medicine because of weak R&D and a lack of capacity to produce patented drugs. And they still rely on hospital sales as a major source of revenue. One way to gauge competitiveness in pharmaceutical quality in a given country is to examine the percentage of companies obtaining GMP certification. By 2007, most of the Chinese pharmaceutical manufacturers had obtained Chinese GMP (Good Manufacturing Practice) certification and the government is in the process of discouraging the operation of non-GMP certified manufacturers (Wikipedia, 2007c). The government's determination to improve quality has shown some results, with sales for the more competitive Chinese companies growing faster than those for Western and smaller companies (Wang, Zhang and Wang, 2007) and smaller companies being forced out of the market. Yet the domestic pharmas still have a long way to go to compete at the same level with their multinational counterparts. For example, the market concentration of the top-tier domestic pharmas is still low in China. The top ten manufacturers now account for 13 percent of the industry's total sales revenue, a much lower share when compared to the top ten pharmas in mature markets (40–50 percent). Nonetheless, if vertical and horizontal integration continues to speed up, as witnessed by the mergers and acquisitions among the local and foreign pharmas, the local companies would gain new momentum in the era of WTO membership.

The silver lining for Chinese domestic pharmas is the production of fine chemicals for pharmaceutical production (Bryant, December 2007, "China emerges in APIs"). It was noted that in the past 25 years, China has developed a competitive chemical industry and is a major supplier of basic intermediates of fine chemicals, which enables China to develop its capacity in advanced pharmaceutical intermediates. For a long time, Chinese producers of advanced pharmaceutical intermediates and formulations have had a stronghold in the domestic market. Starting in 2005, with the Chinese government's regulatory incentives, the sector has started a more global strategy, aiming for the expansion of exports. In this framework, chemical drug manufacturing, which has long been a key part of the Chinese pharmaceutical industry, is now taking a lead in the global market. Chinese chemical makers have also made substantial progress in quality improvement. For example, Chinese plants have obtained 450 active DMFs within the US FDA, compared to Italy's 540 and India's 1350. The DMFs, or the drug master files, are "confidential, proprietary assets about the formulae, processes, test methodology and other data" related to "the manufacture of products used in the composition, packaging, processing of pharmaceuticals or biologics" (quoted from The Center for Professional Innovation and Education, 2008, "Drug master files – understanding and meeting your regulatory and processing responsibilities"). Chinese chemical makers are now able to compete on a global scale. It is noted that there are multiple Chinese producers for the majority of the top-selling advanced pharmaceutical intermediates in the global market (Bryant, 2007). By 2005, the pharmaceutical chemical sector, which includes all types of chemical production and involves more than 3000 manufacturers, accounted for 50 percent of China's total pharmaceutical sales. In 2006, the total sales of bulk drugs and advanced pharmaceutical intermediates were valued at around US$12 billion, of which exports accounted for about 40 percent (ibid.). By 2007, the top-selling advanced pharmaceutical intermediates included citric acid, vitamin C, tetracycline, penicillin, vitamin E, paracetamol (acetaminophen), heparin, erythromycin thiocyanate, monosodium glutamate, and lysine, among which vitamins and food acids account for 30 percent of the total sales (ibid.). The top producers are Shijazhuang Pharmaceutical Group, Zhucheng Xingmao Corn Developing Company, Beijing Double Crane Pharmaceutical, Huadong Medicine, Anhui BBCA Biochemical, Yung Shin Pharmaceutical Industries, Shenzhen Neptunus Bioengineer, and Zhejiang Sunrise Fine Chemicals, with the sales ranging from US$272 million to $US635 million (ibid.). Overall, in 2007, China was already the largest producer and exporter of chemical crude materials and drug preparations and it is estimated that, with a 25 percent annual growth rate in the category of advanced pharmaceutical intermediates, Chinese producers will also take the lead in that field in the near future (ibid.).

Another strength of the Chinese pharmaceutical sector is the production of traditional Chinese medicine (TCM), owing to its wide use in China and its neighboring countries as well as its growing acceptance in the United States and European countries. The fact that since June 2002, China's State Drug Administration has taken concrete steps to standardize production has also helped the sale of traditional Chinese medicine (see Xinhuanet, 13 May 2002, "China standardizes production of traditional Chinese medicine"). By 2005, around 1000 TCM manufacturers in China accounted for approximately 25 percent of China's pharmaceutical sales (Wikipedia, 2007c).

Another fast-growing sector, because of the government's support of it as a strategic investment target, is that of biopharmaceuticals. By 2005, about 400 biopharmaceutical manufacturers had been established in China, including 114 manufacturers of genetically engineered drugs and 28 vaccine manufacturers. The potential of this sector cannot be underestimated because of the Chinese government's encouragement, its abundant human capital, and the increased flow of venture capital into China. It was noted that the biopharmaceutical sector grew by 31.2 percent annually between 2001 and 2005, which propels China toward becoming the largest vaccine manufacturing country in the world, offering 41 vaccines to prevent 26 viral diseases in the domestic as well as international markets. China ranks third in large-scale production of genetically engineered insulin (see Chervenak, Fall 2006, "Industrial biotechnology in China," pp. 174–6).

Imports and exports

The momentum in pharmaceutical growth has increased in both imports and exports, which is directly related to China's WTO membership. In one estimate from China Customs data, total revenue on imports and exports reached US$25.64 billion in 2005 (with exports of $13.80 billion and imports of $11.84 billion). Together, they accounted for a 23.5 percent increase over 2004 (Wikipedia, 2007c). Since China joined WTO in 2001, the tariff rate for imported drugs has reduced from 20 percent in 2001 to 5–8 percent in 2007, and under WTO rules no tariff will be charged after 2008. Import tariffs for such life-saving medicines as ARVs for AIDS have already been completely eliminated. This reduction is beneficial for the imported drugs. For example, according to IMS (2005), since insulin entered into the Chinese market in 1987, more than 1000 imported drugs from over 100 countries became accessible to Chinese consumers. The improved regulatory framework has obviously facilitated imports and it was noted that China's State Food and Drug Administration (SFDA) has granted more than 2000 certificates for imported drug registration and more than 9000 certificates for imported medical device registration (ibid.).

CMOs

Due to regulatory liberalization, China has also gained ground in pharmaceutical contract manufacturing, or CMOs, which started growing in the 1990s and has also expanded to a wide range of production activities, such as API synthesis, peptide synthesis, and recombinant product production. It was noted that starting from 1 January 2006, all GMP-certificated Chinese manufacturers have legal permission to conduct contract manufacturing for overseas consumption for foreign companies, but vaccines, blood products, and Chinese herbal injections are excluded from the production of CMOs. The excess capacity in China's pharmaceutical sector makes it an attractive target for the multinationals for outsourcing (see related discussions in Contract Pharma, June 2006, "Biopharma CMOs in China"; Wikipedia, 2007c).

Pharmaceutical distributors in China

Macroeconomic growth, population health needs, and regulatory change, mainly in the separation of hospital pharmacies from health care services and classification of OTCs, has propelled the growth of business in pharmaceutical distribution, especially the retail pharmacy (see Wang, Zhang and Wang, 2007). Retailers include those with shops, without shops, and retail groups. Despite the fact that hospitals remain the largest pharmacy retailer, the future of health reform is likely to encourage growth in community retail pharmacy. In current situation, hospitals own about 85 percent of retail pharmacy business (Wikipedia, 2007c).

Other potential business in retail pharmacy includes e-business and the setting up of pharmacy retailing chain stores. Although the percentage of such e-business as, for instance, B2B, a new business tool for Internet pharmacy, is small, its potential is unlimited because of the rapid development of the Chinese information technology market (see Qayyum, 2003, "eBusiness technologies and trends in pharmaceutical industry"). In one estimate, China now has the largest population using Internet services and B2B e-pharmacy commerce has increased by 300 percent yearly. It was estimated that in 2003, the trade volume of internet pharmacy sales was 10 percent of the total. The combination of IT and pharmacy sales has attracted investment from some local groups, such as Fang Zheng Group's US$363 million investment; Guangzhou Bai Yun Shan Pharmaceutical Manufactory's US$12 million external-use medicine project, on the top of its US$48 million antibiotics project.

The population trend also bodes well for large pharmaceutical distributors. It was estimated that by 2005, there were 16,500 pharmaceutical wholesalers and 140,000 retailers in China (Wikipedia, 2007c). In this picture, according to an estimate by the China Pharmaceutical Distributor Association, 56 distributors exceeded US$128 million

(1 billion RMB) in revenue, 13 exceeded $382 million (3 billion RMB), and 8 exceeded US$637 million (5 billion RMB) in sales (see the statistics in ibid.). Yet when compared to developed markets, the concentration rate for large distributors is still low in China. For example, in 2005, the market share of sales volume by the top three largest Chinese distributors, China National Pharmaceutical Group, Shanghai Pharmaceutical, and China Jointown Group, was only US$1.3 billion (10 billion RMB), or only 17 percent of the total market. In contrast, the three leading distributors in the United States account for 90 percent of the US domestic market (Wang, Zhang and Wang, 2007).

The major challenge facing domestic pharmaceutical distributors in China is that the sector is not efficient and has a low profit margin. It is in urgent need of integration because about 80 percent of Chinese drug distributors are small-sized, over-represented, and disorganized, despite an effort to streamline operations in 2004. In one estimate, the average gross profit rate for China's drug-distributing companies has decreased to 8 percent, with net profits at 0.5 percent (Wang, Zhang and Wang, 2007; see also Wikipedia, 2007c). The trend for integration is inevitable. For example, on 26 April 2005, an alliance was forged among the major distributors when the five large Chinese distributors of Shanghai Pharmaceutical, Guangzhou Pharmaceutical, Chongqing Medicine, Beijing Pharmaceutical, and Tianjin Taiping Group combined to form China Pharmaceutical Commercial Economic Alliance, to improve efficiency and profit margins. Additionally, a partnership was formed between Sinopharm Medicine Holding and Tianjin Taiping Group to compete with the Alliance (PriceWaterHouseCoopers, March 2006).

Distributors with foreign-investment

China's membership in the WTO is a major incentive for the multinationals. The WTO requires a gradual opening of China's distribution sector to foreigners and foreign companies began their entry in 2003. For example, in December 2003, with a total investment of US$15.3 million (120 million RMB), the first Sino-foreign joint-venture China Zuellig Xinxing Pharmaceutical was established between Zuellig Pharma headquartered in Swiss and China Xinxing Group. By 2005, this market had completely opened up to foreign businesses. In September 2005, the Chinese Ministry of Commerce and Trade gave approval to a US company, Beijing Med-Pharm (BMP), and allowed it to acquire a Chinese drug distributor, Wanwei in Beijing (Genetic Engineering and Biotech News, 2007). BMP became the first wholly foreign-owned pharmaceutical distributor in China, with additional business in drug registration and market research service; and another company also entered China in October 2005 as a wholly Japanese-owned drug wholesale company registered in Guangzhou, China.

Overall assessment. China has demonstrated some strengths in meeting the supply and demand of pharmaceutical provision. These include the largest population in the world, rapid macro-economic growth, graying of the population, health care as a major social and political concern, the increase of health insurance coverage, the emergence of a wide range of diseases and illnesses, the government's incentive of building pharmaceuticals and biotechnology as a new economy, improvements in quality control and the intellectual property rights environment, and ethno-medical knowledge. China has at the same time offered very large opportunities on the supply and demand sides.

Growth strategies

In this picture, there are several growth areas. Chinese medicine, a stronghold for domestic producers in the domestic market, is also likely to be a profitable area for all stakeholders. Chinese domestic producers' potential in this area has not been fully realized when their foreign counterparts, especially the Japanese and Korean companies, have actually been more competitive in exporting Chinese herbal medicine to Western countries.

The pharmaceutical distribution business is another area that has not been fully realized. According to one estimate, in 2003, only 15.1 percent of total drug expenditure was incurred at pharmacy stores (Meng et al., 2005). Regulatory relaxation in 2003 for foreign ownership in pharmaceutical distribution has provided opportunities for foreign distributors and some, such as Alliance Boots, have either operated on their own or formed retail and distribution joint ventures (Alliance Boots, 29, January 2007, "Alliance Boots to enter Chinese pharmaceutical market through joint venture"). Among the possibilities in this area, the growth of the rural retail pharmacy has large potential. It was estimated that due to inadequate supply of pharmaceuticals, about 80 percent of counterfeit products are consumed in rural areas. With the Chinese government's new agenda in its development program focusing on rural reconstruction, rural pharmaceutical distribution is likely to be a major area of growth. This probably explains the promise of such joint efforts by Huanan Pharmaceutical Group, Guangzhou Ruobei Huale, Baiyunshan Pharmaceutical Group, and others to grow their business in this area (Wikipedia, 2007c). In this area, the local players have a major advantage in distribution because most Chinese companies have a niche in low-cost generics. They not only produce the dosage forms (such as tablets), they also own the pharmacies where the drugs are dispensed. The local pharmas also own the distribution networks with the hospitals (see Wang, Zhang and Wang, 2007).

Another area of sales growth in China's pharmaceutical sector is that of dietary supplements, which has grown from US$3 billion in 1998 to a total sales volume of $6 billion in 2001 and is likely to reach US$10 billion in annual sales by 2010 (Natural Products Insider, 2008, "Global market growth for dietary supplements"; Euromonitor International, September 2007b, "Vitamins and dietary supplements in China"). It has been noted that just calcium alone is a 1 billion US dollar business in China annually. Due to the changing lifestyles and increasing prevalence of chronic problems such as obesity or imbalance of nutrition, the demand for supplements is growing in China as well as in industrialized countries. In China, over 3000 domestic manufacturers of dietary supplements produce more than 4000 different types of products (USA Commercial Service, 2008, "Health care products and services"). Foreign products have more credibility despite their small market share, about 10 percent. With less credibility of product quality, China's domestic manufacturers rely on advertising to generate sales (Wikipedia, 2007c). The room for growth and improvement in this area is extensive because China is also the largest producer of some major food supplements, such as vitamin C in the world (Wang, Zhang and Wang, 2007).

On outsourcing, China shares many similarities with India. To begin with, China has abundant skilled and unskilled labor, low-cost facilities, improved infrastructure, and government incentives. As mentioned earlier, contracted manufacturing organizations are a major growth area, which promises opportunities for both domestic as well as foreign players. This potential has been noticed by foreign pharmaceutical companies. For example, in 2006 Pfizer developed a partnership with Shanghai Pharmaceutical Group and is likely to develop another partnership with Harbin Pharmaceutical Group (see BNET, 2006, "Pfizer gives OEM orders to Shanghai Pharm Group"; *Genetic Engineering and Biotechnology News*, 15 February 2008, "Top Chinese biopharms propel industry forward").

Given the urgent need for cost-cutting in pharmaceutical manufacturing in developed markets, this trend is inevitable. Outsourcing in pharmaceutical business foresees positive business potential in China. A major growth area of outsourcing is clinical trials. Examples include NexMed's cream to treat impotence; Therapeutics' cancer treatment; FeRx liver cancer treatment (BIT Life Sciences, 2008, "BIT's world cancer congress"; see also PreventDisease, 2008, "Anti-impotence cancer cream to take on Viagra"; SiniWest, 2001, "Study marks the first time an investigative therapy has been approved for clinical trials in China prior to regulatory approval in the West").

On research and development, China's membership in the WTO has also led to an improvement of its intellectual property rights environment for foreign pharmas and their increasing collaboration with Chinese research institutes and local pharmas for drug development. This factor has facilitated the venture of foreign pharmas in R&D. For example, GSK's establishment of its OTC research and development center in Tianjin, has been followed by similar moves by Pfizer and Janssen Pharmaceutical (Johnson & Johnson), AstraZeneca, Bayer, Eli Lilly, Tiens Biotech Group (USA) (for nutritional supplements and personal care products), Novo Nordisk, Lonza (Basel, Switzerland), and Chiral Quest (biotechnology). Hoffman-La Roche have also set up R&D and clinical trial centers in China (*Genetic Engineering and Biotechnology News*, 2007). As mentioned earlier, a major growth area is biotech and it was noted that some global biopharmaceutical companies see China as a major emerging market. For example, according to James Ward-Lilley, president of AstraZeneca, China grew at about an average of 30 percent from 2003–05. AstraZeneca plans to increase its $40 million investment in manufacturing facilities in Wuxi between 2006 and 2010 (ibid.).

A large potential for foreign companies consists in R&D for Chinese traditional medicine. Despite Chinese domestic makers' long history in this area, they are not competitive in the international market. It is estimated that about 10,000 patents for traditional Chinese medicines belong to Western companies (cited from Wikipedia, 2007c). Roche's move into this area is considered to be entirely rational given the promising conditions. In January 2004, Roche of Switzerland opened its first research and development center in China. In addition to targeting pharmaceutical chemistry, Roche also aims to develop traditional Chinese medicine research. This is Roche's fifth R&D center in the world (see Roche, 2004, "At its 10th anniversary celebration, Roche opens new R&D Center in China").

Overall, in terms of product differentiation, the growth areas are likely to be food supplements, antibiotics, drugs for chronic illnesses, and drugs for infectious diseases. Drugs for the treatment of cancers is an area likely to grow at a very fast pace because of the increasing prevalence and incidence of malignant tumors in the world. In this context, foreign pharmas are well-positioned at every stage of the supply chain and a number of options are open to them; they could take advantage of the downstream of labor supply by using China as a manufacturing base; they could take advantage of China's high-skill labor by leading R&D collaboration; they could be part of the distribution chain; and they could participate in the food supplement business. The foreign pharmas are also well-positioned in both the domestic and export market if they could fully take advantage of the liberalized environment in the wake of China's WTO membership. They could focus on niche markets or they could have a long-term, comprehensive strategy.

The multinationals in China have used a wide range of strategies. For example, Degussa is transferring a large percentage of its pharmaceutical chemicals production from Europe to China and, similarly, the Japanese company Terumo plans to use China as a manufacturing base (with 1362 employees in manufacturing), aiming mainly at exporting to the Japanese market and, to a lesser extent, to the American and European markets (statistics cited from Wikipedia, 2007c). In contrast, Bayer has taken a gradual, long-term strategy since its entry into China. It has grown from a step-by-step investment in the early 1990s to large-scale, world-class facilities today. Bayer's investment in the Shanghai Chemical Industry Park employs around 2800 people across a wide range of functions (BNET, 2004, "Bayer signed agreement with Shanghai Chemistry Industry Park"). In addition to manufacturing and sale, Bayer China has also developed R&D collaboration with major research institutes, such as the Chinese Academy of Science, the Institute of Materia Medica, and the Kunming Institute of Botany in Yunnan as well as with universities in the areas of innovative materials, health care, and crop science. Bayer is strongly motivated to identify new compounds in the health care and crop science field. Some other companies focus on niche markets. For example, Rhodia focuses on the production of analgesics, paracetamol (acetaminophen or APAP), mainly in Wuxi, China (facts cited from Wikipedia, 2007c).

In terms of the format of collaboration, partnership between foreign and domestic pharmas through joint ventures has been used effectively since the opening of the Chinese market. A good model of the joint venture is provided by Xian-Janssen Pharmaceutical in Xi'an (Xian-Janssen, 2004, "Johnson and Johnson and YAES"), which ranks as one of the top ten joint ventures in revenue since 1991. The success of the partnership lies in its focusing on the niche markets and producing treatments for gastrointestinal problems, fungi, allergies, and pain, as well as drugs for psychosis and epilepsy.

Africa

Africa is a continent that embodies diversities, extremes, and contradictions. Africa, with about 922 million people, is the world's second-largest and second most populous continent, after Asia. With 30.2 million km², it covers 6 percent of the earth's total surface or 20.4 percent of the total land area (as of 2005) (Wikipedia, 2008, "Africa"). African countries encompass a wide array of GDP capacities, ranging from the well-endowed South Africa and Botswana to the group of 25 poorest countries in the world (UNDP, 2008, "Human development report"). South Africa, a leading producer of gold and diamonds, is equipped with first-world infrastructure and skilled labor, has one of the largest stock exchanges on the continent, Johannesburg Stock Exchange, and has easy access to financial capital (Wikipedia, 2008). In contrast, 36 percent of the people in Africa live on under $1 a day (see UNDP, 2008; Wang and Nantulya, 2008).

Despite the lack of analyses and information about the pharmaceutical demand and supply chain in Africa, Africa holds large potential for pharmaceutical innovation for several reasons. First of all, the African bloc is likely to become a major economic power on the global scene if there is improved political and financial governance and social stability. The supporting facts are self-evident. It has the largest reserve of natural resources, such as oil, gold, and copper. Given the abundance of Africa's hydraulic power and solar resources, it has large potential for developing alternative energy. With efficient modern farming methods, Africa also has large potential in increasing its agricultural output. In the face of rising agricultural prices, this advantage will become even more influential on the global scene. Second, in terms of population health profiles, Africa presents the richest amount of population informatics for pharmaceutical innovations. Indeed, Africa is faced with the largest challenges to global health because of the prevalence of a wide range of neglected diseases and illnesses, such as HIV, malaria, TB, sleeping sickness, blindness, parasitic diseases, and so on. Nevertheless, the existence of these health challenges has also provided a major source of therapeutics and diagnostics. The continuous invention of new drugs, such as anti-retrovirals (ARVs) to treat HIV is a relevant case in point. Since the inception of the HIV/AIDS epidemic, the new pipelines of HIV/AIDS drugs have gradually improved the morbidity and mortality status of the infected populations. The health challenges in Africa have also brought about new drugs to treat malaria, trachoma, leprosy, and some parasitic diseases. Third, Africa is a virgin land in terms of the pharmaceutical supply and demand chain. Given the improvement of its economic prospects, increasing multilateral aid for global health, and increasing investment in local health infrastructure to improve population health, the demand for quality pharmaceuticals is likely to increase. This bodes well, especially for the generic makers in the region and foreign producers, particularly those in Brazil, India, and China.

The major pharmaceutical production capacity is in South Africa and Nigeria, with South Africa usually the focus of discussion in Africa. Despite the impression that South Africa is hostile to Western pharmaceutical companies, some research does not support the view that the industry is a monopoly that fixes the prices on the supply (manufacturing) side with diminished consumption on the demand (consumer) side (see related discussions in Djolov, June 2004).

In fact, South Africa has a major opportunity in the growth of pharmaceutical supply and demand because of its existing capacity. Compared to other African countries, South Africa has a relatively developed pharmaceutical industry, with a complex network of pharmaceuticals manufacturers, distributors, and dispensers (Mbendi, 2000, "Information for Africa"). The local pharmaceutical manufacturers have some capacities in producing generic active ingredients and formulation, while, in contrast, the multinationals or their subsidiaries are able to produce last-step synthesis. The network of pharmaceuticals distribution is composed of companies and affiliates, dispensing doctors, pharmacists with wholesale licenses, and wholesalers. Dispensers are made up of private channels, dispensing doctors, retail pharmacies, retail chains, private and public institutions, industrial clinics, and private and government hospitals. There is only limited local production of generic active ingredients, formulation and last-step synthesis is common among the local subsidiaries of multinational drug companies (Ibid.).

The negative assessment of South Africa's pharmaceutical industry in the past does not preclude its future growth. Indeed, the controversies surrounding the HIV/AIDS epidemic in the 1990s and early 2000s have caused a setback to the development and growth of the pharmaceutical industry. In order to provide affordable medicines to the HIV/AIDS infected, the South African government enforced compulsory licensing, which had invoked a strong reaction from the large multinationals. The Clinton government in the United States, originally siding with American pharmas, had to modify its position in the face of the accusation of human rights violation from global health activists, such as the Médicines sans Frontière. Future development still hinges on the political will of the leadership in South Africa, as well as on global stakeholders to improve pharmaceutical access and quality for Africans affected by HIV/AIDS and other infectious and chronic diseases. First of all, South Africa has major potential in the growth of health care related business because only 20 percent of the population has private insurance (National Center for Policy Analysis, 2000, "Medical savings account in South Africa"). There is room for business growth within the remaining population, which at present relies on the public health system. This growth is likely to increase given South Africa's present favorable position in the global economy these days. The government's determination to improve population health through a series of policy measures is also conducive to the growth of the pharmaceutical industry. These measures include the Pharmacy Act in 1974 and its amendment in 1999, which improves the quality of pharmacy service to the population (Republic of South Africa, 2000, "Pharmacy Amendment Act"). The government has also initiated a number of programs to improve maternal and child health and the health of the underprivileged. These include a program of free medical care for pregnant women and children under the age of six years, and the provision of free primary health care services to the general population (Mbendi, 2000).

The advantages of South Africa lie in the fact that its populations are facing a wide range of diseases that reflect the health challenges of both developed and developing countries. Disease profiles in South Africa reflect its bi-polar socioeconomic distribution; the affluent population is affected by lifestyle diseases while the poor majority are still fighting against poverty-related or infectious diseases. For example, in addition to HIV, South Africa is also in growing need of drugs for such chronic diseases as diabetes. The need for diabetic therapeutics has been increasing (*Medical News Today*, 2008, "South African diabetes market growing significantly due to improved diagnosis rates").

An estimate in 2006 showed that 43.0 per cent of Type II diabetics were using the more expensive insulin in addition to the oral treatment, which has helped increase the revenues of the anti-diabetic pharmaceutical market. In 2006, these revenues reached US$53.2 million and are projected to reach US$82.7 million in 2012 (Frost & Sullivan, 2008). On the whole, it was also pointed out that because of its heavily regulated environment, low-cost generics are likely to do better than the expensive brands. Yet given the rising prices of commodities, which provide a major source of revenue for South Africa's economy and are likely to improve its macro-economic prospects, there will also be some room for expensive brands to grow. It is important, though, for stakeholders who plan to stay in the market for the long haul to recognize the government's policy priorities of improving equity and access in health care and cost-containment. This assessment is also true for other countries in the region.

This chapter has presented an analysis of the unique positions of the BRICA countries in the global pharmaceutical supply and demand chain, examining their macro-economic conditions, population profiles, and health needs, the status of pharmaceutical development, the positions of local vis-a-vis global stakeholders, and growth areas. Now, the question is how their strengths can be fully realized in global health partnerships to contribute to the future growth of the pharmaceutical industry as well as securing improvements in global health. This question will be answered in the following chapter.

4
Global Health Partnerships between Multinationals and BRICA: A Planting Strategy

Global health challenges have taken a severe toll on economic development in resource-rich as well as resource-poor countries. Yet they have also brought about a unique opportunity to rethink a global strategy for a new kind of partnership between the large multinational pharmaceutical companies and the BRICA stakeholders for a win-win situation.

The analysis in the previous chapters suggests that the major concern for pharmaceuticals is their capacity to meet the demands and needs of global populations. That is, the global community needs innovative, effective, safe, and affordable medicine to address both prevalent illnesses and diseases as well as neglected diseases. So far, no single stakeholder could claim leadership in meeting all of these criteria. The large multinationals have known strengths in financing, technology, research and development, quality control and standard-setting, and marketing and distribution. In contrast, the domestic pharmaceutical companies in BRICA have advantages in the size of populations, unmet needs and demands, market potential, diverse disease profiles, low production cost, distribution, and ethnomedical knowledge as sources of innovation.

The need for collaboration between these stakeholders has never been greater because of several factors. First of all, the pharmaceutical markets in developed countries are growing at a much slower rate than those in BRICA. As mentioned earlier, in 2005 alone pharmaceutical sales across the BRIC economies grew by 22.3 percent (Business Insights, August 2006, "Pharmaceutical growth opportunities in BRICA"; see also Kermani, October 2005, "Contract Farma"; Research and Markets, March 2006, "The image of the pharmaceutical industry in Brazil: Challenges and opportunities"). In contrast, the rate of growth in developed markets is lower than 8 percent. For example, in 2007 Latin America grew at a rate of 12.7 percent to $33.6 billion, while Asia Pacific (outside of Japan) and Africa grew 10.5 percent to $66 billion. China alone has grown at a rate of 12–18 percent since the beginning of the 2000s (IMS, 2007b, "IMS Health Reports Global Pharmaceutical Market Grew 7.0 Percent in 2006, to $643 Billion"). A related issue is that the stagnant population growth in developed countries is affecting pharmaceutical demand. Second, pharmaceutical innovation and development in developed countries has become more expensive and uncertain than ever before. Third, the need for low-cost medicine is omnipresent in the globe, and this has already exerted pressure on the pharmaceutical companies to lower their prices. And this pressure is reflected in increasing legislative initiatives in both developed and developing countries to force the pharmaceutical sector to cut prices. In this picture, the pharmaceutical sector in developed countries needs to employ a different strategy for growth to be sustainable.

Planting strategy versus plucking strategy

This global strategy requires a different conceptual and operational framework for conducting pharmaceutical business in the future. That is, it requires the use of a planting strategy instead of a plucking strategy, the latter of which has been the dominant mode of thinking in the pharmaceutical sector since the 1980s. A planting strategy nurtures the soil to help the plant grow well so that the plant bears abundant fruit; while, in contrast, the plucking strategy takes away all the fruit on the trees without nurturing the soil. In this metaphor, the soil is population health, the nutrients are therapeutics, and the fruit is the profit.

There are several characteristics that identify a plucking strategy. Most importantly, it sets a profit threshold aiming to maximize the profits of a given drug by setting the highest price possible and therefore it has to cater to the needs of those who can afford the drug; and it focuses on diseases mainly in the developed countries or the resource-rich in developing markets because of the assumption that drugs for rare diseases would not meet the investment-return ratio competition. This strategy also requires efforts to deflect any possible attempts to challenge the pharmaceutical companies' dominant position by the use of "influence-buying" tactics, such as through lobbying efforts, legal maneuvers, or intensive marketing. Marketing is considered to be an important part of this existing strategy. For example, it was noted that in 2005, there were 100,000 pharmaceutical sales representatives in the

United States pursuing some 120,000 pharmaceutical prescribers, mainly physicians (Ebisch, March 2005, "Prescription for change"). On business strategy, as mentioned earlier, a common practice of some pharmaceutical companies is to extend the patent life of a blockbuster or deter price controls from the public sector through legal or political maneuvers. The other heavily criticized tactic is to influence the conditions of bilateral trade through the use of technical barriers to trade to maintain market advantages, such as prolonged IPR rights and data exclusivity (see CAPTH, 2008, "Center for policy analysis of trade and health: Thailand's compulsory licenses for medicines").

The promise of planting

In contrast, the premise of a "planting" strategy is that pharmaceutical development can address population health needs and at the same time generate a reasonable level of profit in the global markets. This strategy sees it as possible for the pharmas to support the health of a given population without having to create a sick culture. This illustrates the difference between the "Nieman-Markus stores" approach and the "dollar stores" approach to pharmaceutical business. The planting strategy would not ignore the fortunes of those at the bottom of the population pyramid and sees the business of their health as a sustainable pharmaceutical business. A planting strategy also sees the possibility of collaboration between the multinationals and local pharmaceutical companies in BRICA countries at various levels and stages of pharmaceutical production and distribution. This division of labor can be conceptualized in terms of efficient supply chain management, preferential pricing and market sharing (such as advanced commitments), and patent solutions. A planting strategy aims for a creative and innovative use of market mechanisms in the pharmaceutical business to meet both profit and population health goals at the same time.

In this framework, the multinationals and the locals can collaborate in a number of areas in which their strengths complement each other, such as innovation, cost and quality control, and supply chain management.

Innovation

The key to growth for the pharmaceutical sector on the whole is innovation, that is, whether the industry can generate truly innovative, effective, and safe products to meet the needs and demand of the populations (IMS, 8 March 2007a, "IMS Reports U.S. Prescription Sales Jump 8.3 Percent in 2006, to $274.9 Billion"). That is the real challenge facing the industry. Historically, innovation has played a role in the sector's growth and it was noted that the innovative products launched between 2001 and 2005 were worth about US$13.5 billion in 2006; innovation accounted for the increase of prescription sales to 8.3 percent in 2006, or the total of $274.9 billion; and innovative research has contributed to the emergence of four to seven blockbusters in 2007 (ibid.). As mentioned earlier, innovation can no longer derive solely from developed markets for a number of reasons. One of the most frequently mentioned is the maturation of developed markets (see Silva, 6 March 2008). Second, since the beginning of the 2000s there has been the phenomenon of the drying up of innovative ideas that could be translated into blockbuster molecules. Third, the promise of biotechnology to deliver new drugs is highly uncertain because of both the formulation challenges (the instability of the chemistry and physical chemistry of such products) and challenges of pharmacogenetic sampling (resulting in side-effects) (ibid.). Fourth, pharmaceutical innovation can no longer be based on the disease profiles of those populations in industrialized countries only. Their disease profiles are often limited to certain lifestyle-related problems.

The problem for the pharmaceutical sector of lacking innovative ideas in the developed market can be remedied by the BRICA nations because of the rising of the "creative" class, or the mind workers, in these countries (Silva, 2008). This is a phenomenon often ignored by the multinationals in deploying a global strategy. When discussing the global factor, the conventional wisdom, such as that conveyed by the report by International Marketing Services (IMS, 2007a), often focused on the potential of the markets outside the United States, such as the Chinese, South American (Brazil), and Indian. Indeed, most of the industrialized markets are now facing a low-growth scenario. Even with the boost of Medicare Part D, the United States reached only 8.3 percent growth. In Japan, total pharmaceutical sales were US$64.0 billion in 2006, a decrease of 0.4 percent from 2005, because of the government's biennial price cuts. In contrast, as mentioned earlier, the sales record in the emerging markets presents a totally different picture. For example, as mentioned earlier, in 2006 China experienced a growth rate of 12.3 percent to US$13.4 billion in 2006, compared with a 20.5 percent increase in the previous year. Even with the government intervention of price controls, the growth in 2006 was robust. Similarly, India has experienced fast growth of 17.5 percent, to US$7.3 billion (IMS, 2007b).

The IMS further elucidates the market potential of the developing markets by pointing out that in 2006, 27 percent of the global pharmaceutical market growth comes from countries with a per capita gross national income of less than $20,000, a sharp increase over the 13 percent share by these countries in total growth in 2000 (IMS, 2007b; see also FierceBiotech, 6 December 2007, "Say goodbye to Big Pharma's gilded age"). While the conventional wisdom focuses on the market size of the BRICA nation, what is less apparent is their innovative potential. China's and India's true potential comes with their WTO membership, which provides patent protection for innovative ideas. This forms a large incentive for pharmaceutical stakeholders to engage in collaborative research on innovative drugs in these countries.

In the global picture, what is going to determine the growth momentum for the sector will be whether the industry can generate "relevant" innovation in the pharmaceutical sector. That is, the true test is whether the industry can answer to the needs and demands of the world's patients. In BRICA, the potential of accessing effective and safe medicines for most of the populations is likely to play an increasing role in effecting pharmaceutical companies' bottom lines. A patient-centered approach is critical for innovation in this discussion. The need for comprehensive assessment of companies' R&D and portfolio strategies to support opportunities in both emerging and mature markets that the IMS mentioned was part of this patient-centered approach (IMS, 2007b).

This patient-centered approach requires the dominant pharmaceutical companies to gain better understanding both of the diseases facing populations in the developing countries and their ethnomedical system, from which future innovations could possibly derive. Although the disease distribution shows a bipolar distribution in BRICA, the disease burden is largely in the area of infectious or parasitic diseases, such as HIV, TB, hepatitis, and neglected tropical diseases. These offer rich sources of innovation in diagnostics or therapeutics. The BRICA nations are known for the possession of rich knowledge in their traditional or ethnomedical medicines, which have been their only source of treatment for thousands of years prior to the arrival of biochemical medicine. This knowledge contains valuable information about the therapeutic effects of natural plants in treating infectious or chronic illness.

Success with the development of co-artem illustrates the potential of traditional or indigenous ethnomedical knowledge in drug development. Co-artem is a synthetic derivative of artemisinin, which can be extracted from a traditional Chinese medicinal plant, *Artemesia annua* or sweet wormwood (New Technology for Malaria, 2006, "Artemisinin derivatives"). *Annua*, or qinghao in Chinese, is the active ingredient in artemisinin, or the Chinese term "qinghaosu," known for thousands of years. Qinghaosu has been used by Chinese healers for the treatment of malaria and other similar problems since at least the second century BC. In 1967, under Chairman Mao Tse-Tung, in a systematic examination of the traditional Chinese herbal pharmacopoeia, Chinese scientists were able to isolate the compound qinghaosu/artemisinin in 1972. Artemisinin-derived compounds were then developed in China in the 1980s (ibid.). It is noted that artemisinin derivatives, such as artesunate, arteether, artemether, and dihydro-artemisinin (DHA) are potent anti-malarials that act rapidly against the parasite's asexual erythrocytic (red blood cell) stage. They are noted for having helped to reduce the rate of malaria transmission due to their strong activity against the parasite blood-stage gametocytes (sexual stage). Artemisinin-derived drugs are proven to be highly efficacious for patients who develop parasite resistance to other first-line anti-malarial drugs (ibid.). With the endorsement of the World Health Organization (WHO) in 2004 approving the use of artemisinin-based therapies for the treatment of malaria and its recommendations later in 2005 to use artemisinin derivatives for first-line malaria treatment, the potential of the traditional ethnomedical system is coming into focus. Similar discoveries have also been reported in the ethnomedical systems in India and the indigenous cultures in Brazil.

The discovery of Taxol from the Yew tree is another example showing the promise knowledge of medicinal plants holds in discovering innovative pharmaceuticals. Given the long history of the ethnomedical systems in the BRICA cultures, this knowledge could play a crucial role in discovering innovative medicines. This ethnomedical knowledge is critical for the pharmaceutical industry, which finds itself facing the dilemma of running out of innovative ideas. It has been observed that the rate of discovery of innovative drugs has slowed since the beginning of the 2000s. Between 2002 and 2006, pharmaceutical companies rolled out 43 percent fewer medicines based on new chemicals, compared with the last five years of the 1990s and it was also noted that development in certain areas has been discontinued (FierceBiotech, 2007).

Cost control

The cost of pharmaceuticals has aroused the most intense debate in relation to global health. Indeed, the issue of pricing is complex and cannot be subject to an oversimplified solution. As mentioned earlier, the cost of pharmaceuticals is often considered to be the combined cost of innovation and drug development, marketing, distribution, and stimulating customer demand. In fact, the issue of pricing and the cost of pharmaceuticals should also be discussed as an issue of supply-chain efficiency in division of labor, manufacturing, market segmentation, and effective market competition. As Angell (2004) argued, one of the major issues of pricing is supply chain management. She pointed out that between manufacturers and consumers, the transitional cost increases as pharmaceuticals pass through middlemen, retailers, health facility purchasers, and so on (ibid.).

These layers of cost create inefficiencies as well as inevitable increases in pharmaceutical costs. For example, estimates on the cost of developing an innovative pharmaceutical often vary widely, with estimates ranging from $30 to $800 million, as mentioned in Chapter 1. And the drug development process is often carried out in developed countries with inevitable consequences for costs. When it comes to large-scale manufacturing, most of the pharmaceutical plants are in developed countries, exceptions being those in Brazil, India, and China. Very few are in other resource-poor countries, especially those in Africa. The comparatively higher labor and facility cost in developed countries has also contributed to the relatively higher cost of drugs in those markets. The lack of public sector participation in investment and sustained funding in drug development and production in most developed countries leaves the burden of pharmaceutical provision solely on the shoulders of the private sector. The high amount of initial investment as a requirement for entry into the pharmaceutical industry presents a high barrier that makes it difficult for stakeholders who have fewer means to participate. This lack of participation by new stakeholders makes it impossible for the emergence of a competitive market, a prerequisite for lower drug prices. In the end, the large pharmas have to rely on mergers among the stakeholders in the developed markets to increase efficiency. It was noted that starting from the 1980s, the large pharmas have taken a vertical or horizontal approach to improve efficiency. For example, a vertical integration approach to drug making involves integration of the flow from upstream to downstream, such as from broad drug discovery and development, to manufacturing and quality control, and then to marketing, sales, and distribution. In contrast, horizontal integration entails integration on the basis of complementarity. For example, smaller companies, especially biotech companies, could bring value to large companies in the provision of drug development capacities that the large companies lack, such as identifying potential drug candidates or developing formulations (Wikipedia, 2007, "Pharmaceutical companies"). Conversely, a large company could complement a small biotechnology company in the areas of marketing and distribution because of the large sales force employed under the umbrella of a large pharmaceutical company. These mergers are expected to bring about various *synergy* benefits.

As population growth in the developed markets becomes stagnant, this stagnation is also likely to be reflected in the market and profit growth of the pharmaceutical companies based in developed countries. In a stagnant picture, the only way to increase profit or just maintain the same profit levels is through the raising of pharmaceutical prices, which is reflected in the annual price increases of popular branded drugs such as Claritin. This exhibits the symptoms of a plucking strategy. Yet this strategy has the downside of that when economic growth is slow, the customer base is likely to shrink in response to the scenario of high costs.

In this picture, the only way to maintain the growth and competitiveness of the multinationals is through partnerships with those stakeholders in BRICA at every stage of the pharmaceutical supply and demand chain, in a complementing and decentralized strategy. This means that working with local pharmas, the multinationals can take advantage of the lower costs in labor, materials and facilities, as well as their rich ethnomedical knowledge, and access to diverse disease profiles in drug innovation, development, manufacturing, and packaging. The partnership is likely to gain on several fronts. First, the pharmaceutical companies would gain because of the large market potential in the BRICA nations due both to their population sizes and increasing health challenges in the areas of chronic as well as infectious diseases. Second, macro-economic growth is also likely to increase the consumer power of affluent customers in BRICA, who are already demanding higher-priced, better pharmaceuticals. Third, increasing funding and investment in the health of the underprivileged in those countries, as well as other developing countries, creates a demand for low-price medicines. Fourth, reduced manufacturing cost can be translated into lower pharmaceutical cost for customers in developed markets. This global health partnership framework creates a win-win situation for both the pharmaceutical sector and populations in developing and developed countries. Increased partnership is an inevitable trend for large multinationals to survive in an increasingly challenging regulatory and economic environment.

The growth of the production of generics in meeting global health needs is a reflection of the growing momentum of this trend. For a long time, generics have been seen as a threat to the global pharmaceutical industry's bottom line. For example, generics are expected to cut a total of US$67 billion from the top drug makers' annual US sales between 2007 and 2012, equivalent to half of those companies' total US revenues. In this scenario, industry revenue is expected to drop between 2011 and 2012, the first decrease in 40 years and it has been suggested that the competition in generics will end the large pharmas' gilded age (FierceBiotech, 2007).

In contrast, manufacturers of generics in BRICA are discovering an immense opportunity to meet the large demand in the developing markets. The story of Laboratorio Cristalia, in Brazil, typifies the untapped market potential in the global markets and the generics makers have never found themselves in a better position than now (CBS News, 23 September 2005, "Brazil's drug copying industry"). The need for generics has propelled Laboratorio Cristalia's growth in a span of three decades from that of a small producer of one cloned anti-hyperactivity medication to a firm with 1200 workers producing 150 drugs (ibid.). The company was originally founded in 1972 by Dr Ogari de Castro Pacheco as an auxiliary laboratory to produce cheaper drugs for the mental patients at his private clinic. As discussed in Chapter 2, the WTO's DOHA Declaration and 30 August liberalizing decision made it possible for the production of generics, especially for neglected infectious diseases such as AIDS, TB, or Malaria, in the form of compulsory licensing or parallel imports. These makers of generics in Brazil, India, and China are an indispensable operation for the populations in developing countries because of the low cost of their products and their agility in meeting local demands. For example, Laboratorio Cristalia is able to meet the level of demand for the AIDS cocktail in Brazil in a three- to six-month production run, and its facilities even have the capacity to meet the pharmaceutical needs of HIV/AIDS in South Africa if they are given longer production time. Despite the thin profit margins, the enormous volume for meeting the needs of the patients in developing markets makes it a worthwhile business to pursue.

From this angle, generics are not a threat but an opportunity for the multinationals. This opportunity lies in the large number of diseases and health problems that remain intractable and the large volume of future sales that can occur in the developing markets. In this respect, the strategy of Novartis is worth noting. Novartis has expanded its reach into the generics business as well as increasing its R&D

collaboration in developing countries, such as China, and in areas that have been traditionally ignored by the large pharmaceutical companies.

Quality control

While innovation and manufacturing are potential areas of global partnerships between the multinationals and BRICA for the long term, quality control, especially in substandard medicines (including counterfeits), is an urgent problem that requires immediate partnership between these stakeholders. Since the 1980s, the sale of unsafe medicines has become a serious challenge facing pharmaceutical makers and populations in developing countries and it requires immediate attention and resolution.

According to the WHO (2003), counterfeit medicines, as part of the broader phenomenon of substandard pharmaceuticals, deliberately and fraudulently mislabel with respect to identity and/or source. And this practice, currently affecting both branded and generic products, includes products with the correct ingredients but fake packaging, with the wrong ingredients, without active ingredients, or with insufficient active ingredients (World Health Organization, 2003, "Substandard and counterfeited medicines"). This phenomenon also occurs both in developed as well as developing countries. A WHO report (2003) pointed out that in developed countries the most frequently counterfeited medicines are new, expensive lifestyle medicines, such as hormones, steroids and antihistamines while in developing countries the most counterfeited medicines are those used to treat prevalent, life-threatening, and infectious diseases, such as malaria, tuberculosis and HIV/AIDS (World Health Organization, 2003 "Substandard and counterfeited medicines"). Recently, this list has been expanded. Another report showed that the counterfeits now cover a wide range of drugs and even electronic medical equipment. For example, it was noted that in Myanmar (Burma), the Lao PDR, Cambodia, and Vietnam, which have a high malaria incidence, about 50 percent of all artesunate tablets, an effective anti-malarial drug, are counterfeits. Most of these counterfeits did not only contain the active ingredient but also have toxic, wrong ingredients. Even those counterfeits that contain small amounts of artesunate, may do more harm than good as they could contribute to the resistance of malaria parasites to this class of drugs (TOPNEWS, 12 February 2008, "Fake anti-malarial drugs investigation highlights threat to global health"). Overall, an OECD report pointed out, genital-urinary medicines appear to be by far the most commonly counterfeited. The OECD report also indicated that there had been 253 reported incidents of counterfeiting involving this class of medicines, with the number jumping to 401 in 2005. Following this class of drugs, the other drugs that are most counterfeited are the anti-infectives and central nervous system (CNS) drugs (172 and 147 incidents respectively) (Barnes, 7 November 2007). In another report, paracetamol and the antibiotic amoxicillin were also cited as the most widely counterfeited medicines in the world (*New Scientist*, 8 September, 2006b, "The medicines that could kill millions"). In the United States, the most counterfeited are believed to be human growth hormone; atorvastatin, which is used to lower cholesterol and treat heart disease; erythropoietin, to alleviate anemia; filgrastim, to treat either leukemia or a bone marrow transplant; and the anti-cancer drugs germcitabine and paclitaxel.

The momentum of trafficking in unsafe medicines has increased rapidly across national boundaries. In one estimate, counterfeits accounted for 40–50 percent of total pharmaceutical supply to Nigeria and Pakistan; some products had 50–85 percent counterfeit prevalence in China; around 36.5 percent of antibiotics and anti-malaria drugs on the WHO essential drugs list are substandard in Thailand and Nigeria. A survey of seven African countries found that 23–38 percent of chloroquine-based syrup and tablets and 90 percent of sulphadoxine/pyrimethamine tablets, the major anti-malarials used in the region, failed quality testing. In Cambodia, approximately 71 percent of the artemisinin-derived drug artesunate sold was counterfeit and across South-East Asia, the counterfeiting rate for this drug was 53 percent in 2002 and 2003 (see New Scientist, 2006). The WHO pointed out that in April 1999, 771 cases of substandard medicines had been reported to the WHO, of which 77 percent came from developing countries and in 60 percent of the 325 cases an active ingredient was found to be missing from the product (World Health Organization, 2003).

Another survey by the WHO (World Health Organization, 2003) in 20 countries between January 1999 and October 2000 found that 60 percent of counterfeit cases occurred in poor countries and 40 percent in industrialized countries. By 2003, WHO, referring to a report by the Food and Drug Administration in the United States, pointed that about 10 percent of the medicines sold in the global markets were counterfeits and 25–50 percent of the medicines consumed in resource-poor countries were counterfeit or substandard (see International Narcotics Control Board, 2 March, 2007). In 2002, GlaxoSmithKline in the United States discovered misleading labels for HIV medicines used as part of a "cocktail treatment." The bottles that were supposed to contain 60 tablets of Combivir (lamivudine plus zidovudine) actually contained another medicine, Ziagen (abacavir sulfate). It was pointed out that the mixing can cause potentially life-threatening hypersensitivity reactions in patients taking other medicines in the combination regimen (ibid.). In 2006, the British authorities intercepted 846 pounds of unsafe medicines, mostly counterfeits of the products of Merck, Novartis, AstraZeneca, Pfizer, and Procter&Gamble, for the treatment of high blood pressure, high cholesterol, osteoporosis, acid reflux, and other major illnesses (Bogdanich, 17 December 2007b, "Counterfeit drugs' path eased by free trade zones"). In the same year, in the United States, officials arrested 124 individuals associated with a 27-state underground network for the sale of steroids and human growth hormone in a massive clean up in "Operational Raw Deal" (ibid.). Testimony by Mr Theriault, a former Pfizer official, that there has been an exponential increase in "the importation of counterfeit, infringing, misbranded and unapproved pharmaceutical products in the United States" shows the seriousness of this problem even in the developed countries (ibid.).

The production activities of counterfeiters occur in almost every continent (Morris and Stevens, 2006). The major operators are those in Cambodia, India, China, Nigeria, and Latin America (Argentina, Brazil, Colombia, Venezuela, Mexico, Peru, and Guatemala). Among these countries, counterfeits from India, China, Mexico, and Russia have aroused most attention. An estimate by the OECD showed that India has emerged as the largest base for the manufacture of counterfeits, accounting for the origin of 75 percent of all counterfeits in the world, followed by 7 percent from Egypt and 6 percent from China (Barnes, 2007).

The effects of consuming unsafe medicines range from therapeutic failure or drug resistance in the most benign scenario to a disastrous outcome, such as widespread deaths, at the other end of the spectrum. The insufficient dosage of active ingredients, inappropriate delivery channels, or the wrong active ingredients could make the patients sicker or encourage the development of drug resistance (Morris and Stevens, 2006). The recent increase of new drug-resistant strains of viruses, parasites, and bacteria is suspected to be a direct result of the use of unsafe medicines (ibid.).

The population in developing societies has become the major victims of these negative effects. It was noted that in China, 200,000 to 300,000 individuals die every year due to unsafe medicines (Morris and Stevens, 2006). In another example, the unsafe medicines received to tackle the meningitis epidemic in Niger in 1995 caused 2500 deaths. The consumption of paracetamol cough syrup prepared with diethylene glycol (a toxic chemical used in antifreeze) has led to at least eight mass poisonings around the world in the past 20 years (Bogdanich, 2007b). These include 29 deaths in Argentina in 1992; 188 deaths, mainly children under two in Haiti in 1991; 89 deaths and 30 infant deaths in India in 1998; 138 deaths in Panama in 2006 (ibid.). It was noted that 200,000 malaria deaths annually could have been avoided if effective and safe medicines had been taken (World Health Organization, 2003).

The business of producing unsafe medicines is enabled to continue because of the deficiency of several factors in supply chain control and demand/need management of safe medicines. The most important factors are the limited access to health care systems and the persisting high cost of medicines produced by conventional pharmaceutical suppliers (see World Health Organization, 2003; International Narcotics Control Board, 2007). This high-cost scenario of the pharmaceuticals sold through conventional channels leaves wide open a niche market for unsafe medicines. The high demand for low-cost pharmaceuticals has boosted the production of unsafe medicines, and this phenomenon is not limited to developing markets. In an investigation conducted by the *New York Times*, the Canada-based RxNorth, the first major online pharmacy in the world, was also associated with the sale of counterfeits. Ironically, the pharmacy was known for its claim to serve the pharmaceutical needs of two million uninsured and underinsured Americans, mainly the elderly, by providing heavily discounted drugs. The drugs were supposed to have been produced in Canada (Bogdanich, 2007b). In 2005, the company's total sales were $800 million (ibid.). The counterfeits found on sale from RxNorth included Lipitor, Crestor and Zetia (for cholesterol control), Diovan and Hyzaar (for controlling high blood pressure), Actonel (for osteoporosis), Nexium (for reflux disease), Celebrex (for arthritis pain), Arimidex (for breast cancer), and Propecia (for baldness) (ibid.).

Another factor explaining the increase of unsafe medicines in the world is the ease with which substandard medicines have been sold through both the Internet pharmacies and the global trade framework, such as the free trade zones. The borderless global trade phenomenon leads to such problems as uncontrolled imports; illicit manufacture of controlled, patented drugs; counterfeits infiltrating licit market; infiltrating illicit or wrong active ingredients in licit drugs; poor storage conditions and administrative controls in the wholesale or retail sector; repetitive trading of medicines to obscure their source, storage conditions or previous ownership that might be illicit; and poor enforcement of prescription-only requirements in dispensing medicines (see related discussions in International Narcotics Control Board 2007). In 2006, a survey of 185 Internet pharmacies in one country by the International Narcotic Control Board showed that 89 percent did not require a prescription and that the risks of getting counterfeits or substandard medicines from the Internet pharmacies could be high (ibid.). An investigation by the *New York Times* demonstrated how the free trade zones, characterized by no tariffs and minimal regulatory oversight, have inadvertently facilitated the efficiency of the counterfeited medicines supply chain (Bogdanich, 2007b). The same report also showed that the counterfeited or substandard drugs originating from Asia have traveled through Hong Kong, the United Arab Emirates, Britain, and the Bahamas and landed in the warehouse of an Internet pharmacy for North American customers. It was estimated that a third of all counterfeit drugs confiscated in Europe in 2006 were shipped from the United Arab Emirates, a free trade zone (ibid.). Other factors that have led to the increase of counterfeits include a lack of public awareness and a lack of consistent enforcement of drug control regulations (see related discussions in International Narcotics Control Board, 2007).

The economic incentive is a key factor for the boom in unsafe medicines. WHO (2003) noted that by 2003, the profits from counterfeit and substandard medicines reached more than US$32 billion globally (World Health Organization, 2003). And counterfeit sales could reach $75 billion by 2010 (*New Scientist*, 25 February 2006a, "Global task force to target fake-drug peddlers"). The aforementioned report by the *New York Times* clearly showed that there was a strong profit incentive for the counterfeit makers. For example, the Internet pharmacy Personal Touch Pharmacy in Freeport in the Bahamas, a major buyer of counterfeits, easily grossed US$8 million in their annual sales (Bogdanich, 2007b). What is alarming is that the counterfeit makers in developing markets have infiltrated into the pharmaceutical supply and demand chain in developed countries. The Personal Touch Pharmacy in Freeport in the Bahamas was also connected to the Canadian Internet pharmacy RxNorth. This phenomenon has aroused attention from global stakeholders, especially the WHO and governments, but so far both are limited by their enforcement powers and their efforts have been insufficient to stem the trade.

In the United States, despite the fact that the number of investigations by the FDA of possible counterfeit drugs has increased from about five per year in the 1990s to more than 20 per year in the early 2000s, this activity has not curtailed the growth in counterfeits. And despite help from US FDA, the Chinese regulatory authorities also face a similar dilemma. In China, it was estimated that about 80 percent of pharmaceuticals consumed in rural areas are counterfeits (Cockburn et al., 2005, "The global threat of counterfeit drugs: Why industry and governments must communicate the dangers").

Collaboration against counterfeits

Since the early 2000s, there have been some efforts at the global level to increase international collaboration to crack down on the counterfeits, and bring them into regulatory oversight. These efforts extend the progress made in existing international agreements in this area, which includes the Single Convention on Narcotic Drugs of 1961 and the Convention of Psychotropic Substance of 1971 (International Narcotics Control Board, 2007). Following upon the existing framework, the new efforts include the establishment of the West African Drug Regulatory Agencies Network, aiming at combating counterfeit and fake drugs, and most importantly, the setup of IMPACT, a new task force against substandard and counterfeit medicines at the World Health Organization. The WHO task force aims to provide a global platform for collaboration in this area but given WHO's limited capacity, WHO sees the strengthening of government capacity as a key element in dealing with unsafe medicines. Government capacity includes political will, relevant legislation, appropriate organizational capacity and skilled professionals, financial resources, and well-structured and motivated drug inspectorate services (ibid.).

For now, the best that WHO and country governments can do is to arouse the attention of the stakeholders involved. At the country level, WHO encourages intersectoral cooperation among regulatory authorities, police, customs services, and the judiciary to effectively control the drug market and enforce drug regulation; strengthen pharmaceutical regulation; support Good Manufacturing Practices (GMP); assess national drug regulatory capacity and performance; promote information exchange among drug regulatory authorities; and increase drug procurement safety (World Health Organization, 2003). At the international level, the WHO advocates a collaborative platform for timely exchange of information and harmonized action to deter the spread of unsafe medicines (ibid.). The WHO itself provides technical assistance to ensure that quality assurance is integrated into the pharmaceutical supply chain.

Facing the counterfeit challenge, leadership from the United States is indispensable. And the United States have taken concrete steps toward bilateral collaboration in this area. The US FDA has proved that it remains a global leader in terms of taking concrete actions in cracking down on the counterfeits. For example, in December 2007, an agreement reached by American and Chinese regulators could strengthen regulation of drugs and medical devices exported to the United States, especially atorvastin, the generic form of Lipitor; sildenafil, the generic for Viagra; and the antibiotic gentamicin sulfate (see Bogdanich, 12 December 2007a "Agreement with China to regulate some drugs"). These measures have produced some tangible results. For example, in 2002 China's State Drug Administration closed 1300 illegal factories and investigated cases of counterfeit drugs worth US$57 million (WHO, 2003). In 2008, collaboration among International Criminal Police Organization (INTERPOL), the World Health Organization's Western Pacific Regional Office, the Wellcome Trust-University of Oxford SE Asian Tropical Medicine Research Program, and Chinese authorities also facilitated investigation of the counterfeits in China (TOPNEWS, 2008). In 2008, the US FDA requested the US Congress to increase funding of US$275 million on the top of its proposed $2.4 billion budget, mainly to focus a plan to set up surveillance and investigation offices in China, India, and Central America (A&A Contract Customs and Brokers, 23 May 2008, "FDA to set up food and drug offices in China"; see also China Knowledge, 2008). According to Michael Leavitt, Secretary of the US Department of Health and Human Services, this effort is designed to further enhance the safety and quality of food and drugs exported to the United States. This plan includes an initial effort to place ten FDA staff at three sites in China, including the US embassy, Shanghai, and Kwanzhou.

After China, the US FDA's next target country is India because, according to Leavitt, there are more than 100 FDA-inspected facilities in India and most of the imported medical equipment and therapeutics in the United States come from India. The US FDA also plans to set up similar operations in Central America (see World Journal, 24 May 2008, "FDA awaits China's permission to set offices in Beijing, Shanghai and Kwanzhou", B-7). This strategy is farseeing because instead of stationing the investigators at the borders, this plan tackles the problem at the source (see related analysis in ibid.). However, this move is also believed to be a reaction against the discovery of tainted heparin, a blood thinner, in 11 countries. Both Chinese and American officials insisted on their right to inspect the others' plants involved in the production of the blood product. In this case, the initial phase of heparin production was carried out in China and the finished heparin vials were made at an

American plant (see *New York Times*, 22 April 2008, "FDA identifies tainted heparin in 11 countries"). Finger pointing does not help in this or other cases of tracing the origin of unsafe medicine because they have become a global phenomenon.

These efforts are a good first step to address the problem of counterfeits, but the constraints of governments' financial capacity often make it difficult to equip countries with an effective infrastructure because of a lack of funding, safety systems, trained officials, and sufficient laboratory capacity to contain unsafe medicine. Today, almost all governments are facing major challenges in stifling the growth of counterfeits on the market and in preventing them from entering into the global supply chain. In other words, this is truly a challenge in supply chain management (see related discussions in Morris and Stevens, 2006).

To tackle the supply chain problem in unsafe medicine requires the participation of the multinationals and the local pharmaceutical companies in the BRICA countries. In terms of collaboration with regulatory authorities, the multinationals and BRICA pharmaceutical makers must work in the existing global regulatory framework to limit the possession, use, distribution, import, export, manufacture and production of, and trade in, drugs exclusively to medical and scientific purposes, and to address drug trafficking through international cooperation in different areas, especially in regulation on pharmaceutical sales on the Internet. One recent example in public-private collaboration in this area is the agreement between US pharmaceutical companies with the US FDA in 2003 that US pharmaceutical companies would report suspected counterfeit drugs to the FDA within five days of discovery, despite the fact this agreement really hinges on the companies' voluntary action to report (see PLOS, 2003, "Companies that have warned").

In terms of other micro-level activities, multinationals and the BRICA pharmaceutical companies can collaborate in a wide range of areas in the supply chain process, such as procurement of raw materials, manufacturing, distribution, labeling, packaging, marketing, and surveillance. First, the multinationals could support the building of safety mechanisms in the procurement of raw materials. Most of the raw material used by pharmaceutical manufacturers comes from the BRICA nations, especially China. To ensure safety and quality, the large multinationals could use their quality control expertise to help BRICA suppliers establish and enforce Good Manufacturing Practice at the source of the supply chain. Both the multinationals and BRICA pharmas have to come to a consensus that they have to purchase raw material from certified producers. And this action can be part of their marketing strengths. Both parties also have to collaborate to establish an inspection system for import/export authorization, similar to the pre-export notifications in international precursor control for narcotic surveillance.

Second, monitoring the "change of hands" in the distribution process is also critical to ensure supply chain safety and effectiveness. This requires the ability both to track every point at which the pharmaceuticals make their stop before being transported to the next destination and to ensure that adulteration attempts do not seep into this process before medicines reach the hands of credible sellers and patients. This is an area where the multinationals and BRICA can complement each other's expertise because the multinationals have the technology of tracking and identification while the BRICA pharmas are familiar with local distribution networks and channels. Both parties could collaborate to establish pharmaceutical safety in the shipping process and destination safety by improving the safety mechanisms in transportation, warehouse management, and increasing the technical capacity of local suppliers to distinguish safe medicines from unsafe ones. A related issue is that both parties need to work on improving distribution efficiency and effectiveness in remote or rural regions, where pharmaceutical access is often difficult. They should also increase collaboration in establishing a post-sale surveillance system, in which the public could report suspected products to the drug makers, distributors, and regulatory authorities.

Third, on marketing, both parties could learn from each other in their expertise to protect the trade marks of legitimate goods. In addition, both parties could support the marketing efforts of credible, safe suppliers as legitimate suppliers in their communities. Alternatively, the multinationals and BRICA could jointly support the establishment of pharmaceutical outposts in developing countries as the sole legitimate outlets of safe pharmaceuticals, integrating this idea in their already functioning pharmaceutical sale networks. This collaboration will prove beneficial because both the multinationals and BRICA pharmas are more likely to use the same retail stores in most of the countries. Boosting the credibility of local distributors is a win-win situation for both parties.

Overall, tackling counterfeits in the long term requires partnership between the multinational and BRICA pharmas by the use of preventive information technology network in identification, scanning and intercepting. The US FDA's move to set up offices in China, India, and Central America to prevent the trafficking of unsafe medicine illustrates the importance of collecting information as a preventive measure. As noted by WHO (2003), the technology for counterfeits has become more sophisticated. Some fake medicines now even carry holograms like those on the originals (see Mukhopadhyay, 1 April 2007, "The hunt for counterfeit medicine"). The types of technology that have potential to effectuate the detecting of counterfeits are as follows: the FDA's radio frequency identification (RFID), using electronic devices to track and identify items from the radio waves emitted by the goods; assigning individual serial numbers to the containers holding each product; the FDA's ePedigree system to track drugs from factory to pharmacy to prevent diversion or counterfeiting of drugs by allowing wholesalers and pharmacists to determine the identification and dosage of individual products; high-tech methods such as HPLC, MS, GC, or optical spectroscopy (such as Raman spectroscopy and Energy Dispersive X-Ray Diffraction (EDXRD)). The EDXRD technology allows for the discovery of counterfeits when they are still inside their packaging (see ibid.). For example, researchers have used the fingerprinting technology invented by Pavel Matousek and Charlotte Eliasson of the Rutherford Appleton Laboratory in Didcot, UK, which is a variant of Raman spectroscopy, to detect the infrared radiation of the counterfeits inside the package (New Scientist Tech, 3 February 2007, "Lasers spot fake drugs in the packet"). The RFID has the potential to be of wide use in the United States. In one estimate, META Group predicts that RFID use by pharmaceutical companies will exceed that of packaged goods by the beginning of 2006. It was also pointed out that in February 2004, the US Department of Agriculture had instructed the industry to start using RFID technology to detect and protect against counterfeit drugs (Ebisch, 2005).

There is other technology to fight against counterfeits. Many have used thin-layer chromatography (TLC) or colorimetric tests (Sherma, 2007). TLC can be carried out by inspectors of limited expertise by using portable kits with standard reference tablets. The suspected samples are compared to reference standards in terms of whether the active ingredients are within a certain specification range. Colorimetric tests measure the color frequency distribution of the reds, blues, and yellows. Yet TLC and colorimetric tests are time-consuming. For the sake of efficiency, some have tried the combination of FTIR (Fourier transform infrared imaging) and DESI MS (Desorption Electrospray Ionization Mass Spectrometry) or the use of a forensic approach to examine organic materials in the matrix of the tablet (such as pollen or insect remains) to trace medicines back to their creators (see Mukhopadhyay, 2007). It was found that Fourier transform infrared imaging and Raman spectroscopy could generate detailed information about a tablet's composition in a matter of a few seconds (RSC, 2007, "Forging ahead of the counterfeiters"). The Desorption Electrospray Ionization Mass Spectrometry (DESI-MS), invented by Dr Facundo M. Fernandez and colleagues, is a one-step process that does not require extensive sample preparation. It is mainly used to determine the authenticity of large amount of products, especially large batches of Tamiflu samples, and it is said to be 20 times faster than conventional methods (News-Medical. Net, 2008, "New method to detect fake Tamiflu"). The use of a forensic approach, such as forensic palynology, also has some potential. This approach studies pollen contamination within the fake tablets in order to track down the likely location of the manufacturer (TOPNEWS, 2008). The WHO's IMPACT also suggests the option of giving drugs a code name that can only be read when the seal is broken (*New Scientist*, 2006b).

In the long term, using advanced technology against counterfeiting is the most effective method to prevent them getting into the global supply chain, but this calls for investment that is capital and labor-intensive and it could also result in inefficiency in the delivery of life-saving medicines. In contrast, the use of effective information networks is an efficient short-term solution to reduce the impact and prevalence of counterfeits. To achieve the information network necessary for monitoring the procurement, preparation, manufacture, distribution, and advertisement of counterfeits needs immediate partnership among all pharmaceutical manufacturers. The multinationals and BRICA stakeholders should establish their role in the WHO-supported Rapid Alert System, which allows the public to report suspected counterfeiting activities. This system should be enlarged to include rapid exchange of information, sharing experiences, use of standardized data, and tracking of counterfeits (World Health Organization, 2003).

One area that allows for immediate collaboration is the supply chain information network. The large multinationals already have their proven expertise and an extensive network in this area in the developed markets. For example, in one estimate, the global pharmaceutical industry spends between $100 million and $250 million of its IT budget on supply chain management. Part of it was what the large pharmas call customer relation management (CRM). CRM examines general prescription behavior, the characteristics of patient flow and patient needs, and related marketing and demographic information (Ebisch, 2005). In one estimate, the international market for CRM tools in the pharmaceutical industry was believed to be about $455 million in 2003 and was projected to reach almost $625 million by 2008, with the

United States dominating the market expansion, followed by the 30 percent market share in Europe and 8 percent by Japan by 2008 (ibid.).

This focus on customer relations management has also pointed to the need for better consideration of the demand-driven process, or the demand-driven supply network (DDSN), into the supply chain. The multinationals' expertise in this network could be extended to trace the volume and destination of the products in the invention, in the shipping process, as well as on retail shelves. This information allows the detection of illegal infiltration of the counterfeits in the normal supply chain and can save a large amount of time in tracking the counterfeiters (for discussion of DDSN, see Ebisch, 2005).

Another strategy to effectively tackle counterfeits is for the partnerships between the multinationals and BRICA pharmas to establish a culture of safe and rational use of medicine by effective communication and education at the population level. This is the most cost-effective way of preventing the counterfeits in developing countries. Effective communication requires public health education in schools and the diffusing of information within the social networks to create an effective process of both sending alerts and raising vigilance. It also requires patient education in health care settings. The fact that most countries already have an established public health system in place makes this strategy most feasible in the short term.

The fundamental solution

The discussions so far point out a number of possible areas of partnership for multinational and BRICA pharmaceuticals. Yet the fundamental issue is the imbalance of supply and demand/need in the global pharmaceutical provision chain at the macro level. That is, global pharmaceutical stakeholders need an answer to the following question: "Who is going to do what in the global pharmaceutical division of labor?" Or to put it in a different way: "How are we going to satisfy the pharmaceutical needs for every population?" All the problems of pricing, innovation, and unsafe medicines point to the gap between supply and demand/need in terms of the provision of safe, effective, and affordable medicines for the populations in developed and developing countries.

That said, macro-level solutions are by no means simple and it requires the configuration of a global strategy to consummate partnership on the basis of a division of labor between the multinationals and the BRICAs. This strategy will require a thoughtful framework to tackle major challenges in the global pharmaceutical supply and demand chain.

On the issue of innovation, there is a severe imbalance in terms of innovation and needs/demand, as mentioned in Chapter 1. For example, heightened competition has emerged for producing similar-class products or treatments for certain health problems, such as erectile dysfunction; while at the same time there exists a wide range of threatening diseases or health problems that have been ignored on the innovation radar screen of the large pharmas. The neglected tropical diseases are a relevant case in point. These diseases effect a large number of populations in the world, but most of them are curable. For example, trachoma, the leading cause of preventable blindness, has caused 15 percent of all blindness in the world (Caines, 2004). Yet the effort in treating trachoma apart, there has been little research and development to generate effective pharmaceuticals to treat other neglected diseases (ibid.).

The pharmaceutical industry would benefit from following a planting strategy in which the customer-centric pull strategy in planning is a part (Ebisch, 2005). That is, global innovation priorities should be determined by the range of health problems facing the population/customers in the developed and developing countries. For example, in addition to focusing on blockbusters, global pharmas should also seek diversification through a global division of labor with the BRICA pharmas (see the related discussion in ibid.).

A related debate concerns the funding of innovations. For now, most of the burden of drug development falls on the shoulders of the private sector, which has to answer to their stockholders, while most people recognize that pharmaceutical provision has a public health component and is therefore part of the responsibility of the public sector. The critical issue facing the global pharmas is indeed to figure out "who is going to pay for what?" For example, global multinationals could team up with local BRICA countries to research on new drugs for neglected diseases which are prevalent in developing countries but rare in developed markets, while the individual governments, global charities, and multilateral or bilateral aid agencies pay for the development, marketing, and distribution cost. The suggestion of a collaborative partnership to fund pharmaceutical innovations is relevant to this discussion and could apply for both developing and developed countries (Knowledge Ecology International, 2008, "Prizes to stimulate innovation"). Since the drugs developed this way are mainly used to treat the populations in developing countries, they rarely pose a threat to the bottom line or the market share of the multinationals, which derive their major profit from the developed markets. The large pharmas could be rewarded by sharing the patents or having the right to patent certain molecules developed in the process.

Other methods of funding R&D include global tax, direct public funding, tax credits or other expenditures, philanthropic spending, research funding obligations imposed on sellers of medicines, purchases or relevant medical products (as a condition to induce R&D investment), and innovation prizes (to the degree that such prizes induced R&D investment) (World Health Assembly Executive Board, 24 February 2005, "World Health Organization Commission on Intellectual Property, Innovation and Health"). The idea of using a global framework has received some attention. For example, the proposed Global Medical R&D Treaty requires members states to forgo dispute resolution over IPR issues related to the products covered by the agreement; R&D for NTDs and other priority research products; open public goods (free and open source public databases; technology transfer and capacity building; preservation and dissemination of traditional medicine; and exceptionally useful public goods) (World Health Assembly Executive Board, 24 February 2005, "World Health Organization Commission on Intellectual Property, Innovation and Health"). The idea of a global tax, as proposed by France's ex-president Jacques Chirac for global aid, might be applied to the development of life-saving medicines (BNET, 2005, "Chirac proposes global tax; Gates bets against dollar").

Some have put these ideas into practice and have actually produced positive results, the collaboration between WHO, Novartis, and Chinese scientists on the development of co-artem is a successful example and is worth further study.

The case of Coartem: A partnership between China, the WHO, and Novartis

The coartem partnership between WHO and Novartis provides a unique model for developing a win-win situation between large pharmas and developing countries (PAHO, 2003, "An Update on Quality Assurance and Procurement through WHO for Improving Access to Artemisinin-based Combination Treatments (ACTs) for Malaria"). As mentioned earlier, the natural form of coartem has been used in the Chinese pharmacopeia as an effective anti-malarial for more than four thousand years. Coartem is considered to be the most effective medicine against malaria. In order to reduce risks and costs, the WHO chose to collaborate with Novartis and provides expert reviews (reducing scientific risk); provides funding and technical assistance to make the product suitable for target markets (e.g., appropriate packaging and partial funding of Phase IV trials to determine appropriate dosage); monitors leakage; assists with collecting pharmaco-vigilance and post-marketing surveillance data; and helps with the transaction costs that Novartis would otherwise incur from having to manage a business relationship with multiple purchasers. In addition, WHO is also involved in forecasting demand and providing a credit fund to support effected countries to pay for coartem. The extent of the WHO's contribution enables those countries to have a greater purchasing leverage due to the reduced price of the malaria medicine (Grace, 2004, "GHP study paper: Global health partnership impact on commodity pricing and security").

For Novartis, involvement in the project has not only helped it gain a positive reputation, it also gained some new knowledge and markets (Laverty, 10 December 2007). According to Novartis, based on its knowledge of traditional medicine the Chinese government developed a combination drug that was found to be effective for malaria during the Vietnam War, China did not have the technology at the time to move into production. During the 1990s, some collaboration was developed between Novartis and China, with Novartis transferring the technology of manufacturing the malaria drug out of artemisinin to China and helping China with GMP standards, along with agreements with the Chinese to manufacture the product. Both Novartis and China co-own the patent. By the end of the 1990s, an effective drug was successfully made. But it was clear to Novartis that it was not possible to profit from the drug because most malaria victims were poor, with the situation of children especially difficult. Because of the personal conviction and leadership of Daniel Vasella, CEO and Chair of Novartis AG and also a physician, Novartis decided to proceed with the decision. Dr Vasella himself feels strongly about the issue and support the development of the drug.

In 2001, the partnership was made possible because of a donation from the Global Fund, which enabled the WHO to form a partnership with Novartis and the Medicines for Malaria Initiative. The key leaders at the time were Silvio Gabrielle of Novartis (partnership management, forecasting, budgets, manufacturing, and related duties), Arata Kochi from the WHO; and Dr Chris Hentschel from the Medicine for Malaria Initiative. In terms of the division of labor, Novartis has been committed to devoting some of its resources (human capital, paying for manufacturing) to provide coartem at the cost of production. It would also help distribute and make use of vendors' networks. Later, Novartis also began to support the development of the pediatric version of coartem, taking in such considerations as taste and the need to dispense the drug in water quickly, on the basis of experience gained in the field. It is anticipated that at some time in 2008, Novartis will move into production of this new formulation for children. Novartis also helps in the creation of educational material, especially the pictorial dispenser sheets for children, and MMI has also provided some advice/expertise for pediatric formulation. The technical assistance provided by the WHO helps coordinate the supply and demand chain for the needy countries. For patients treated by the public sector, the fees are $1 for adults and 45 cents for children, while Novartis can also sell the drug at a higher price to those populations who can afford it. Initially, no orders for the drug came in to Novartis, then, in 2004, an article was published in *The Lancet* that provided a positive assessment of the drug for clinicians and policy makers. This evaluation in turn then stimulated demand for coartem and orders started increasing.

The outcome of this partnership has generated concrete success for all parties. The WHO has successfully achieved the goal of reducing malaria morbidity and mortality by improving access to coartem. Novartis has also gained in various ways to do with supply chain management issues in global health. The company has also acquired valuable knowledge about the drug. First of all, coartem takes 14 months to make (from planting seeds, extraction, and manufacturing) and involves the process of transforming a plant-based medicine into synthetic molecules. The shelf life is 24 months. Second, to meet the needs of malaria patients requires an accurate forecast, which later became a challenge to both the WHO and Novartis. In 2004, there was an estimate of 40–60 million tablets being needed but only 4 million coartem were shipped. In 2005, given the criticism voiced about the length of the production time, Novartis had to rapidly increase production to 33 million tablets when only 9 million had been shipped. Novartis was undaunted by the challenge and still went ahead with a higher forecast of demand and in 2006, 62 million tablets were produced; increasing in 2007, to more than 70 million. The valuable insights about supply chain issues gleaned from this case are important because they have enabled Novartis to become very efficient with production. The time lag between order and shipping has shortened from 14 weeks to 6–7 weeks. During the 2005 supply challenge, the company was able to generate an emergency response team to increase production. Now, Novartis has the capacity to meet with any emergency situations with this drug. It makes coartem regularly and always ensures that there is enough stock on hand to avoid shortage given the production cycle of this particular drug. The company also supports patient education issues by facilitating workshops twice a year on best practices, in which national coordinators participate. Some of the central issues in supply chain management in this case are record keeping, patient impact data, impact assessment, and so on. Novartis has also acquired information unique in the African context, such as the need for trained health care professionals, the brain drain phenomenon, the need to update lab practices and the like. In addition, Novartis has gained information about distribution networks in Africa, which is a new skill for the company. Other positive outcomes include that the partnership has enhanced Novartis' reputation and has increased employee education on the issue as well as increasing their pride in working for Novartis. Most importantly, this partnership has enabled Novartis to become one of the leaders in meeting global health needs. It was able to share expertise with other global health stakeholders in several areas. These include how to use expertise in a positive way; how to work with developing countries; and how to work with local authorities. The fact that coartem is on the formularies in 84 countries also suggests that it could be bringing about some company from sales of the drug in the more affluent markets. This case shows that despite the many disputes between the pharmaceutical sector and other global health stakeholders, an innovative partnership can meet the objectives of all the parties involved.

Since the early 2000s, partnerships like the coartem project have increased to address the lack of innovation in meeting population health needs and demand in the areas of neglected diseases, and international donors have provided technical support, pharmaceuticals, and in a few cases, funding (Caines, 2004). These partnerships have provided positive impact, especially in raising awareness, synergizing resources, and accelerating progress, despite the problem of lacking sustainable funding (see related discussions in ibid.). These efforts have covered 80 percent of the 15 most neglected diseases, that is, Buruli ulcer, Chagas disease, congenital syphilis, cysticercosis, dengue fever, guinea worm, leishmaniasis, leprosy, lymphatic filariasis, maternal and neonatal tetanus, onchocerciasis, rabies, schistosomiasis, sleeping sickness and trachoma, with the exeption of congenital syphilis, cysticercosis, and rabies which are yet to benefit (ibid.).

The WHO has played an important role in increasing these global health partnerships, such as for the treatment of HIV, malaria, TB, Chagas disease, dengue and dengue hemorrhagic fever and leishmaniasis, and can also be instrumental in brokering partnerships between multinationals and BRICA stakeholders. As in the coartem partnership, the WHO provides the framework for accelerating collaboration to ensure the regular availability and accessibility of affordable medicines of good quality (World Health Organization, 2003). The WHO's effort often adds value to existing efforts, such as the UNICEF-UNDP-World Bank-WHO Special Program for Training and Research in Tropical Diseases (TDR) established in 1975, which was created to support global efforts to fight against such infectious diseases as Chagas' disease, dengue, sleeping sickness, leishmaniasis, lymphatic filariasis, malaria, onchocerciasis, schistosomiasis, tetanus, and TB (Caines, 2004).

Most partnerships, as indicated earlier, have borne concrete fruits. Successful examples abound and they point to a new way of improving pharmaceutical innovation. One of the most celebrated examples was the treatment of river blindness through various onchocersiasis control programs, such as the African Program for Onchocerciasis Control (APOC). APOC, which covered 11 countries in West Africa, was considered by the World Bank to be one of the most successful disease control programs in the history of development assistance (World Health Organization, 2008, "African Program for Onchocerciasis Control"; Caines, 2004). In 2002, after 30 years of effort, the program had reached its target of eliminating onchocersiasis. Some of its achievements included protecting 40 million people from blindness; preventing 600,000 cases of blindness, and sanitizing 25 million hectares of arable land supporting the feeding of 17 million people free of onchocerciasis; and achieving a 20 percent economic rate of return on the US$556 million committed by donors to the program (World Health Organization, 2008; Caines, 2004). The key to this success is Merck's ivermectin. In 1975, ivermectin was found to be effective against parasite worms and in the 1980s, Merck and Company used this knowledge to make Mectizan, a human formulation of ivermectin. Despite the lack of profit prospects, in 1987 Merck, working with the WHO, decided to donate the medicine to anyone needing it, for as long as needed to treat the disease (Sturchio, 2001).

Other successful examples have also made concrete improvements in global health. For example, the Global Alliance to Eliminate Leprosy (GAEL), formed in 1999 and supported by Nippon Foundation/Sasakawa Memorial Foundation and the multi-drug donation program by Novartis, aimed at elimination of leprosy by 2005. Novartis has also embarked on a patient assistance program, GIPAP™, to provide eligible patients Glivec®. Glivec® was found to be a potent treatment for patients with certain forms of chronic myeloid leukemia (CML) and gastrointestinal stomal tumors (GIST). Novartis started the GIPAP™ program in 2002 to provide Glivec® at no cost to those who were inflicted with certain forms of CML and GIST in countries with no comprehensive reimbursement system or available generics. It is noted that by the end of 2006, Novartis had provided Glivec® valued at US$362 million free to those needy patients and the drug is said to have helped 21,000 cases and is now available in 80 countries (IFPMA, 2008, "Glivec International Patient Assistance Program"). Novartis also supports the treatment of TB and malaria through its Access to Medicine projects.

Similarly, the DNDi (Drugs for Neglected Disease Initiative) partnership in 2003 is another example that provides a forum for collaboration among the public sector, the pharmaceutical industry, and other stakeholders to develop effective drugs or new formulations of existing drugs for sleeping sickness, leishmaniasis (kala azar), and Chagas disease for sufferers of these neglected diseases (see DNDi, 2008). Specifically, in March 2008, DNDi and GSK announced a collaborative research effort to identify and develop compounds from existing GSK programs and to leverage the expertise of researchers from GSK at its Tres Cantos facility along with leading academic centers like the London School of Hygiene and Tropical Medicine (LSHTM). This partnership aims to address the barriers in current pharmaceutical development in treating these diseases, these barriers including drawbacks such as difficulty of administration, severe side-effects, length of treatment, cost, and emerging parasitic resistance (ibid.). Overall, these partnerships have opened a new path for collaboration between large pharmas and developing countries, but most of them rely on donation programs and are not sustainable in the long run. The key barrier for long-term development in producing pharmaceuticals to meet global demand is the controversy of intellectual property rights.

Since the inception of the AIDS epidemic, the controversy surrounding intellectual property rights, or the patents, requires an urgent solution so that it will not hamper the production of life-saving medicine to improve global health. The solution requires an improvement in the current oversimplified patent framework implemented by the TRIPS regulation of the World Trade Organization. The global pharmaceutical stakeholders need to generate a more creative patent system to reward innovation that also meets population health needs. For now, there is no lack of solutions. For example, Love's (Knowledge Ecology International, 2008) proposal of a prize fund is most relevant here. The proposal allows the public sector or the global governance body to support pharmaceutical research by rewarding innovators who choose to open their licenses and patents to needy populations (see CPTECH,

2007, "The medical innovation prize fund"). These discussions also suggests that consideration needs to be given to different types of patents for the different types of pharmaceutical innovation. These discussions have raised certain questions about the issue of pharmaceutical patents in protecting global health. For example: Are there other ways of protecting intellectual property rights that could protect the profits position of the pharmaceutical companies as well as meeting the population health objectives? Could governments use the public patents to ensure the wider availability of life-saving medicines by actively participating in the innovation and development process, as the governments of Thailand and Brazil have done in various forms? Could stakeholders in the public and private sectors and academe share the patents? In addition. a more practical reward scheme needs to be configured in relation to global pharmaceutical partnerships. And, in this discussion, the collaboration of the BRICA stakeholders is indispensable, as this also involves discussions about the division of labor in global pharmaceutical development.

Division of labor

On the issue of the manufacturing of medicines to meet all health needs, there needs to be an effective and efficient division of labor in a decentralized operation model between the multinationals and BRICA nations. A division of labor in manufacturing would save on production costs for the multinational pharmas because, at present, pharmaceutical production costs outweigh the transportation costs. Certainly, a safety mechanism has to be included in a decentralized framework for the division of labor. Although most of the large pharmas claim to have production facilities around the world, the major facilities are still concentred in developed countries. For example, as Angell (2004) pointed out, Pfizer claimed to have 60 manufacturing plants in 32 countries, while in actuality, most of the manufacturing is still in the United States and Europe. This is also evidenced by the fact that half of the large pharmas are based in Europe (ibid.). Manufacturing in BRICA countries would reduce production costs significantly and would also make maximal use of BRICA facilities as regional centers/hubs for the onward transportation of pharmaceuticals to adjacent regions or countries. For example, the case of Brazil, where a treaty to improve political and economic integration in the South American region – signed by 12 UNASUR (la Unión de Naciones Sudamericanas) countries in the third week of May 2008 – makes Brazil even more important in its position as the driver of the pharmaceutical conveyor belt in the region (see EuroNews, 24 May 2008, "Doce países latinoamericanos se integran en la UNASUR").

The case of vaccine production is relevant to this discussion. Concern for vaccine shortage has increased in both developed and developing countries, given the increase of the outbreaks of influenzas, epidemics, pandemics, and terrorist threats. In the United States, this concern has been acutely felt. The United States experienced a shortage of vaccines in 1994 when the Center of Disease Control capped the prices of vaccines for children, which lead some companies to stop selling the vaccines to the government (Angell, 2004). Since 2004, worry about the insufficient supply of vaccines to counter influenzas, sparked by the unusual case of bird flu, is another relevant case in point. In 2004, a severe shortage of a new vaccine, Prevnar, had caused a delay in giving the last two doses in a four-dose regimen because of production problems at Wyeth Vaccines, the world's sole manufacturer of the vaccine (*New York Times*, 3 March 2004, "A shortage of meningitis vaccine"). The company attributed the shortage to a supply and demand gap, that is, demand for the vaccine had increased since it appeared on the market in 2000. In 2003, the company provided 18 million doses, which was an increase of 33 percent from 2002. A full four-dosage Prevnar is 97 percent effective in preventing the seven strains of the pneumococcal bacterium that causes meningitis, blood and ear infections, and other conditions. This vaccine is recommended for children under two years because of their high susceptibility to such infections.

Another shortage of vaccine also occurred, but on a larger scale, in the United States. In October 2006, America's supply of flu vaccine was cut nearly in half as the world's second-leading supplier of the flu vaccine, the Chiron Corporation was forced to shut down by the British government because of suspected problems at its Liverpool, England, manufacturing plant (National Public Radio, 6 October 2006, "US faces flu vaccine shortage"). The timing of the suspension of license was inopportune because the company was about to ship 48 million doses of vaccine to the United States.

This vaccine shortage has again raised issues about the relationship between global pharmas and the public good called "population health." In the current mode of operation and regulation, the multinational pharmas have no obligation and have no incentives to produce vaccines. As Angell (2004) pointed out, the large pharmas can stop producing any drugs, even for critical needs, at any time by notifying the FDA of their intentions six months in advance. These "medically necessary" drugs include anesthetics, anti-venins for poisonous snakebites, steroids for premature infants, antidotes for certain drug overdoses, an anti-clotting drug for hemophilia, an injectable drug for cardiac resuscitation, an antibiotic for gonorrhea, a drug to induce labor in childbirth, and vaccines against flu and pneumonia in adults. Yet this shortage of vaccines can easily be addressed if there is an effective partnership between global, multilateral, and governmental oversight, the multinational pharmas and BRICA producers. The BRICA facilities can be put to good use because of their production capacities.

This example clearly shows that the BRICA stakeholders are likely to play a crucial role in the global division of labor in the pharmaceutical manufacturing chain. Thus, the solution is obvious. That is, the BRICA stakeholders can make efficient use of their facilities by producing the therapeutics that support the public health objectives for the resource-poor populations. At the same time, the multinationals can continue to take advantage of their manufacturing capacity and technology in the developed markets to produce medicines catering to the local needs and/or to the more affluent markets. Yet there should also be a collaborative strategy supported by the public sector and intergovernmental agencies among these stakeholders so that they can maximize their strengths in the manufacturing process.

Conclusion

Confronting the dilemma of both increasing global health challenges and the challenges to the growth of the pharmaceutical business, the global pharmaceutical industry is at a crossroads. The solution requires a rethinking of its current global strategy.

This writing has illustrated that in the face of these formidable challenges, the future of the pharmaceutical sector lies in its ability to use a farseeing, sustainable planting strategy in conducting its global business. This new strategy requires a collaborative partnership between the multinationals and BRICA pharmas. Unlike the conventional plucking strategy of operating in the global health care business, this planting strategy supports global health objectives without sacrificing the profit bottom line of the industry.

The starting point to figure out a planting strategy requires the global pharmaceutical and related health care industries to see their business as part of "global health business." The crux of the global health challenge is the imbalance in the global supply and demand/need chain, which gives rise to other related problems of lack of access, lack of affordability, the controversy of price controls, the prevalence of unsafe medicines, and the increasing morbidity and mortality of chronic and infectious diseases. A planting strategy requires global pharmaceutical makers to be cognizant that all the stakeholders involved need to restore the balance of the global supply and demand/need chain in a multilateral, multilevel, and collaborative environment. All stakeholders need to recognize that the objective of supporting "everyone's health" is the business of the pharmaceutical business. It is also important to see that poor, ill populations are not the problem, but are also part of the solution because they are sources of information about how to generative affordable, effective products to eliminate diseases and improve health. In carrying out this planting strategy, there needs to be an effective partnership between the multinationals and BRICA stakeholders in various areas of the pharmaceutical business.

In mapping out the partnership potentials, this book has demonstrated that there exist abundant possibilities for collaboration. Overall, the multinationals could offer their technical expertise in drug development, clinical trials, patents, marketing expertise, patient education, and so on. In contrast, BRICAs can complement this partnership by offering ethnomedical knowledge, raw materials, low-cost manufacturing facilities, distribution networks, clinical trial populations, and consumer markets. But these ideas are not mutually exclusive and they require a constant exchange of ideas and dialogue to generate a mutually beneficial outcome. Or to put it more bluntly, this synergy would lead to the reduction of production costs, a widening of the innovative repertoire, and most importantly, efficient and balanced supply and demand/need chain management.

In particular, one of the most important contributions from the BRICA countries is their offering of cultural knowledge that would broaden and complement the expertise of the multinationals. The BRICA nations have already demonstrated the strength of their cultural knowledge in many areas of business operation beyond pharmaceutical knowledge. For example, these markets have demonstrated intelligent entrepreneurial skills in creating business opportunities and products, agile response to consumer needs, and adaptive methods to cope with business climate changes. The success of TATA in India is the most relevant case in point.

Today, TATA seems to occupy the attention of global business leaders all the time. Established by Jamsetji Tata in the second half of the nineteenth century, TATA is a true global business leader (see TATA, 2008b, "About us"). The TATA Group is an India-based conglomerate that has the largest market capitalization and also the largest revenues in India. Its core businesses focus on, but are not limited to, steel, automobiles, information technology, communications, power, tea, and hotels (see facts about TATA in Wikipedia, 2008, "TATA group"; see also TATA, 2008c, "Good to great"). With 98 companies in more than 85 countries across six continents, market capitalization of $66.26 billion as of 30 April 2008 (or 3.2 percent of India's GDP), with revenues in 2006–07 of $28.8 billion, and employing 289,500 people, it is no exaggeration to say that TATA is a giant success amongst global businesses. Nevertheless, what truly distinguishes TATA from other companies is its creative use of its cultural knowledge in its business operations and reinvestment of its wealth. For five generations, TATA has used a set of five core values: integrity, understanding, excellence, unity, and responsibility to guide and drive the business decisions of Tata companies (Wikipedia, 2008). In practice, the Tata Trusts have come to control 65.8 percent of the shares of Tata Sons, the holding company of the TATA group, and put their dividends into community and human capital building, such as poverty reduction, education for underprivileged children, health improvement, and so on (see TATA, 2008a, "A tradition of trust"). TATA's business tradition reflects a planting strategy in global business operations. That is, it creates a business that caters for all of people's needs and the fulfillment of these needs feeds back in terms of business growth. TATA sells virtually every kind of product and it is often keyed to the needs of the poorest, which are also the most ignored markets. Poor or rich, TATA serves them all. Its moves in the auto business are perfect examples of this planting strategy. In January 2008, at an auto show in India, Tata Motors unveiled Nano, a super-compact, $2500 car within the economic reach of millions of people in India (PRAVDA, 2008, "TATA motors makes Mercedes for the poor"). Yet at the same time, in late March 2008 TATA purchased Jaguar Land Rover from the Ford Company for around US$2.3 billion (*The Times of India*, 2008, "TATA acquires Jaguar, Land Rover for 2.3 billion"). This acquisition allows TATA to also compete in the up-scale auto market. These strategies allow TATA to serve the transportation needs of both the poor and the rich. TATA has all of their business.

The lessons from TATA are instructive for pharmaceutical business. TATA has not only created a business empire unparalleled by others but a new way of doing business that reflects the core value of a planting strategy. That is, the people's business is the business of all successful businesses. In explaining its success, TATA attributes its creative insights to its cultural knowledge, which creates a different way of conceptualizing businesses and markets. In this regard, the creative potential embodied in BRICA's cultural knowledge should no longer be ignored by global stakeholders in the pharmaceutical industry. The BRICA countries should not be seen as merely passive consumers. They are a critical link to the solution of exploring new therapeutics and new ways of health care to confront the global health challenge. Their potential can only be materialized in an effective, creative global partnership that aims to address the health of the majority of the global populations, that is, the vast number of excluded people who have already proved that they can be the rare source of our inspiration for healthy solutions. The business of these people is everyone's business.

References

Chapter 1

American Diabetes Association (2007) "Diabetes statistics." Available at: http://www.diabetes.org/diabetes-statistics.jsp

American Heart Association (2007a) "Heart attack and angina statistics." Available at: http://www.americanheart.org/presenter.jhtml?identifier=4591

American Heart Association (2007b) "International cardiovascular disease statistics." Available at: http://www.americanheart.org/downloadable/heart/1168612193463INTL07.pdf

American Lung Association (2006) "Lung cancer fact sheet." Available at: http://www.lungusa.org/site/pp.asp?c=dvLUK9OOE&b=669263

Anslem Ministries (2007) "Big pharma: The black box of R&D." Available at: http://www.pharmameddevice.com/App/homepage.cfm?appname=100485&linkid=23294&moduleid=3162#Pharmaceutical

Australia Government Department of Health and Aging (2008) "PBS." Available at: http://www.pbs.gov.au/html/home

Bain & Co. press release (8 December 2003) "Has the Pharmaceutical Blockbuster Model Gone Bust?' Available at: http://www.bain.com/bainweb/publications/printer_ready.asp?id=14243

BDI initiative (2001) "Table 1: Growth of expenditure on health, 1990–2001." Available at: http://www.bdi-initiativ-italegesellschaft.de/home_oecd_daten_aus_health_data_03.pdf

Blankenau, R. (1993). "OTA takes a closer look at cost of drugs." *Hospitals*, vol. 67, no. 7, pp. 48–50.

Borras, J. M., Fernandez, E., Schiaffino, A., Borrell, C., La Vecchia, C. (2000) "Pattern of smoking initiation in Catalonia (Spain) from 1948 to 1992." American Journal of Public Health, vol. 90, pp. 1459–62.

Business Monitor (2006) "United States pharmaceuticals and health care report." Available at: http://www.piribo.com/publications/country/usa_canada/usa/united_states_pharmaceuticals_healthcare_report_q3_2006.html

Cancer Research UK (2007) "UK lung cancer mortality statistics." Available at: http://info.cancerresearchuk.org/cancerstats/types/lung/mortality/

Centers for Disease and Control and Prevention (2005) "Pneumonia among children in developing countries." Available at: http://www.cdc.gov/ncidod/dbmd/diseaseinfo/ pneumchilddevcount_t.html

Centers of Disease Prevention and Control (2006) "U.S. Tuberculosis cases at an all-time low in 2005, but drug resistance increasing." Available at: http://www.cdc.gov/od/oc/media/pressrel/fs060323.html

CNN (31 May 2007) "Man knew he had TB before flying to Europe." Available at: http://www.cnn.com/2007/HEALTH/conditions/05/30/tb.flight/index.html

Davis, K., Collins, S. R., Doty, M. M., Ho, A., and Holmgren, A. L. (August, 2005) "Issue brief: Health and productivity among US workers." Commonwealth

Fund. Available at: http://www.illinoiscovered.com/assets/cover_856_davis_hlt_productivity_usworkers.pdf

DiMasi, J. (May 2001) "New drug development in the United States from 1963 to 1999." *Clinical Pharmacology and Therapeutics,* vol. 69, no. 5. pp. 286–98. Available at: http://www.cchem.berkeley.edu/chem195/Dimasireview.pdf

DiMasi, J. A., Hansen, R. W., and Grabowski, H. G. (2003) "The price of innovation: New estimates of drug development costs." *Journal of Health Economics,* vol. 22, p. 151.

Eisenberg, D. M., Davis, R. B., Ettner, S. L., Appel, S., Wilkey, S., Van Rompay, M., Kessler, R. C. (2001) "Trends in alternative medicine use in the United States, 1990–1997: Results of a follow-up national survey." *Journal of the American Medical Association.* Available at: http://www.ncbi.nlm.nih.gov/pubmed/9820257

EMSNow (18 April 2003) "The cost of SARS—$1.1 billion and rising." Available at: http://www.emsnow.com/newsarchives/archivedetails.cfm?ID=1451

European Cardiovascular Disease Statistics (2005) British Heart Foundation Health Promotion Research Group.

Families USA (September 2005) "The choice: Health care for people or drug industry profits." Available at: http://www.familiesusa.org/issues/prescription-drugs/drug-industry/

Fan, W., Liu, Y, Bhattacharyya, and Hu, L. (5 November 2007) "Equity and efficiency in China's health care delivery system," in the panel "Establishing equitable access to healthcare for 1.3 billion people: Challenges and strategies of health sector reforms in China.' Presentation at the 2007 Convention of the American Public Health Association, Washington, DC.

Far Eastern Economic Review (2003) "The cost of SARS." Issue 166, no. 16, pp. 12–17. *International Journal of Cancer,* vol. 121, no. 2, pp. 462–5. Available at: http://www3.interscience.wiley.com/cgi-bin/abstract/114190249/ABSTRACT?CRETRY=1&SRETRY=0

FierceBiotech (12 December, 2006) "Pozen shares sink on new demand for data." Available at: http://www.fiercebiotech.com/story/pozen-shares-sink-on-new-demand-for-data/2006-12-13

FierceBiotech. (8 June, 2007a) "FDA decision on Trexima may trigger new studies." Available at: http://www.fiercebiotech.com/story/fda-decision-on-trexima-may-trigger-new-studies/2006-06-09

FierceBiotech (July 2007b) "Press release: FDA needs more data on GPC Biotech cancer drug." Available at: http://www.fiercebiotech.com/press-releases/press-release-fda-needs-more-data-gpc-biotech-cancer-drug

FierceBiotech (25 July, 2007c) "GPC cancer drug voted down by FDA committee." Available at: http://www.fiercebiotech.com/story/gpc-cancer-drug-voted-down-by-fda-committee/2007–07-25

FierceBiotech (2 August, 2007d) "Press release: FDA issues second approvable letter for Pozen, Inc. and GlaxoSmithKline's Trexima; Approval delayed." Available at: http://www.fiercebiotech.com/press-releases/press-release-fda-qissues-second approvable-letter-pozen-inc-and-glaxosmithklines-trex

Fiercebiotech. (30 August, 2007e) "Safety concerns force delay for Phase III ED Trial." Available at: http://www.fiercebiotech.com/story/safety-concerns-force-delay-phase-iii-ed-trial/2007-08-30

FierceBiotech (28 November, 2007f) "The top 15 R&D budgets." Available at: http://www.fiercebiotech.com/special-reports/top-15-r-d-budgets

Forbes (2007) "BHP Billiton." Available at: http://www.forbes.com/lists/2007/37/biz_07fab50_BHP-Billiton_6RJ3.html

Giaccotto, C., SanTerre, R. E., and Vernon, J. A. (April 2005) "Drug prices and research and development investment behavior in the pharmaceutical industry." *Journal of Law and Economics*, vol. xlviii. Available at: http://www.journals.uchicago.edu/JLE/journal/issues/v48n1/480109/480109.web.pdf

Gibbs, J. (17 March 2000) "Mechanism-based target identification and drug discovery in cancer research." *Science*, vol. 287, no. 5460, pp. 1969–73. Available at: http://www.sciencemag.org/cgi/content/abstract/287/5460/1969

Global Health Council (30 October 2007) "Access to life saving medicines for the world's poorest: Tariff and non-tariff barriers." Available at: http://www.globalhealth.org/news/article/9246

Grabowski, H. G. and Vernon, J. M. (1990) "A new look at the returns and risks pharmaceutical R&D." *Management Science*, vol. 36, no. 7, pp. 804–21.

Gross, D. J., Ratner, J., Perez, J., and Glavin, S. (Spring 1994) "International pharmaceutical spending controls: France, Germany, Sweden, and the United Kingdom – Prescription Drugs: Payment and Policy Issues." *Health Care Financing Review*. Available at: http://findarticles.com/p/articles/mi_m0795/is_n3_v15/ai_15779283/pg_3

Health Insurance Association of America (HIAA) (2000) "The impact of pipeline drugs on pharmaceutical spending." Available at: http://www.ahipresearch.org/PDFs/25_ExecSumImpactofPipelineDrugs.pdf

Herper, M. and Kang, P. (22 March 2006) "The world's ten best-selling drugs." Available at: http://www.forbes.com/home/sciencesandmedicine/2006/03/21/pfizer-merck-amgen-cx_mh_pk_0321topdrugs.html

Industry Surveys (September 1993) "RX-to-OTC conversions to boost market." *Health Care*, vol. 9.

Hertsgaard M. (1997) "Our real china problem." *The Atlantic Monthly*. Available at: http://www.theatlantic.com/issues/97nov/china.htm

International Federation of Pharmaceutical Manufacturers and Associations (September 2006). "Building healthier societies through partnership." Available at: http://www.ipfma.org/documents/NR1158/BUILDING_HEALTH_ang.pdf

Intercontinental marketing services (IMS) (20 March 2007) "IMS health reports global pharmaceutical market grew 7.0 percent in 2006, to $643 billion." Available at: http://www.imshealth.com/ims/portal/front/articleC/0,2777,6599_3665_80560241,00.html

International Trachoma Initiative (2005) "About trachoma." Available at: http://www.trachoma.org/trachoma.php

Interview with Adam Clark (16 November 2007) "Commentary on supply chain management." Novartis Company, Switzerland.

Ioannides-Demos, L. L., Ibrahim, J. E. and McNeil, J. J. (2002) "Reference based pricing schemes: Effects on pharmaceutical expenditure, resource utilisation, and health outcomes." *Pharmacoeconomics*, vol. 20, no. 9, pp. 577–91.

Japan Pharmaceutical Manufactures Association (2006) "Pharmaceutical administration and regulations in Japan." Available at: http://www.jpma.or.jp/english/parj/pdf/2006.pdf

Lichtenberg, F. R. (2003) "The impact of new drug launches on longevity: Evidence from longitudinal, disease-level data from 52 countries, 1982–2001." Working Paper No. 9754, National Bureau of Economic Research.

Lipsky, M. S. and Sharp, L. K. (2001). "From idea to market: The drug approval Process." *Journal of American Board of Family Practitioners*, vol. 14, no. 5 pp. 362–7. Available at: http://www.jabfm.org/cgi/reprint/14/5/362.pdf

Martin, Khor. (15 February 2007) "Health: WHO DG regrets her reported remarks on Thai compulsory licenses." TWN Info Service on Health Issues. Third World Network. Available at: http://www.twnside.org.sg

Maynard, A. and Bloor, K. (2003) "Dilemmas in regulation of the market for pharmaceuticals." *Health Affairs*, vol. 22, no. 3. Available at: http://www.content.healthaffairs.org/cgi/reprint/22/3/31.pdf

Maynard, A. and K. Bloor ((26 July 1997) "Regulating the pharmaceutical industry." *British Medical Journal*, vol. 315, pp. 200–1.

Mecaskey J. W., Knirsch, C. A., Kumaresan, J. A. and Cook J. A. (2003) "The possibility of eliminating blinding trachoma." *The Lancet Infectious Diseases*, vol. 3, pp. 728–34.

Medical Ecology (2007) "Trachoma." Available at: http://www.medicalecology.org/water/trachoma/trachoma.htm

Microbiologybytes (2007) "Shistomiasis." Available at: http://www.microbiologybytes.com/ introduction/Schisto.html

Morbidity and Mortality Weekly Report (1998) "Surveillance for Asthma – United States, 1960–1995." vol. 47, no. SS-1. Atlanta, Georgia.

Nagle, H. and Nagle, B. (2005) *Pharmacology: An Introduction*. Boston, MA: McGraw Hill.

National Institutes of Health (1999) "National Heart, Lung, and Blood Institute Data Fact Sheet – Asthma Statistics." Washington, DC: National Institutes of Health.

National Public Radio (June 2007) "TB patient sparks public health menace." Available at: http://www.npr.org/templates/story/story.php?storyId=10555481

New York Times (1 May 2003) "The cost of SARS." Available at: http://query.nytimes.com/gst/fullpage.html?res=9E0DE0D91F3DF932A35756C0A9659C8B63

Organization for Economic Cooperation and Development (2002) *OECD Health Data 2002*. Paris: OECD.

Pharmaceutical Manufacturers Association (1989) "Annual survey report, 1987–1989". Washington, DC: PMA.

Pharmaceutical Research and Manufacturers Association (2003) Pharmaceutical Industry Profile, Annual Membership Survey 75.

Pharmaceutical Research and Manufacturers Association (2007) "Innovation." Available at: http://www.phrma.org/about_phrma/

Pharma MedDevice (2007) "Pharmaceutical statistics." Available at: http://www.pharmameddevice.com/App/homepage.cfm?appname=100485 &linkid=23294&moduleid=3162#Pharmaceutical

PharmaDevice (2008) "Pharmaceutical statistics." Available at: http://www.pharmameddevice.com/App/homepage.cfm?appname=100485&moduleID=3162&LinkID=23294#Pharmaceutical

Porter, R. B. (1998) "Global initiative: The economic case." *Community Eye Health*, vol. 11, no. 27, pp. 44–5. Available at: http://www.pubmedcentral.nih.gov/articlerender.fcgi?artid=1706060

Public Citizen (2002a) "Pharmaceuticals rank as most profitable industry, again." Available at: http://www.citizen.org/congress/reform/drug_industry/corporate/articles.cfm?ID=7416).

Public Citizen (26 June 2002b) "Would Lower Prescription Drug Prices Curb Drug Company Research & Development?" Available at: http://www.citizen.org/congress/reform/drug_industry/r_d/articles.cfm?ID=7909

Reed, V. (20 July 2007) "Spectrum plunges on potential drug delay." *Orange County Business Journal.* Available at: http://www.ocbj.com/industry_article.asp?aID=68549769.3400797.1502306.45722.5759531.246&aID2=115553

Redwood, H. (1993) "New drugs in the world market: Incentives and impediments to innovation." *American Enterprise*, vol. 4, no. 4, pp. 72–80

Roll Back Malaria (2001) "Economic costs of malaria." Available at: http://www.rbm.who.int/cmc_upload/0/000/015/363/RBMInfosheet_10.htm

Schweitzer, S. O. (1997) *Pharmaceutical Economics and Policy.* Oxford: Oxford University Press.

Sherer, F. M. (1993) "Pricing, profits, and technological progress in the pharmaceutical industry." *Journal of Economic Perspectives*, vol. 7, no. 3, pp. 97–115.

Sustainable Development (2007) "Malaria control in Mozambique." Available at: http://www.bhpbilliton.com/bb/sustainableDevelopment/socialResponsibility/communityInvestmentPrograms/malariaControlInMozambique.jsp

The Metropolitan Corporate Counsel (June 2004). "BHP Billiton: Globalization's two way street – How a foreign-based company benefits the U.S. and the world." Available at: http://www.metrocorpcounsel.com/current.php?artType=covsel&artMonth=June&artYear=2004

The Parliamentary Office of Science and Technology (June 2005) "Fighting diseases of developing countries." POSTNOTE, no. 241. Available at: http://www.parliament.uk/documents/upload/POSTpn241.pdf

Tufts Center for the Study of Drug Development (2001) "Tufts Center for the Study of Drug Development Pegs Cost of a New Prescription Medicine at $802 Million." Available at: http://csdd.tufts.edu/NewsEvents/RecentNews.asp?newsid=6

The Tufts Center for the Study of Drug Development (2007) Available at: http://csdd.tufts.edu/Research/Milestones.asp

Thylefors, B., Negrel, A. D., Pararajasegaram, R, and Dadzie, K. Y. (1995) "Global data on blindness." *Bulletin of the World Health Organization*, 73, pp. 115–21.

Trouiller, P., Olliaro, P., Torreele, E., Orbinski, J.,Laing, R., and Ford, N. (2002). "Drug development for neglected diseases: A deficient market and a public-health policy failure." *The Lancet*, vol. 359, pp. 2188–94.

UNAIDS (2006) "AIDS epidemic update." Available at: http://data.unaids.org/pub/EpiReport/2006/2006_EpiUpdate_en.pdf

US Congressional Budget Office of Research and Development in the Pharmaceutical Industry (October 2006) "A CBO Study: Research and Development in the Pharmaceutical Industry." Available at: http://www.cbo.gov/ftpdocs/76xx/doc7615/10-02-DrugR-D.pdf

US Food and Drug Administration (2007) "Frequently asked questions." Available at: http://www.fda.gov/opacom/faqs/faqs.html

US Food and Drug Administration (2008) "FDA." Available at: http://www.fda.gov/

US Congress Office of Technology Assessment (1993) *Pharmaceutical R&D: Costs, Risks and Rewards*. Washington, DC: US Government Printing Office.

Vidyasagar, D. (2002) "A global view of advancing neonatal health and survival." *Journal of Perinatology*, vol. 22, pp. 513–15. Available at: http://www.nature.com/jp/journal/v22/n7/full/7210797a.html

Wall Street Journal (1 August 2007) "Cancer regression." Available at: http://online.wsj.com/article/SB118593325021784255.html?mod=dist_smartbrief

Walters, P. G. (1992) "FDA's new drug evaluation process: A general overview." *Journal of Public Health Dentistry*, vol. 52, pp. 333–7.

Wang, M. L. and Nantulya, V. (2008) *Social Exclusion and Community Capital: The Missing Link in Global Partnerships of Health for All*. Lanham, MD: University Press of America.

Wang, Zheng and Wang (2007) *WTO, Globalization and China's Health Care System*. Basingstoke: Palgrave Macmillan.

Wikipedia (2007) "European Medicines Agency." Available at: http://en.wikipedia.org/wiki/European_Medicines_Agency

Wikipedia (2007a) "Pharmaceutical company." Available at: http://en.wikipedia.org/wiki/Pharmaceutical_companies#_note-2

Wikipedia (2007b) "Pharmacology." Available at: http://en.wikipedia.org/wiki/Pharmacology

World Health Organization (2004) World Health Report. Available at: http://www.who.int/whr/en/

World Health Organization (2007a) "Control of neglected tropical diseases." Available at: http://www.who.int/neglected_diseases/en/

World Health Organization (2007b) "Cardiovascular diseases." Available at: http://www.who.int/cardiovascular_diseases/en/

World Health Organization (2007c) "Malaria." Available at: http://www.who.int/mediacentre/factsheets/fs094/en/

World Health Organization (2007d) "Stop TB partnership: 2007 tuberculosis facts." Available at: http://www.who.int/tb/publications/2007/factsheet_2007.pdf 2004 QuickFacts. Heart and Stroke Foundation of Canada. Available at: http://www.heartandstroke.ca.

Chapter 2

AAAS (2008) "NIH wins $1 billion funding but veto looms." Available at: http://www.aaas.org/spp/rd/nih08c.htm

American Medical Student Association (13 April, 2008) "Prescription drug importation: A short-term effort to reduce drug prices." Available at: http://www.amsa.org/hp/reimportation.cfm

Angell, M. (2004) *The Truth about the Drug Companies*. New York: Random House.

Barry, P. (April 2003) "More Americans go North for drugs." AARP Bulletin. Available at: http://www.aarp.org/bulletin/yourmoney/a2003-06-25-moreamericans.html

Bayer (2007) "Bayer: Science for a better life." Available at: http://www.bayer.com/en/History.aspx

BBC (10 December 2003) "Aids activists say GlaxoSmithKline is to allow the manufacture of cheap generic drug versions in South Africa." Available at: http://news.bbc.co.uk/2/hi/business/3306079.stm

Bekelman, J. E. et al. (22 January 2006) "Scope and impact of financial conflicts of interest in biomedical research." *Journal of the American Medical Association*, p. 454.

Bioanalytical Systems Inc. (2007a) Bayer corporation. Available at: http://www.bioanalytical.com/info/calendar/99/01bayer.htm

Bioanalytical Systems Inc. (2007b) Eli Lily and Company. Available at: http://www.bioanalytical.com/info/calendar/99/04lilly.htm

Bioanalytical Systems Inc. (2007c) Hoechst Marion Roussel. Available at: http://www.bioanalytical.com/info/calendar/99/03hoech.htm

Bioanalytical Systems Inc. (2007d) Merck and Company Inc. Available at: http://www.bioanalytical.com/info/calendar/99/05merck.htm

Bioanalytical Systems Inc. (2007e) "The pharmaceutical industry: A history and calendar." Available at: http://www.bioanalytical.com/info/calendar/99/07.html

Bioanalytical Systems Inc. (2007f) Pfizer. Available at: http://www.bioanalytical.com/info/calendar/99/07pfizer.htm

Bioanalytical Systems Inc. (2007g) SmithKline Beecham. Available at: http://www.bioanalytical.com/info/calendar/99/09smith.htm

Bioanalytical Systems Inc. (2007h) Wyeth Ayerst. Available at: http://www.bioanalytical.com/info/calendar/99/10wyeth.htm

Bristol-Myers Squibb (2006) "A Brief History of Bristol-Myers Squibb." Available at: http://www.bms.com/aboutbms/content/data/ourhis.html

Cauchon, D. (25 September 2000) "FDA advisors tied to industry". *USA Today*, 1A.

Center for Policy Alternatives (2000) "Playing fair: State action to lower prescription drug prices." Available at: http://www.stateaction.org/issues/issue.cfm/issue/PrescriptionDrugPricing.xml

Centre of Public Integrity (7 July 2005) "Drug lobby second to none." Available at: http://www.publicintegrity.org/rx/report.aspx?aid=723

Cptech (2001) "Pharmaceutical industry R&D costs: Key findings about the Public Citizen Report." Available at: http://www.cptech.org/ip/health/econ/phrmaresponse.pdf

Darwin, C. (2003). *The Origin of Species*. New York: Signet Classics.

Denning, B. P. (2003) "The Maine Rx prescription drug plan and the ormant Commerce Clause Doctrine: The case of the missing link." *American Journal of Law and Medicine*. Available at: http://papers.ssrn.com/sol3/papers.cfm?abstract_id=355303

Dictionary.com Unabridged, v 1.1 (2007) Random House.

Dobson, R. (28 April 2001) "Drug company lobbyist joins Oxfam's cheap drugs campaign." *British Medical Journal*, vol. 322, p. 1011.

Ebisch, R. (March 2005) "Prescription for change" *Teradata Magazine* on-line. Available at: http://www.teradata.com/t/page/131951/

Eli Lilly Company (2007) "History." Available at: http://www.lilly.com/about/history.html.

European Commission (2007) "The 2007 EU industrial R&D investment scoreboard". Available at: http://iri.jrc.ec.europa.eu/research/scoreboard_2007.htm

European Public Health Alliance, 2008, "UK parliamentarians put the pharma industry under the spotlight." Available at: http://www.epha.org/a/1773

FDA Magazine (2006) "Wiley W. Harvey: Pioneer consumer activist." Available at: http://www.fda.gov/fdac/features/2006/106_wiley.html

FDA (1997) "Food And Drug Administration and Modernization Act of 1997." Available at: http://www.fda.gov/cder/guidance/105–115.htm

FDA (1983) "Orphan Drugs." Available at: http://www.fda.gov/cder/handbook/orphan.htm

FierceBiotech (2007a) "The top 15 R&D Market." Available at: http://www.fiercebiotech.com/special-reports/top-15-r-d-budgets

FierceBiotech (28 November 2007b) "Schering-Plough – Top 15 R&D Budgets." Available at: http://www.fiercebiotech.com/special-reports/15-schering-plough-top-15-r-d-budgets

FierceBiotech (28 November 2007c) "Amgen – Top 15 R&D." Available at: http://www.fiercebiotech.com/special-reports/9-amgen-top-15-r-d-budgets

FierceBiotech (28 November 2007d) "Eli Lilly – Top 15 R&D." Available at: http://www.fiercebiotech.com/special-reports/11-eli-lilly-top-15-r-d-budgets

FierceBiotech (28 November 2007e) "Merck – Top 15 R&Ds." Available at: http://www.fiercebiotech.com/special-reports/7-merck-top-15-r-d-budgets

FierceBiotech (28 November 2007f). "Novartis – Top 15 R&D budget." Available at: http://www.fiercebiotech.com/special-reports/6-novartis-top-15-r-d-budgets

FierceBiotech (28 February 2008a) "AstraZeneca may shake up R&D with spin-off." Available at: http://www.fiercebioresearcher.com/story/astrazeneca-may-shake-up-rd-with-spin-off/2008–02-12

FierceBiotech (15 November 2008b) "Abbott – Top 15 R&D Budgets." Available at: http://www.fiercebiotech.com/special-reports/14-abbott-top-15-r-d-budgets

FierceBiotech (28 November 2008c) "Bristol-Myers Squibb – Top 15 R&D Budgets." Available at: http://www.fiercebiotech.com/special-reports/13-bristol-myers-squibb-top-15-r-d-budgets

Franklin Pierce Law Center (2008) "Overview of federal technology transfer." Available at: http://www.fplc.edu/risk/vol5/spring/rudolph.htm

Fundinguniverse (2008) "Wyeth." Available at: http://www.fundinguniverse.com/company-histories/Wyeth-Company-History.html

Gagnon, M.-A. and Lexchin. J. (3 January 2008) "The cost of pushing pills: A new estimate of pharmaceutical promotion expenditures in the United States." *PLOS Medicine Journal.* Available at: http://medicine.plosjournals.org/perlserv/?request=get-document&doi=10.1371/journal.pmed.0050001&ct=1

Goozner, M. (2004) *The $800 Million Pill: The Truth behind the Cost of New Drugs.* Berkeley, CA: University of California Press.

Gribbin, A. (18 June 2001) "House investigates panels involved with drug safety." *Washington Times.*

Gribbin, J. and Hook A. (2004) *The Scientists: A History of Science Told Through the Lives of Its Greatest Inventors.* New York: Random House.

Griffiths, S. (March 2004) "Betting on biogenerics." *Nature* Reviews Drug Discovery, vol. 3, pp. 197–8. Available at: http://www.nature.com/nrd/journal/v3/n3/full/nrd1333.html

GSK (2007) "Our company." Available at: http://www.gsk.com/about/company.htm

GSK (2008) "Research and development." Available at: http://www.gsk.com/research/about/index.html

Harris, G. (23 October, 2003) "Cheap drugs from Canada: Another political hot potato." *New York Times.* Available at: http://biopsychiatry.com/pharmacy/canada.html

Hensley, S. and Martinez, B (15 July 2005) "To sell their drugs, companies increasingly rely on doctors." *Wall Street Journal*, p. A1.

Herper, M. and Kang, P. (22 March 2006) "The world's ten best-selling drugs." Available at Forbes: http://www.forbes.com/home/sciencesandmedicine/2006/03/21/pfizer-merck-amgen-cx_mh_pk_0321topdrugs.html

Hoechst AG (2008) "Hoechst A.G." Available at: http://www.fundinguniverse.com/company-histories/Hoechst-AG-Company-History.html IMS Reports (17 February 2004) "11.5 Percent Dollar Growth in '03 U.S. Prescription Sales." IMS Health. Available at: http://www.imshealth.com/ims/portal/front/article C/0,2777,6025_3665_44771558,00.html

IMS Reports (2007a) "IMS Health reports global pharmaceutical market grew 7.0 percent in 2006, to \$643 Billion." Available at: http://www.imshealth.com/ims/portal/front/articleC/0,2777,6025_3665_44771558,00.html

IMS Reports (8 March 2007b) "U.S. Prescription Sales Jump 8.3 Percent in 2006, to \$274.9 Billion." Available at: http://www.imshealth.com/ims/portal/front/a rticleC/0,2777,6025_3665_44771558,00.html

Ismail, M. A. (7 July, 2005) "Drug lobby second to none." The Center for Public Integrity. Available at: http://www.publicintegrity.org/rx/report.aspx?aid=723

Johnson & Johnson (2007). "Innovations." Available at: http://www.jnj.com/innovations/pharma_pipeline/index.htm

Kaufman, M. (6 May 2005) "Merck CEO Resigns as Drug Probe Continues." A-1. Available at: http://www.washingtonpost.com/wp-dyn/content/article/2005/05/05/AR2005050501115_pf.html

Lamberti, M. J. (2001) *An Industry in Evolution*, 3rd edn. Boston, MA: CenterWatch, p. 22.

Larson, R. (2005) *Bioinformatics and Drug Discovery*. New York: Humana Press.

Le Monde (19 October 2007) "Pfizer et Novartis souffrent du succèss des mèdicaments gènètique." Available at: http://www.lemonde.fr/web/article/0,1-0@2-3234,36-968860@51-968475,0.html

Lichtenberg, F. R. (11 July 2007) "Yes, new drugs save lives." *Washington Post*, A15. Available at: http://www.washingtonpost.com/wp-dyn/content/article/2007/07/10/AR2007071001468.html.

Long, S. H. (Spring 1994) "Prescriptions drugs and the elderly: Issues and options." *Health Affairs*, vol. ii, pp. 157–74."

Mantone, J. (6 December 2007) "Big Pharma's Bitter Pill." *Wall Street Journal*. Available at: http://blogs.wsj.com/health/2007/12/06/big-pharmas-bitter-pill/?mod=WSJBlog

Martinez, B., and Goldstein, J. (6 December 2007) "Big Pharma Faces Grim Prognosis." *Wall Street Journal*. Available at: http://online.wsj.com/article/SB119689933952615133.html?mod=WSJBlog

Martino, M. (2007) "Comments on top-15 R&D budget." Available at: http://www.fiercebiotech.com/special-reports/top-15-r-d-budgets

McKinzie Productview (March 2007) "Global company sales summary." Available at: http://www.p-d-r.com/ranking/2006_Company_Sales.pdf

Merck and Company (2002) "History of Merck." Available at: http://www.msd.com.hk/about_us/e_history_of_merck.html

Moynihan, R. (31 May 2003a) "Drug company sponsorship of education could be replaced at a fraction of its cost." *British Medical Journal*, vol. 326, no. 7400, p. 1163. Available at: http://www.bmj.com/cgi/content/full/326/7400/1163

Moynihan, R. (31 May 2003b) "Who pays for the pizza? Redefining the relationships between doctors and drug companies." 2: "Disentanglement." *British Medical Journal*, vol. 326, no. 7400, pp. 1193–6.

Moynihan, R. and Alan Cassels (2005) *Selling Sickness: How Drug Companies are Turning Us All Into Patients*. New York: Allen & Unwin.

Myers, Kelly D. (1 January 2007) *Marketing to Professionals: Tomorrow's Changes Today*. Available at: PharmExec.com

National Cancer Institute (2007) "Menopausal hormone replacement therapy use and cancer: Questions and answers." Available at: http://www.cancer.gov/cancertopics/factsheet/Risk/menopausal-hormones

Nature Reviews Drug Discovery (July 2006) "Editorial: Keeping sight of the goal." *Nature*, vol. 5, p. 525. Available at: http://www.nature.com/nrd/journal/v5/n7/abs/nrd2102.html

Nelson, G. (1983) *Pharmaceutical Companies Histories*. Bethesda, MD: Woodbine House Publishing.

Newton, D. Thorpe, A. and Otter, C. (2004). *Revise A2 Chemistry*. New York: Heinemann Educational Publishing, p. 1.

No Free Lunch (2008) http://www.nofreelunch.org/

Osterloh, I. (June, 2007) "How I discovered viagra." (An account by the executive director of discovery research at Pfizer Global Research & Development's Sandwich Laboratories, England). *Cosmos*, issue 15. Available at: http://www.cosmosmagazine.com/node/1463

Oversteegen , L., Rovini, H., and Belsey, M. J. (September 2007) "Respiratory drug market dynamics." *Nature* Reviews Drug Discovery, vol. 6, pp. 695–6. Available at: http://www.nature.com/nrd/journal/v6/n9/full/nrd2401.html

Ozols, R. F. (1 January 2007) "Clinical cancer advances 2006: Major research advances in cancer treatment, prevention, and screening – A report from the American Society of Clinical Oncology." *Journal of Clinical Oncology*, vol. 25, no. 1, pp. 146–62. Available at: http://www.cancer.org/docroot/NWS/content/NWS_1_1x_Targeted_Therapies_Vaccines_Among_Major_Cancer_Advances_in_2006.asp

Pagnamenta, R. (12 February 2008) "AstraZeneca may spin off drug research unit to venture capitalists." Times on-line. Available at: http://business.timesonline.co.uk/tol/business/industry_sectors/health/article3352968.ece

Pear, R. (25 December 2002) "Law requiring lower drug prices is struck down." Available at: http://query.nytimes.com/gst/fullpage.html?res=9E0CE7D9133CF936A15751C1A9649C8B63&sec=&spon=&pagewanted=all

Pfizer (2008a) "About Pfizer." Available at: http://www.pfizer.com/about/history/2000_present.jsp

Pfizer Inc. (2008b) "Pfizer Inc and Hoechst Marion Roussel to co-develop and co-promote inhaled insulin." Available at: http://www.prnewswire.com/cgi-bin/stories.pl?ACCT=104&STORY=/www/story/11–04-1998/0000793273&EDATE=

Pfizer (2008c) "Pfizer pipeline – new medicine in development." Available at: http://www.pfizer.com/research/pipeline/pipeline.jsp

PLOS Medicine (2006) *A Collection of Articles on Disease Mongering*. Public Library of Science. Available at: http://collections.plos.org/plosmedicine/diseasemongering-2006.php

Prescription Access Litigation (2007) Available at: http://www.prescriptionaccess.org/

Privitera, M. D. (2003) "Phase IV trials: A wolf in sheep's clothing?" *The Annals of Pharmacotherapy*, vol. 37, no. 5, pp. 741–3. Available at: http://www.theannals.com/cgi/content/full/37/5/741

Public Citizen Report (23 July 2001) "Rx R&D myths: The case against the drug industry's R&D 'scare card'." Available at: http://www.tradewatch.org/documents/ACFDC.PDF

Quintiles Transnational (2001) "Promoting drugs through physician meetings and events: Pfizer leads the way; antidepressants are top category." Available at: http://www.quintiles.com/products_and_services/informatics/scott_levin/press_releases/press_release/1,1254,209,00.html

Rang, H. P. (2006) "The receptor concept: Pharmacology's big idea." *British Journal of Pharmacology*, vol. 147, Suppl., pp. S9–S16.

Robinson, J. T. (November 2003). *Changing the Face of Detailing by Motivating Physicians to See Pharmaceutical Sales Reps*. Health Banks. Available at: http://www.healthbanks.com/PatientPortal/Public/support_documents/PMT_Robinson.pdf

Roche Pharmaceuticals (2008) "Innovative R&D." Available at: http://www.rocheusa.com/r&d/overview.html

Schweitzer, S. O. (1997) *Pharmaceutical Economics and Policy*. Oxford: Oxford University Press.

Schweitzer, S. (2006) *Pharmaceutical Economics and Policy*. Oxford: Oxford University Press.

SciDeve (2008) "Universities urged: 'Share benefits of health research'." Available at: http://www.scidev.net/en/news/universities-urged-share-benefits-of-health-rese.html

Seppa, N. (18 and 25 December 1999) "With new vaccine, scientists prevent rabies in boys." *Science News*, vol. 156, nos 25 and 26, p. iv.

Swann, J. (2007) "History of FDA." US Department of Health and Human Services. Available at: http://www.fda.gov/oc/history/historyoffda/default.htm)

The American Heritage Science Dictionary (2007) Houghton Mifflin Company, dictionary.com.

The World Medical Association (2004) "Declaration of Helsinki." Available at: behttp://www.amsa.org/hp/reimportation.cfm

Trombetta, B. (1 September 2005) "2005 Industry Audit." Pharmaceutical Executive. Available at: http://www.pharmexec.com/pharmexec/article/articleDetail.jsp?id=177964

US Department of Health and Human Services (August 1999) "FDA Guidance for Industry on Consumer-Directed Broadcast Advertisements." Available at: http://www.fda.gov/cder/guidance/1804fnl.htm

US Department of Health and Human Services (29 September 2006) "News release: Medicare release data on 2007 drug plan options." Available at: http://www.hhs.gov/news/press/2006pres/20060929.html

US Department of Health and Human Services (2007a) "Regulating Cosmetics, Devices, and Veterinary Medicine After 1938." Available at: http://www.fda.gov/oc/history/historyoffda/section4.html

US Department of Health and Human Services (2007b) "The 1906 Food and Drugs Act and Its Enforcement". Available at: http://www.fda.gov/oc/history/historyoffda/section1.html

US Government Technology Administration (9 May, 2002) "Testimonies on the virtue of the Bayh-Dole Act." Available at: http://www.technology.gov/Speeches/BPM_020509_PCAST.htm

USA Today (2002) "How to buy prescription drugs at over 50 percent off US prices." Available at: http://www.kirknews.com/newpage1.htm

Visongain (May 2006) "World generics market: 2006–2011." Available at: http://www.piribo.com/publications/generic_drugs/world_generics_market_20062011.html

Watson, J. (2001) *The Double Helix: A Personal Account of the Discovery of the Structure of DNA*. New York: Touchstone.

Wikipedia (2007a) "History of medicine." Available at: http://en.wikipedia.org/wiki/History_of_medicine#Modern_medicine

Wikipedia (2007b) "Pharmaceutical companies." Available at: http://en.wikipedia.org/wiki/Pharmaceutical_companies

Wikipedia (2007c) "Pharmacology." Available at: http://en.wikipedia.org/wiki/Pharmacology

Wood McKinzie Productview (March 2007) "Global company sales summary." Available at: http://www.p-d-r.com/ranking/2006_Company_Sales.pdf

Chapter 3

Alliance Boots (29 January 2007) "Alliance Boots to enter Chinese pharmaceutical market through joint venture." Available at: http://www.allianceboots.com/main.asp?nid=400&pid=1494

Anon (2000) "National AIDS drugs policy." Ministry of Health, Brazil. Available at: http://www.brasilemb.org/social_issues/social3.shtml

Anon (23 August 2001) "Brazil to break AIDS patent." *BBC News*. Available at: http://news.bbc.co.uk/1/hi/business/1505163.stm

Anon (5 August 2002) "Brazil's looming economic crisis." *BBC News*. Available at: http://news.bbc.co.uk/1/hi/business/2173296.stm

Anon (2003a) "Generics take off in Brazil." IMS Health. Available at: http://open.imshealth.com/webshop2/IMSinclude/i_article_ 20030123a.asp

Anon (12 September 2003b) "Pfizer, Schering, Boehringer Ingelheim, Bristol Myers-Squibb, Novartis e Organon são empresas TOP 100, segundo o Guia Exame." Interfarma Press Release. Available at: http://www.interfarma.org.br/

Anon (29 January 2004) "ANVISA estudia reglas para ensayos clínicos con voluntaries. Estado de Minas." *Boletin Farmacos*. Available at: http://www.boletinfarmacos.org/

Anon (February 2005a) "IMS Retail Drug Monitor: Pharma sales growth continues at 6 percent pace in 13 major markets." IMS Health. Available at: http://www.imshealth.com

Anon (2005b) Ministério da Saúde. Available at: http://portal.saude.gov.br/saude/

Anon (March 2005c) "Brazil's economy." *The Economist*. Available at: http://www.economist.com/research/backgrounders/displayBackgrounder.cfm?bg=616685

Asia Times (19 June 2007) "India's blossoming biotech boom." Available at: http://www.atimes.com/atimes/South_Asia/IF19Df01.html

AstraZeneca (2006) "AstraZeneca in China." Available at: http://en.astrazeneca. com.cn/article/502748.aspx

Bailey E. (2003) *The Pharmaceutical Pricing Compendium.* Urch Publishing. Available at: http://www.urchpublishing.com/

BBC (20 April 2008) "Heparin contaminated on purpose." Available at: http:// news.bbc.co.uk/2/hi/asia-pacific/7375057.stm

Bharat Book Bureau (November 2007) "Booming Clinical Trials Market in India." Available at: http://www.bharatbook.com/detail.asp?id=70010

Bioportfolio (2008) "Chinese pharmaceutical industry." Available at: http:// www.bioportfolio.com/cgi-bin/acatalog/Chinese_Pharmaceutical_Industry. html

Biospace (1 April, 2008) "Boehringer Ingelheim corporation profits from Sinopharm deal." Available at: http://www.biospace.com/news_story. aspx?NewsEntityId=91275

BIT Life Sciences (2008) "BIT's world cancer congress." Available at: http://www. bitlifesciences.com/cancer2008/Sponsorship%20Brochure-WCC.pdf

Biztradeshows (2008a) "Pharmaceutical industry." Available at: http://www. biztradeshows.com/trade-events/apteka-moscow.html

Biztradeshows (2008b) "Health industry." Available at: http://www.biztradeshows. com/trade-events/health-industry.html

BNET (2004) "Bayer signed agreement with Shanghai Chemistry Industry Park." Available at: http://findarticles.com/p/articles/mi_hb048/is_200405/ai_ hibm1G1117681957

BNET (2006) "Pfizer gives OEM orders to Shanghai Pharm Group." Available at: http://findarticles.com/p/articles/mi_hb5562/is_200608/ai_n22734943

Boehringer Ingelheim (2002) "Boehringer Ingelheim opens new production plant in China." Available at: http://www.boehringeringelheim.com/ corporate/news/press_releases/detail.asp?ID=220

Bryant, R. (December 2007) "China emerges in APIs." *Specialty Chemicals Magazine.* Available at: http://www.brychem.co.uk/docs/RJBSpecChem200712.pdf

Business Insights (August 2006) "Pharmaceutical growth opportunities in Brazil, Russia, India and China: Healthcare reform, market dynamics and key players." Available at: http://www.piribo.com/publications/country/latin_america/ brazil/pharmaceutical_growth_opportunities_brazil_russia_india_china.html

Business Week (22 August 2005) "The rise of Chindia." Editor's memo. Available at: http://www.businessweek.com/magazine/content/05_34/b3948012.htm

CBS News (23 September 2005) "Brazil's drug copying industry." Available at: http://www.cbsnews.com/stories/2003/09/25/health/main575168.shtml

Chervenak, M. (Fall 2006) "Industrial biotechnology in China." *Industrial Biotechnology,* pp. 174–6. Available at: http://www.liebertonline.com/doi/ pdf/10.1089/ind.2006.2.174?cookieSet=1

China Daily (24 January 2008) "GDP expands 11.4 percent, fastest in 13 years." Available at: http://www.chinadaily.net/china/2008-01/24/content_6418067. htm

Contract Pharma (June 2006) "Biopharma CMOs in China." Available at: http:// www.contractpharma.com/articles/2006/06/biopharma-cmos-in-china

Dance with Shadows Communication. (2 April 2006) "Pharma markets in China, Korea, Mexico, Russia & Turkey gather pace." Available at: http://www. dancewithshadows.com/hara/pharma-markets-china-korea.asp

Datamonitor Report (2005) "India's growth prospects in pharma." Available at: http://www.datamonitor.com/Products/Free/Report/DMHC2152/010DMHC2152.pdf

Department for International Development Health Resource Centre (2004) Brazil health briefing paper, Department for International Development Health Resource Centre, UK. Available at: http://www.dfidhealthrc.org/shared/know_the/publications.html

Djolov, G. G. (June 2004) "Market power and the pharmaceutical industry in South Africa." *Economic Affairs*, vol. 24, no. 2, pp. 47–51. Available at: http://papers.ssrn.com/sol3/papers.cfm?abstract_id=556899

Economic Times (26 April 2007) "Mr Re gets India $1 trillion gang." Available at: "http://economictimes.indiatimes.com/Mr_Rupee_pulls_India_into_1_trillion_GDP_gang/articleshow/1957520.cms

Economist (December 1998) "Keep taking the tablets: Russian pharmaceutical industry suffering in economic crisis." Available at: http://findarticles.com/p/articles/mi_hb5037/is_199812/ai_n18282554

Economist (12 April 2007) "Land of promise." Available at: http://www.economist.com/surveys/displaystory.cfm?story_id=E1_RJVNQGG

Economist (23 April 2008) "Country briefings: Brazil." Available at: http://www.economist.com/countries/Brazil/profile.cfm?folder=Profile%2DEconomic%20Data

Engardio, P. (22 August 2005a) "A new world economy." *Business Week*. Available at: http://www.businessweek.com/magazine/content/05_34/b3948411.htm

Engardio, P. (22 August 2005b) "Crouching tigers, hidden dragons." *Business Week*. Available at: http://www.businessweek.com/magazine/content/05_34/b3948411.htm

Euromonitor (2007a) "OTC health care in China." Available at: http://www.euromonitor.com/OTC_Healthcare_in_China

Euromonitor International (September 2007b) "Vitamins and dietary supplements in China." Available at: http://www.euromonitor.com/Vitamins_And_Dietary_Supplements_in_China

Finance Management Weekly (16 Jan 2008) "BRIC 4 and BRIC 11." Part III, vol. 386. Available at: http://magazine.sina.com.tw/winmoney/386/2008-01-16/180746476.shtml

Frost & Sullivan (2008) "Strategic analysis of the South African diabetes markets." Available at: http://www.pharma.frost.com

Genetic Engineering and Biotech News (1 March 2007) "China pharma basking in its spotlight." Clinical research and diagnostics channel. Vol. 27, no. 5. Available at: http://www.genengnews.com/articles/chitem.aspx?aid=2049&chid=4

Genetic Engineering and Biotechnology News (15 February 2008) "Top Chinese biopharms propel industry forward." vol. 28, no. 4. Available at: http://www.genengnews.com/articles/chitem.aspx?aid=2367&chid=0

Global Information Inc. (December 2004) "Strategic analysis of the Brazilian pharmaceutical markets." Available at: http://www.the-infoshop.com/study/fs25625_strategic_analysis.html

Global Technology Forum (9 January 2003) "*The Economist*: Indian software firms prosper due to outsourcing business." Available at: http://globaltechforum.eiu.com/index.asp?layout=rich_story&doc_id=6298&categoryid=&channelid=&search=prosper

Goldman Sachs (October 2003) "Dreaming with BRICs: The path to 2050." Global Economics Paper No. 99. Available at: http://www2.goldmansachs. com/ideas/global-growth/dreaming-with-brics.html

Goldman Sachs (1 December, 2005) "How solid are the BRICs?" Global Economics Paper 134. Available at: http://www2.goldmansachs.com/hkchina/insight/ research/pdf/BRICs_3_12-1-05.pdf

Goldman Sachs (2007) "India's rising growth potential." Global Economics Paper No. 152. Available at: http://www.usindiafriendship.net/viewpoints1/ Indias_Rising_Growth_Potential.pdf

IMS (2005) "IMS Health Reports Global Pharmaceutical Market Grew 7 Percent in 2005, to $602 Billion." Available at: http://www.imshealth.com/portal/site/ imshealth/menuitem.a46c6d4df3db4b3d88f611019418c22a/?vgnextoid=2bc a1d3be7a29110VgnVCM10000071812ca2RCRD&vgnextchannel=41a67900b 55a5110VgnVCM10000071812ca2RCRD&vgnextfmt=default

Johnson, Steve (11 December 2006) "Emerging Markets: BRICs sceptics have their backs to the wall." *Financial Times*. Available at: http://www.ft.com/ cms/s/7761deb2-88bc-11db-b485-0000779e2340,dwp_uuid5cc9f419c-4bb1-11da-997b-0000779e2340,Authorised5false.html?_i_location5http%3A%2F%2Fwww. ft.com%2Fcms%2Fs%2F1%2F7761deb2-88bc-11db-b485-0000779e2340%2Cdwp_uuid%3Dcc9f419c-4bb1-11da-997b-0000779e2340. html&_i_referer5http%3A%2F%2Fen.wikipedia.org%2Fwiki%2FBRIC

Kermani, F. (October 2005) "Contract Farma." Available at: http://www. contractpharma.com/articles/2005/10/regional-roundup-brazil

Kumar, P. (31 May 2007) "India's GDP expanded at fastest pace in 18 years." *Market Watch*. Available at: http://www.marketwatch.com/news/story/indias-economy-grows-best-pace/story.aspx?guid=%7BDD148070-EA3F-4E40-AAEB-A9B6A96868F4%7D

Langley, A. (25 September 2006) "Russia's pharmaceutical market gains appeal." *Wall Street Journal*. Available at: http://online.wsj.com/article/ SB115914471238872669.html?mod=health_home_stories

Lobato L. (2000) "Reorganizing the health care system in Brazil." In *Reshaping Health Care in Latin America: A Comparative Analysis of Health Care Reform in Argentina, Brazil, and Mexico*. Ed. S. Fleury, S. Belmartino and E. Baris. International Development Research Centre, ch. 5. Available at: http://web. idrc.ca/en/ev-9421-201-1-DO_TOPIC.html

Love, James (4 May 2007) "Brazil puts patients before patents." The Hufftington Post. Available at: http://www.huffingtonpost.com/james-love/brazil-puts-patients-befo_b_47651.html); http://www.keionline.org/ index.php?option=com_content&task=view&id=41&Itemid=1

Mbendi (2000) "Information for Africa." *South Africa – Chemicals: Pharmaceutical and Medicine Manufacturing*. Available at: http://www.mbendi.co.za/indy/ chem/phrm/af/sa/p0005.htm

Medici, A. C. (November 2002) *Financing Health Policies in Brazil: Achievements, Challenges and Proposals*. The UN Development Programme Poverty Centre. Available at: http://www.undp.org/povertycentre/publications/

Medical News Today (2008) "South African diabetes market growing significantly due to improved diagnosis rates." Available at: http://www.medicalnewstoday. com/articles/105860.php

Meng, Q., Cheng, G., Silver, L., Sun, X., Rehnberg, C., and Tomson, G. (2005) "The impact of China's retail drug price control policy on hospital expenditures: A case study in two Shandong hospitals." Oxford: Oxford University Press. Available at: http://heapol.oxfordjournals.org/cgi/reprint/20/3/185.pdf

Ministry of External Relations, Brazil (2005). "Frequently asked questions about regional integration and Mercosur." Available at: http://www.mre.gov.br/ingles/faq/p_mercosur.asp

National Center for Policy Analysis (2000) "Medical savings account in South Africa." Available at: http://www.ncpa.org/studies/s234/s234.html#C

Natural Products Insider (2008) "Global market growth for dietary supplements." Available at: http://www.naturalproductsinsider.com/articles/market-growth-supplements-international.html

Natural Resources Defense Council (2002) "Consequences of nuclear conflict between India and Pakistan." Available at: http://www.nrdc.org/nuclear/southasia.asp

Nhlapo, W. (21 January, 2008) *Economic Roundtable with Ambassador Welile Nhalpo of South Africa*. Philadelphia: Global Interdependence Center.

Norbrook, N. (October–December 2007) "Interview: Obiageli Ezekwesili." *Jeune Afrique*, p. 91.

Oliveira, J. (2003) "Brazil: Market overview of drugs and pharmaceuticals." US & Foreign Commercial Service and US Department of State. Available at: http://strategis.ic.gc.ca/epic/internet/ inimr-ri.nsf/en/gr118345e.html

Pharmabiz (2006) "Moving towards a quality culture." Available at: http://www.pharmabiz.com/article/detnews.asp?articleid=32246&sectionid=50

PRAVDA (23 January 2008) "Mafia dominates Russian pharmaceutical industry." Available at: http://english.pravda.ru/main/18/88/351/14652_pharmaceutics.html

PreventDisease (2008) "Anti-impotence cancer cream to take on Viagra." Available at: http://preventdisease.com/news/articles/anti-impotence_cream.shtml

PriceWaterHouseCoopers (March 2006) "Investing in China's pharmaceutical industry." Available at: http://www.pwchk.com/webmedia/doc/632785588008556096_ts_invest_pharm_mar2006.pdf

Qayyum, I (2003) "eBusiness technologies and trends in pharmaceutical industry." Massachusetts Institute of Technology. Available at: http://dspace.mit.edu/bitstream/1721.1/16997/1/54106677.pdf

Republic of South Africa (2000) "Pharmacy Amendment act." Available at: http://www.doh.gov.za/docs/legislation/acts/2000/act1.pdf

Research and Development (2008) "Clinical trials in Latin America: Why Latin America." Available at: http://www.rd-latam.com/web724/cro/latin-america/english/06_porque_rd/03_latino.html

Research and Markets (2004) "BioMed Outsourcing Report – Drug Discovery Partnerships – The Indian Biopharmaceutical Outsourcing Sector." Available at: http://www.researchandmarkets.com/reportinfo.asp?report_id=228073

Research and Markets (2005a) "Indian biotech industry." Available at: http://www.researchandmarkets.com/reportinfo.asp?report_id=307530

Research and Markets (2005b) "Indian pharmaceutical and healthcare market annual review, 2005." Available at: http://www.researchandmarkets.com/reportinfo.asp?report_id=300716

Research and Markets (March, 2006a) "The image of pharmaceutical industry in Brazil: Challenges and opportunities." Available at: http://www.researchandmarkets.com/reportinfo.asp?report_id=335963

Research and Markets (May 2006b) "Russian Pharmaceutical Industry Trails West." Available at: http://findarticles.com/p/articles/mi_hb5243/is_200605/ai_n19566157

Research and Markets (2007a) "Chinese pharmaceutical industry." Available at: http://www.researchandmarkets.com/reportinfo.asp?report_id=237931

Research and Markets (2007b) "Indian pharmaceutical industry: Issues and opportunities." Available at: http://www.researchandmarkets.com/reportinfo.asp?report_id=35229

Research and Markets (2007c) "The pharmaceutical market: Brazil 2007." Available at: http://www.researchandmarkets.com/reportinfo.asp?report_id=54509

Research and Markets (2007d) "The Russian pharmaceuticals & healthcare market is expected to increase by 10.5% in 2007." Available at: http://findarticles.com/p/articles/mi_hb5243/is_200705/ai_n19725381

Reuters (28 March 2007) "Update1-Brazil revises 2006 GDP growth upward to 3.7 percent." Available at: http://uk.reuters.com/article/marketsNewsUS/idUKN2828177720070328

RNCOS (2007) "Russian pharma sector analysis." Available at: http://www.investorideas.com/News/r011108a.asp.

Roche (2004) "At its 10th anniversary celebration, Roche opens new R&D Center in China." Available at: http://www.roche.com/med-cor-2004-11-01b

Sandullo E. (2003) "Latin America lagging behind in health care provision." IMS Health. Available at: http://www.ims-global.com/insight/ news_story/0312/news_story_031217.htm

Segatto, C. (2 May 2005) "Super remédios para quem?" *Época*. Available at: http://revistaepoca.globo.com/

Silva, R. (6 March 2008) *Commentary on Brazil's Pharmaceutical Industry.* Philadelphia, PA: University of Sciences in Philadelphia.

Sina News (19 December 2008) "Survey shows that health care is on the top of government's concerns." (Tiao tsa hsien shih: chung kuo kwan dzong kwan dzu shih tan jiao tien, yih liao jiu shou). Available at: http://news.sina.com.tw/society/xinhuanet/cn/2007-12-19/161412787756.shtml

SiniWest (2001) "Study marks the first time an investigative therapy has been approved for clinical trials in China prior to regulatory approval in the West." Available at: http://www.siniwest.com/new/FeRx.htm

Strada, M. J. (2007) "Brazil faces global economic and environmental pressures." Available at: http://www.polsci.wvu.edu/facdis/stradaoverview.htm

The Center for Professional Innovation and Education (2008) "Drug master files – understanding and meeting your regulatory and processing responsibilities." Available at: http://www.cfpie.com/content.aspx?c=026agenda.html

The World Bank Group (2007) "Brazil – Inequality and Economic Development." Available at: http://wbln1018.worldbank.org/LAC/LAC.nsf/ECADocbyUnid/28840FED2FE42C2A85256E4D00661B68?Opendocument

UNDP (2008) "Human development report." Available at: http://hdr.undp.org/en/

UNESCO, (2005), "UIS statistics in brief." Available at: http://stats.uis.unesco.org/unesco/TableViewer/document.aspx?ReportId=121&IF_Language=eng&BR_Country=760

USA Commercial Service (2008) "Health care products and services." Available at: http://www.buyusa.gov/china/en/healthcare.html

Wang, M.L. and Nantulya, V. (2008) *Social Exclusion and Community Capital: The Missing Link in Global Partnerships of Health for All.* Lanham, MD: University Press of America.

Wang, M. L., Zhang, S. and Wang, X. (2007) *WTO, Globalization and China's Health Care System.* Basingstoke: Palgrave Macmillan.

Wikipedia (2007a) "Brazil." Available at: http://en.wikipedia.org/wiki/Brazil

Wikipedia (2007b) "BRIC." Available at: http://en.wikipedia.org/wiki/BRIC#_note-6

Wikipedia (2007c) "Pharmaceutical industry in China." Available at: http://en.wikipedia.org/wiki/Pharmaceutical_industry_in_China#_note-0

Wikipedia, (2007d), "Russian financial crisis." Available at: http://en.wikipedia.org/wiki/Russian_financial_crisis

Wikipedia (2008) "Africa." Available at: http://en.wikipedia.org/wiki/Africa

World Intellectual Property Rights Organization (2008) "Brazilian university leads the way in patent licensing." Available at: http://www.wipo.int/sme/en/best_practices/unicamp.htm

World Journal (11 March 2007) "From the gold BRIC four to the new diamond of eleven" (You jing dzwan shih kwo bien shing dawn shih yih kuo). A-3.

Worldwatch Institute (6 May 2006) "China's pharmaceutical industry lacks innovation, lags behind." Available at: http://www.worldwatch.org/node/3923

Xian-Janssen (2004) "Johnson and Johnson and YAES." Available at: http://www.xian-janssen.com.cn/default.aspx?menu_uid=110204

Xinhuanet (13 May 2002) "China standardizes production of traditional Chinese medicine." Xinhua News Agency. Available at: http://news.xinhuanet.com/english/2002–05/13/content_391052.htm

Chapter 4

A&A Contract Customs and Brokers (26 August 2008) "FDA to set up food and drug offices in China." Available at http://www.irishtimes.com/newspaper/health/2008/082/1219679936900.html

Angell, M. (2004) *The Truth about the Drug Companies.* New York: Random House.

Barnes, C. (7 November 2007) "New counterfeit report highlights worrying trends." Available at: http://www.outsourcing-pharma.com/news/ng.asp?n=81178-oecd-counterfeit-drug-supply-chain

BNET (2005) "Chirac proposes global tax; Gates bets against dollar." Available at: http://findarticles.com/p/articles/mi_m0JZS/is_4_21/ai_n25105111

Bogdanich, W. (12 December 2007a) "Agreement with China to regulate some drugs." Available at: http://www.nytimes.com/2007/12/12/business/worldbusiness/12safety.html?_r=1&oref=slogin

Bogdanich, W. (17 December, 2007b) "Counterfeit drugs' path eased by free trade zones." *New York Times.* Available at: http://www.nytimes.com/2007/12/17/world/middleeast/17freezone.html?_r=1&partner=rssnyt&emc=rss&oref=slogin

Business Insights (August 2006) "Pharmaceutical growth opportunities in Brazil, Russia, India and China: Healthcare reform, market dynamics and key players." Available at: http://www.piribo.com/publications/country/

latin_america/brazil/pharmaceutical_growth_opportunities_brazil_russia_ india_china.html

Caines, K. (2004) "GHP study paper: Global health partnerships and neglected diseases." DFID Health Resource Centre. Available at: http://www.ohchr.org/ english/issues/development/docs/WHO_4.pdf

CAPTH (2008) "Center for policy analysis of trade and health: Thailand's compulsory licenses for medicines." Available at: http://www.cpath.org/id27. html

CBS News (23 September 2005) "Brazil's drug copying industry." Available at: http://www.cbsnews.com/stories/2003/09/25/health/main575168.shtml

China Knowledge (2008) Available at: http://www.chinaknowledge.com/; or http://www.aacb.com/news/press.asp?id=3819).

Cockburn, R., Newton, P. N., Agyarko, E. K., Akunyili, D. and White, N. J. (2005) "The global threat of counterfeit drugs: Why industry and governments must communicate the dangers." PLoS Med, vol. 2, no. 4. Available at: e100 doi:10.1371/journal.pmed.0020100; or http://medicine.plosjournals.org/ perlserv/?request=get-document&doi=10.1371/journal.pmed.0020100&ct=1

CPTECH (2007) "The medical innovation prize fund." Available at: http://www. cptech.org/ip/health/prizefund/other-articles.html

DNDi (2008) "GlaxoSmithKline, Drugs for Neglected Diseases Initiative to Collaborate on Research Projects to Meet Public Health Needs in the Developing World." Available at: http://www.dndi.org/cms/public_html/ insidearticleListing.asp?CategoryId=166&SubCategoryId=167&ArticleId=46 3&TemplateId=1)

Ebisch, R. (March 2005) "Prescription for change." *Teradata Magazine* on-line. Available at: http://www.teradata.com/t/page/131951/

EuroNews (24 May 2008) "Doce países latinoamericanos se integran en la UNASUR." Available at: http://www.euronews.net/index.php?page=info&arti cle=489167&lng=5

FierceBiotech (6 December 2007) "Say goodbye to Big Pharma's gilded age." Available at: http://www.fiercepharma.com/story/say-goodbye-big-pharmas-gilded-age/2007-12-06

Grace, C. (2004) "GHP study paper: Global health partnership impact on commodity pricing and security." DFID Health Resource Centre. Available at: http://www.ohchr.org/english/issues/development/docs/WHO_3.pdf

IFPMA (International Federation of Pharmaceutical Manufacturers and Associations) (2008) "Glivec International Patient Assistance Program." Available at: http://www.ifpma.org/index.php?id=302

IMS (8 March 2007a) "IMS Reports U.S. Prescription Sales Jump 8.3 Percent in 2006, to $274.9 Billion." Available at: http://www.imshealth.com/ims/portal/ front/articleC/0,2777,6599_3665_8041546500.html

IMS (August 2007b) "IMS health reports global pharmaceutical market grew 7.0 percent in 2006, to $643 billion." Available at: http://www.imshealth.com/ ims/portal/front/articleC/0,2777,6025_3665_44771558,00.html

International Narcotics Control Board (2 March 2007). "International Narcotics Control Board 2006 Report." Vienna: INCB.

Kermani, F. (October 2005) "Contract Farma." Available at: http://www. contractpharma.com/articles/2005/10/regional-roundup-brazil

Knowledge Ecology International (2008) "Prizes to stimulate innovation." Available at: http://www.keionline.org/index.php?option=com_content&task=view&id=4

Laverty, B. Vice President (10 December 2007) *Communications, Malaria Initiatives, Novartis: Commentary On Coartem Partnership.* Philadelphia, PA: University of the Sciences.

Morris, J. and Stevens, P. (2006) *Counterfeit Medicines in Less Developed Countries: Problems and Solutions.* London: International Policy Network.

Mukhopadhyay, R. (1 April 2007) "The hunt for counterfeit medicine." *Analytical Chemistry.* Available at: http://pubs.acs.org/subscribe/journals/ancham/79/i07/pdf/0407feature_mukhopadhyay.pdf

National Public Radio (6 October 2006) "US faces flu vaccine shortage." Available at: http://www.npr.org/templates/story/story.php?storyId=4073505

New Scientist (25 February 2006a) "Global task force to target fake-drug peddlers." Available at: http://www.newscientist.com/channel/opinion/mg18925403.700-global-task-force-to-target-fakedrug-peddlers.html

New Scientist (8 September 2006b) "The medicines that could kill millions." Available at: http://www.newscientist.com/channel/health/mg19125683.900-the-medicines-that-could-kill-millions.html

New Scientist Tech (3 February 2007) "Lasers spot fake drugs in the packet." Available at: http://www.newscientist.com/article.ns?id=mg19325896.100

New Technology for Malaria (2006) "Artemisinin derivatives." Available at: http://www.artemisininproject.org/Malaria/artemisinins.htm

New York Times (3 March 2004) "A shortage of meningitis vaccine." Available at: http://query.nytimes.com/gst/fullpage.html?res=9901E4DE153FF930A35750C0A9629C8B63

New York Times (22 April 2008) "FDA identifies tainted heparin in 11 countries." Available at: http://www.starnewsonline.com/article/20080422/ZNYT04/804220313/0/NEWS

News-Medical.Net (2008) "New method to detect fake tamiflu." Available at: http://www.news-medical.net/?id=37079

PAHO (2003) "An update on quality assurance and procurement through WHO for improving access to artemisinin-based combination treatments (ACTs) for malaria." Available at: http://www.paho.org/English/AD/DPC/CD/mal-acts-update-7-03.htm

PLOS (2003) "Companies that have warned." Available at: http://medicine.plosjournals.org/perlserv/?request=get-document&doi=10.1371/journal.pmed.0020100&ct=1

PRAVDA (2008). "TATA motors makes Mercedes for the poor." Available at: http://english.pravda.ru/business/companies/10-01-2008/103346-tata-nano-0

Research and Markets (March 2006) "The image of the pharmaceutical industry in Brazil: Challenges and opportunities." Available at: http://www.researchandmarkets.com/reportinfo.asp?report_id=335963

RSC (2007) "Forging ahead of the counterfeiters." Available at: http://www.rsc.org/chemistryworld/News/2007/October/29100701.asp

Sherma, J. (2007) "Analysis of counterfeit drugs by thin layer chromatography." Available at: http://www.us.edu.pl/uniwersytet/jednostki/wydzialy/chemia/acta/ac19/zrodla/01_AC19.pdf

Silva, R. (6 March 2008) *Commentary on Brazil's Pharmaceutical Industry.* Philadelphia, PA: University of Sciences in Philadelphia.

Sturchio, J. L. (2001) "The case of ivermectin: Lessons and implications for improving access to care and treatment in developing Countries." *Journal of Community Eye Health*, vol. 14, no. 38, pp. 22–3. Available at: http://www. cehjournal.org/0953-6833/14/jceh_14_38_022.html

TATA (2008a) "A tradition of trust." Available at: http://www.tata.com/0_our_ commitment/community_initiatives/tata_trusts/overview.htm

TATA (2008b) "About us." Available at: http://www.tata.com/0_about_us/ history/index.htm

TATA (2008c) "Good to great." Available at: http://www.tata.com/

The Times of India (2008) "TATA acquires Jaguar, Land Rover for 2.3 billion." Available at: http://timesofindia.indiatimes.com/Tata_acquires_Jaguar_ Land_Rover_for_23_bn/articleshow/2902216.cms

TOPNEWS (12 February 2008) "Fake anti-malarial drugs investigation highlights threat to global health." Available at: http://www.topnews.in/health/fake-anti-malarial-drugs-investigation-highlights-threat-global-health-21020)

Wikipedia (2007) "Pharmaceutical companies." Available at: http://en.wikipedia. org/wiki/Pharmaceutical_companies

Wikipedia (2008) "TATA group." Available at: http://en.wikipedia.org/wiki/ Tata_Group

World Health Assembly Executive Board (24 February 2005) "World Health Organization Commission on Intellectual Property, Innovation and Health." Available at: www.who.int/intellectualproperty/en/

World Health Organization (2003) "Substandard and counterfeited medicines." Available at: http://www.who.int/mediacentre/factsheets/2003/fs275/en/

World Health Organization (2008) "African Programme for Onchocerciasis Control." Available at: http://www.who.int/blindness/partnerships/APOC/en/

World Journal (24 May 2008) "FDA awaits China's permission to set offices in Beijing, Shanghai and Kwanzhou" (FDA jing huei hu ban shih tsu, tai chung kuo heh dwen), B-7.

Index